The Women's Home-Based Business Book of Answers

The Women's Home-Based Business Book of Answers

78 Important Questions Answered by
Top Women Business Leaders

MARIA T. BAILEY

PRIMA PUBLISHING
3000 Lava Ridge Court • Roseville, California 95661
(800) 632-8676 • www.primapublishing.com

Published by Prima Publishing, Roseville, California. Member of the Crown Publishing Group, a division of Random House, Inc.

PRIMA PUBLISHING and colophon are trademarks of Random House, Inc., registered with the United States Patent and Trademark Office.

This book contains information of a general nature regarding starting and operating a business. It is not intended as a substitute for professional, legal, or financial advice. As laws may vary from state to state, readers should consult a competent legal or financial professional regarding their own particular business. In addition, readers should understand that the business world is highly dynamic and contains certain risks. Therefore, the author and publisher cannot warrant or guarantee that the use of any information contained in this book will work in any given situation.

Library of Congress Cataloging-in-Publication Data

Bailey, Maria T.
The women's home-based business book of answers / Maria T. Bailey
    p. cm.
Includes index.
ISBN 0-7615-3413-X
    1. Home-based businesses—United States. 2. Women-owned business enterprises—United States. 3. New business enterprises—United States. 4. Businesswomen—United States.
HD2336.U5. B35 2001
658'.041—dc21
2001-021789

01 02 03 04 HH 10 9 8 7 6 5 4 3 2 1
Printed in the United States of America
First edition

Visit us online at www.primapublishing.com

To Tim—
my best friend and my husband—
and to my children,
Madison, Owen, Keenan, and Morgan.
Dare to dream it and strive to achieve it.

CONTENTS

ACKNOWLEDGMENTS

When I told my mother-in-law and good friend, Patricia Bailey, that I was going to write a book, she asked me how I would figure out where to begin. Now that the book is completed, I'm happy to report that I was never at a loss for words until it was time to write these acknowledgments. What words do I use to adequately thank those who have helped me achieve a dream? This is the only time I've ever sat, staring at my blank computer screen, struggling for words.

The book you hold in your hands is the product of years of support from family, friends, coworkers, and acquaintances that have had more of an impact on my life than they've probably ever realized.

Dr. Jim Garner unknowingly challenged me to write this book in only four months. The thought of his friendly chuckle and "okay, we'll see" kept me writing late at night, even when I was barely able to stay awake.

Jorj Morgan, my friend and now a cookbook author, introduced me to Prima Publishing. She has been an inspiration and one of my best cheerleaders.

Many thanks to Denise Sternad and Michelle McCormack of Prima Publishing for all their patience and guidance throughout the publishing process. I appreciate their faith and have enjoyed our friendship.

Thank you to Dr. Betti Hertzberg, Dr. Roni Liederman, and Randy Prange who have been a big part of BlueSuitMom.com's success.

A business cannot survive without funding, and for that I thank my investors—especially Tim Elmes and Kim Hackett.

A special thanks to Jeff Davis, a man I admire and respect not only for his strategic business thinking but also for his dedication to family and friends. Earning Jeff's respect gave me the confidence I needed to jump into the venture capital arena.

If good friends are a sign of wealth, I am the richest person on earth. My friends not only stand by me when I describe to them my next crazy dream; they also support me with freelance work that is truly free. Thank you to Marti Zenor, Paula Levenson, and Robin Sterne for the countless special favors they do. To Noreen Conroy Dobrinsky, thanks for picking up the slack for me when my late night writing spilled into the daylight hours. Special appreciation goes to Patricia Campbell, friend and executive mom, who is always ready and willing to be a BlueSuitMom.com spokeswoman when the press needs an executive mother to interview.

There are many times when pursuing my dreams requires me to drop out of sight for a while, but true friends understand and support those endeavors. Thank you to Pam Berrard, Paige Hyatt, Nancy DeJohn, and Jill Oman for applauding my efforts and encouraging me throughout the years. To Brenda Kouwenhoven and Jennifer Calhoun who constantly try to convince me to work less and enjoy more of life, for always believing in me. Finally, to Audrey Ring, who has personally survived many of my ambitious endeavors; her friendship is one of the things I value most in life. Every girl should have a friend like her.

It is hard to express my appreciation for my business partner and friend, Rachael Bender. It was her commitment to my dream that made BlueSuitMom.com a reality. We shared more meals together during the launch of our company than we did with our own families. Together we have shared tears, joy, passion, and success. Special thanks to Rachael for all the additional hours she spent proofing and editing this book.

My business experience has been shaped by four incredible men. Few people are as fortunate as I am to have worked for some of the most respected men in South Florida.

Chris Mobley, president of American Lawyer Media, Inc., Florida division, and former *Herald* associate publisher, took a chance on promoting a young, ambitious, twenty-something woman to a management position at the *Herald*. Chris taught me the power of a hand-written note and genuine concern for people.

I was honored to work with Dr. Will Holcombe, president of Broward Community College, who helped me to see in myself what others saw in me. As my self-confidence grew, Will taught me how to manage it so that I would remain grounded. He's a Florida Gator but I forgave him for that a long time ago.

I often say that I learned more about business working for Steve Berrard than I could have by attending Harvard Business school. Steve challenged me for years to write a book but little did he know I'd write one filled with business lessons I learned from him. He promised me that he would teach me about business, and the opportunity to learn from him was a once-in-a-lifetime experience. I especially thank Steve for all the times he pushed me and challenged me intellectually.

Finally, many thanks to Michael Egan, one of the brightest men I know. His sincere interest in supporting women executives sets him apart from others. It was Mike who believed in the concept of BlueSuitMom.com and financially supported us through the Internet crash of 2000. I cannot thank him enough for his advice, insight, and commitment to my dream.

The support of family is a very important ingredient to my professional success. It was my mother who taught me how to write. My earliest memories are of the two us sitting up late at night writing book reports, fiction, and poetry together. She is the master of multi-tasking and it was she who taught me how to fit twenty-six hours into a day. You don't truly appreciate the lessons you learn from your mother until you are a mother yourself; only when you apply them to your own children do you recognize their value. I thank my mother for all the lessons I learned as her daughter.

Thanks to my sister, Debbi Jackson, who tolerates my busy life and reminds me to smell the roses; my stepmother, Susan Telli, who sets a constant example of commitment; my grandfather Louis Telli who has always demonstrated to me that high morals, strong values, and hard work are important to live a good life; and to my grandmother Eleanor Mattar who still has the first story I ever wrote, and reminds me of it often.

To my father-in-law, Patrick Bailey, who is one of my biggest fans, and whose faith and interest in my ambition fuel my passion to succeed. Patrick is a voracious reader and, although my book isn't a crime thriller, I hope he enjoys reading it some lazy Sunday afternoon. And to my mother-in-law, Patricia, whose support and interest in my various endeavors have helped me through the years.

I thank my stepfather, the late Dr. H. Michael Alligood for all his love, support, and encouragement. Although he was a veterinarian, he had a strong interest in business that seemed to rub off on me. My only regret is that I cannot personally give him a copy of this book. I know he would have shared in my excitement.

A special thank you to my father, Bill Telli, for teaching me how to build good relationships with people. I've never known a person not to like my father and I can only hope to one day have the reputation that he possesses in the community.

Finally, thank you to the forty-one women who are the true stars of this book. It has been a remarkable experience getting to know each and every one of them. These women have endured late night e-mails, urgent deadlines, and "just one question" over and over again. I cherish the friendships that I have made through the countless phone interviews and middle-of-the-night instant messaging.

There is not an accomplishment in my life that I do not share with my best friend and husband, Tim Bailey. Whether it's entertaining our four children outside the house so I can write in a quiet environment, or reminding me that rest is necessary, he supports each and every goal I set for myself. We have always shared the dream to write a book and although the words you read here are typed with my fingers, it was definitely a team effort. As I spent four months writing this book, he maintained our family. I sincerely thank him for all he does.

I would be remiss not to acknowledge my children, Madison, Owen, Keenan, and Morgan, who shared their mother's time with the creation of a book. Instead of continually asking me, "Are we there yet?" they repeatedly asked, "What page are you on now, Mom?" Well, kids, I'm done.

INTRODUCTION

The rest of the world is fast asleep as the clock in the living room chimes 2:00. Although fatigue has overtaken your body, your mind races with anticipation. After months of working, a day that will change your life forever is quickly approaching, and your enthusiasm for the moment keeps you awake while your family sleeps. Your imagination visualizes growth, maturity, and moments of success. You know that there will be challenges, but you know in your heart that your struggles will be rewarded by the positive experiences and the happiness you will feel at the end of each day.

If you are a woman, you might think this scene describes a mother anticipating the birth of her child. Think again! I'm describing the feelings of a woman about to launch her own home-based business. Building your own business will be the second most exhilarating, liberating, and exhausting thing you will ever experience. The only life event that comes close is giving birth. By the time you launch your business, you will truly feel that your company is your child. In fact, I often hear women business owners refer to their businesses as their babies.

It's surprising how many parallels there are between parenting a child and building a business. The similarities begin the moment you decide to enter the world of entrepreneurship. The amount of responsibility you assume as a business owner begins immediately with careful preparation, just as an expectant mother begins nesting. The time it takes for a new entrepreneur to research the market, write a business plan, find funding, and market the product may take more than a year. As you go about these tasks, I am hoping that the experiences of successful home-based business owners described by the contributors to this book will decrease your incubation time significantly. That is just the beginning. From then on, you will need to provide constant attention and nurturing so your business can grow and mature just as you need to feed and diaper your baby. Your business plan, customer base, and marketing needs will constantly change with each stage of growth, just like a child. The similarities between the emotional and personal experiences of giving birth and starting a home-based business are remarkable. Perhaps it's no wonder that a large portion of the more than 24 million home-based business owners are mothers of young children.

However, you don't have to be a mother to want to own a home-based business. Women, not all of them mothers, are venturing into the world of self-employment at an incredible rate. A recent study conducted by three sources—the National Foundation for Women Business Owners, the Committee of 200, and Catalyst—reported the number of women-owned businesses in the United States is increasing at nearly twice the number of businesses owned by men. In the same study, women cited the desire for greater flexibility, the need to feel their work is valued, and glass-ceiling issues as the top reasons for moving into entrepreneurship. More than 10 million women start home-based businesses each year. What's more, women-owned businesses employ more people than the top five Fortune 100 companies combined. An observer might conclude, if so many women are doing it, it must be easy to do. Trust me, nothing could be farther from the truth. On average, only 30 percent of small businesses succeed. The failure of the remaining 70 percent can be attributed to lack of preparation, poor management of daily operations, and underestimating the amount of funding required to keep the business alive. Success in operating a home-based business is not an accident. It requires skill, managerial expertise, and attitudinal competencies. Many people have good ideas, enthusiasm, and the best intentions to make a business succeed, yet lack what it takes to build a profitable company.

In this book, I will provide you with the tools, information, and insight you need to become part of the elite 30 percent who succeed. Let me explain what I mean by success. To me, success occurs when your home-based business not only meets your financial expectations but meets your personal lifestyle goals as well. Some high achievers want to build companies that will finance early retirement, exotic trips, luxury cars, and summer houses in Nantucket. Other women

with more modest expectations may want their businesses to supplement the household budget, cover their children's tuition at private schools, or pay for summer vacations. It's up to you to determine your business, lifestyle, and financial goals before you start out. Since you are reading this book, I'm assuming that some personal situation has fueled your desire to start a business. I'd like you to think about the circumstances that have brought you to this point. Do you want the flexibility to travel with your significant other? Do you want to scale back your work hours so you can spend more time with your aging parents? Do you desire to work at home to be near your children? Or, are you one of those women like myself who enjoys the challenge of venturing into uncharted territory and emerging the winner? Whatever the reason, it is important to clearly define both the financial and lifestyle expectations of your business very early in the process.

Seven Reasons Women Begin Home-Based Businesses

- Unhappiness in their present career
- The need to make more money or supplement family income
- Having an idea for a new product or service in the marketplace
- Personal need for a product or service not available
- The need for personal flexibility
- Desire to stay at home with young children
- Choice of a profession traditionally based from a home office
- Other circumstances necessitating the need to be at home

The reasons women choose self-employment are as different as the personality traits of those who successfully build home-based businesses. In this book, I will give you the tools and tips to succeed. I have gathered the insights, advice, and personal stories of more than forty women who are doing it right now. Their advice occurs as

answers to questions I ask throughout each chapter. I selected these particular women because they represent a variety of industries with a wide range of annual gross revenues. You will meet Julie Aigner-Clark whose Baby Einstein videos have won a bundle of national parenting awards and now line the shelves of Target stores. She manages her multimillion-dollar business from her basement. Then there is Alex Powe Allred, a member of the women's Olympic bobsled team and a mother of three who is also a full-time, home-based author. Shannon Rubio runs her gift-basket company, TheSmileBox.com, from her living room and homeschools her four children as well. By the end of this book, I think you will agree that these truly amazing women are just like you. The only difference right now is that they have taken the initiative and are reaching their financial, lifestyle, and personal goals. Over forty different personalities, providing forty different products or services, offer hundreds of lessons for other women in running a home-based business. Since there is value in learning from someone else's mistakes, I've included them as well. Profiles of these remarkable women follow in the next section. I recommend taking a minute to meet our experienced group of home-based business owners. They are a smart and often humorous bunch!

Perhaps this is a good time to introduce myself. I won't bore you with the "I was born in Miami, Florida" details. I'd rather touch on the facts that have led me to write this book. However, I can't completely ignore my personal life because, like so many home-based working women, it has influenced the direction of my professional career. After a ten-year, fast-track career at the *Miami Herald*, I found myself the mother of three children under twenty months—Owen, Madison, and Keenan. How does that happen, you might ask? My husband, Tim, and I were fortunate enough to get pregnant days after learning of the pending adoption of our first child. And, as if having two babies only six months apart was not enough, we decided to repeat our infertility treatments, thinking it would take years to get pregnant again. Surprise! Our third child arrived fourteen months after his big brother. I continued to work full time with the support of an au pair and a lot of help from Tim. Although it was challenging, I enjoyed my job. The year before having my third child, I had

created and produced the South Florida Parenting Conference. It was a one-day educational conference that brought parents and experts together to talk about topics like discipline and education. It was an immediate success, and I loved doing it. My position also allowed me to interact with a number of high-level corporate executives, including Donna Moore, who was then the CEO of Discovery Zone play centers. I spent a lot of time at Discovery Zone with my young brood. During a conversation one night, I proceeded to tell Donna how I would do it if she gave me the opportunity to market her company to mothers. She liked my ideas and told me that if ever I went out on my own, Discovery Zone would be my first client. That was all the security I needed to take the plunge into self-employment. In 1994, I gave birth to Bailey Innovative Marketing, Inc. My second client was my former employer, the *Miami Herald,* which hired me to continue producing the parenting conference. My company grew quickly. The best part of it all was that I was able to balance my three babies and find personal fulfillment in working.

Less than a year after launching, I met, through a client, one of South Florida's most respected businessmen, Steve Berrard. Steve had been the CEO of Blockbuster and Spelling Entertainment and was now launching a new company that promised to revolutionize the car industry, AutoNation USA. Steve recruited me to join his team. His promise to me was simple: "I'll teach you everything you need to know about building a company." The following year, *Forbes* named AutoNation the fastest growing company in America. For me, it was an incredible year of learning. Sitting next to the CEO of a major corporation, I was given the opportunity to work on business development, market research, corporate affairs, and marketing. I can't imagine that a year at Harvard Business School would have taught me more!

Unfortunately, there was a negative side to the experience, and that was a great deal of travel. One year, I earned more than 100,000 frequent flyer miles. To be away that much with a husband and now four children at home was a challenge.

To help me balance my life, I began looking for a publication to give me advice on juggling a career and a family. Although I found a few, none of them seemed to address the specific issues of a female corporate vice president who was also a mother. I wanted advice on stock options, childcare, and dealing with the guilt that came with my long work hours. I knew I wasn't alone in my search for help. Each week, my female peers and I would gather behind closed doors and talk about the challenges we faced as executive mothers.

My search for help soon turned into a passion to provide other executive mothers with information on how to balance work and family. I began talking to women in airports and on playgrounds. One day, I started writing my business plan on an airplane. I'm also a marathoner, and it was while on one of my training runs for the New York marathon that I thought of the name BlueSuitMom.com.

On February 1, 2000, I once again stepped into the world of self-employment and began working full time on my new venture. This time I needed investors, employees, business partners, and a good product. I found my best resource in my business partner, Rachael Bender, and together we worked eighteen-hour days for three months to build our company. On Mother's Day 2000, we pushed "enter" on our keyboard and BlueSuitMom.com was born. The response was overwhelming. Our company, during the first week of business, made the news in over twenty national and local newspapers. We appeared in *USA Today, Working Woman,* and *SELF.* My children suddenly thought they were famous because we were all in the local newspapers and on the nightly news. Today, our Web site is the leading provider of work and family balance information to executive mothers and the companies who employ them. You can find us on Discovery.com and AmericanBaby.com among hundreds of other sites. It was all an incredibly positive experience for my family and me. Michael Egan, chairman of Certified Vacations, ANC Rental Group, and theglobe.com, a well-respected businessman who founded, among other companies, Alamo Rent A Car, recognized our efforts. In December 2000, he acquired BlueSuitMom.com, of which I remain president. The entire sequence of events fell directly in line with the business plan I created and followed.

It is hard to describe the feeling of accomplishment and personal fulfillment when you can look at something you have built, see how successful it is, and then have those feelings validated when someone of Mr. Egan's stature likes your concept enough to buy it. To be sure, I have stubbed my toe along the way and made more blunders than I can count. It is for that reason that I think I have valuable insights and experiences to offer other women looking to make the same big move. I don't know any magic formulas or shortcuts. I do know what it feels like to push all the chips to the center of the table, and I mean all of them, and announce publicly, "I'm in." I am certain my having personally tasted the fear and jubilation of the whole crazy ride will help me to help you.

A long time ago, I learned that there is always more than one way to do something. Whether it's wrapping a present, organizing a garage, or starting a business, each of us has her own way of getting the job done. Individual experience, personal preferences, and the opportunities we create for ourselves all contribute to how we accomplish our personal and professional goals. I've always been interested in how certain people actually do the things they do. For many years, I've read with interest the personal stories behind successful entrepreneurs, and it's always amazed me that there are so many different paths to success. When I was approached to write a book on how to build a business, I thought it was important to tell more than one person's story. Sure, I have built two companies, but if I had all the answers, I wouldn't read the histories of other entrepreneurs with such intent to learn. I want to deliver to the reader of this book the most valuable insights and information possible about how to start a home-based business.

The best way to accomplish my goal, I believed, is to assemble an experienced team of home-based business owners who are women. The group members must have diverse backgrounds and represent a variety of industries, annual sales, and business philosophies. I also needed my women to be both married and single, with children and without, because I know from experience that home life influences professional life. I am happy to say that I found them. They are a group of forty-one dynamic, knowledgeable, and successful home-based business owners. Cumulatively, they represent over $30 million in annual sales, 300 years of business experience, and employ more than 250 people. Their businesses educate, entertain, and do e-commerce. The locations of their home-based businesses range from a log cabin in Utah to a farm in upstate New York to a condo on Miami Beach. Personally, it has been a fulfilling experience getting to know each of these talented women. I hope that I adequately describe them throughout the book so that you get to know them the way I do. They have so much to offer both professionally and personally.

I asked each of them to put themselves back at the beginning and provide the insight they wished they had when they were building their home-based businesses. This was their chance to reflect on "If I knew then what I know now" and pass it along to other women just getting started. Now, meet the women.

CONTRIBUTOR BIOGRAPHIES

ALEX POWE ALLRED is an author and gold medalist on the U.S. bobsled team. Her sport may be downhill, but the success of her home-based business has gone nowhere but up. In 1996, Alex was in the U.S. Nationals as part of the U.S. bobsled team. Four months pregnant, she thought she was on her way to the Olympics. Unfortunately, the International Olympic Committee decided to eliminate women's bobsledding from the winter games. This twist of fate created a new career for the mother of three. Disappointed and frustrated, Alex began writing. Her first book, *The Quiet Storm: A Celebration of Women in Sport*, contains personal interviews with athletes such as Mary Lou Retton and Bonnie Blair and describes the challenges faced by female athletes in male-dominated sports. Alex works out of her Ohio office and is presently writing her fourth book during her children's nap times.

E-mail: REDBURN4@aol.com

AMILYA ANTONETTI created her company, SOAPWORKS, because of her infant son's frantic cries for help. After her son came home from the hospital, he began screaming nonstop, had breathing difficulties, and broke out in rashes. After countless hospital visits with no diagnosis, Amilya began to do some good old-fashioned detective work and discovered David's screams were an allergic reaction to the chemicals in her brand-name household cleaners. Determined to find a nonallergenic product to keep her house clean, Amilya spent days talking with her grandmother and other senior citizens, asking them to describe the products they cleaned with in their younger days. They told her they had used basic compounds like vinegar and baking soda. Soon, Amilya turned her home kitchen into a lab for creating nonallergenic natural cleaners. Today, her northern-California-based company employs over 75 people, boasts sales of $5 million, and sells product in over 2,500 stores nationwide.

E-mail: amilya@soapworks.com

DIANE BALLARD went from the semi-conductor industry to the printing industry before she decided to explore entrepreneurship. As a graduate of the University of Wisconsin-Platteville in industrial technology with a master of science degree from Central Michigan University, Diane felt she was well-equipped to build her own home-based consulting business. DKB Associates provides a comprehensive development process to small manufacturing facilities in all industries. Her process focuses on application and measurable bottom-line results, which separates it from standard training programs. A mother, Diane lives in Wisconsin.

E-mail: dballard@scc.net

RACHAEL BENDER is cofounder of BlueSuitMom.com. After enjoying a career in Web design and content management for Cox Interactive Media and other Internet companies, Rachael decided to venture out on her own. Although not yet a mom herself, Rachael had a strong desire to be her own boss and apply her talents to her own venture. Today, the site designed for executive working mothers and the companies that employ them licenses work and family balance content to Discovery.com and over twenty Fortune 100 companies. She has a journalism degree from the University of Florida. Rachael and her husband reside in South Florida with their cats and iguana.

E-mail: rachael@bluesuitmom.com

KIT BENNETT is the founder of Amazingmoms.com and the mother of four children. Using her fifteen years experience as a music/art teacher, children's entertainer, and, most of all, a mother, she created the leading Web site for birthday, craft, and family activity ideas for busy mothers. She is a featured contributor on About.com, Discovery.com, and BlueSuitMom.com. Prior to starting Amazingmoms.com, Kit owned and operated Party Sensations, a children's entertainment business, until the computer bug bit her in 1998. In her new company, Kit created an innovative way to share her unique ideas and participate in the issues facing the modern family. She runs her business with her husband from her southern Oregon home and still finds time to do volunteer teaching in elementary art classes.

E-mail: mom@amazingmoms.com

BETH BESNER, a lawyer, felt inspiration strike as she watched her infant son eat chicken off a dirty restaurant table. She saw the need for a simple product to protect her son from germ infestation. Putting her New York know-how and creative streak to work, Beth began talking to people who could take her concept from idea to product. The result was Table Topper, a clear plastic mat with brightly colored animal designs and two strips of adhesive tape on the back. Today, Beth's product is carried by Toys R Us, Babies R Us, and Kmart. She also has licensing agreements with Sesame Street and Disney. Beth, her husband, and two sons reside in South Florida.

E-mail: BesnerB@aol.com

JULIE AIGNER-CLARK is the proud mother of two daughters and the founder of the Baby Einstein Company. Her multimillion-dollar business, located in the basement of her Littleton, Colorado, home, has become the leading provider of developmental media products for babies and toddlers. Julie uses her experience as a former teacher to create books, videotapes, DVDs, and CDs that introduce children to the arts and humanities. Large retailers such as Target and The Right Start stores now carry her Baby Mozart, Art Time Classics, and Baby Bach products. *Working Woman,* Ernst & Young, and *Entrepreneur* have recognized Julie for her entrepreneurial accomplishments.

E-mail: julie@babyeinstein.com

NANCY CLEARY did what most people do not have the courage to do. When the design studio she worked for in Providence, Rhode Island, closed, she launched her own graphic design studio in a location which she describes as "better suited for her spirit," Deadwood,

Oregon. That was nine years ago. Today, the company's growth has provided her with the financial means to launch her second company, Wyatt-McKenzie Publishing. The company, named after her two children, Wyatt and McKenzie, creates promotional products. Her signature product is the Box-is, which is a concept-to-doorstep packaged prototype of new products, complete with a print and online marketing campaign. Nancy takes an idea and proposes a design concept for the product, the packaging, and brochures for the product. Nancy has found a niche for her product among young entrepreneurs and women who want to create a personalized box containing legacy elements for their children.

E-mail: nancy@box-is.com

JEANNINE CLONTZ asked herself with her tongue in her cheek, what could be more exciting than a career in the seafood distribution industry? Owning your home-based business, of course, she answered seriously. After twenty-seven years as an administrative and customer service professional, Jeannine decided to apply her skills to her own benefit and in 1997 in Missouri founded Accurate Business Services, which provides business support services to companies of all sizes. Jeannine's company offers mail processing, database management, desktop publishing, and general bookkeeping and has experienced a 150% growth rate since its inception. Jeannine is a mother and wife.

E-mail: Accbizsvc@aol.com

DIANE DESA is the owner of A Virtual Assistant, a long-term, online support provider of professional assistance for small-business owners, law offices, and independent professionals. The company operates out of her Texas home where she lives with her twin teenage boys. Prior to being self-employed, Diane's career included fifteen years in high-level administrative positions in government, medical, and legal offices. She also served in the U.S. Air Force where she held a number of managerial positions before being honorably discharged in 1985. Diane's goal is to have A Virtual Assistant double in size by the end of 2001.

E-mail: diane@dianedesa.com

DEE ENNEN was no stranger to being her own boss when she started Ennen Computer Services. The owner and operator of a word processing business since 1985, she expanded her professional role in 1996 to include writing and has authored *Success from Home: The Word Processing Business*, published by Adam-Blake Publishing. Today, she provides word processing and computer tutoring services from her home in Florida. She is a wife and the mother of three children.

E-mail: DeeEnnen@aol.com

SANDI EPSTEIN has an MBA from Columbia University and over fifteen years experience in marketing and business management. She has worked inside large U.S. and international businesses, including Johnson & Johnson, Hearst/ABC, and Ferrero, as well as small, under-$10-million businesses, providing engineering services and catalog sales. Her home-based consulting and coaching practice started in 1992. As a wife and mother of two, balancing life and work and creating and running businesses have been a subject of thought, study, and successful practice for Sandi.

E-mail: SLSE123@aol.com

DEBBIE GIOQUINDO is a graduate of SUNY College of Buffalo with a degree in business. She began her career as an office manager for a group of radio stations. Later, her love of travel led her to pursue her certification as a travel counselor from the Institute of Certified Travel Counselors. In 1997 she founded Personal Touch Travel in her New York home. The agency specializes in, but is not limited to, family and honeymoon travel and has expanded to include a network of independent contractors. Debbie is the mother of two children.

E-mail: dlgioquindo@juno.com

MOLLY GOLD is a former meeting planner who knows firsthand the importance of organization. Faced with the scheduling challenges of a mother with two toddlers, Molly in 1999 created Go Mom !nc to provide a calendar solution for mothers everywhere. The Go Mom !nc Planner is a unique day-planner system with a three-part calendar that enables moms to focus on the big picture. All three components—an eighteen-month flip calendar, weekly scheduler, and to-call and to-do pads—are visible simultaneously and are complementary in their functions. The weekly planner allows moms to schedule takeout dinners, grocery lists, and extracurricular activities. Molly works from her Virginia home.

E-mail: mgold@gomominc.com

MERYL GUERRERO is a Florida mother of three and parenting educator. While serving more than twelve years as the director of communications for the National Safety Council, South Florida chapter, she was an integral part of the growth of Safety First, a national safety program created to teach parents the importance of child safety. In 1996 she shared her passion by producing Parenting 101, a day-long parenting conference for parents and childcare providers. Now held twice a year, the conference presents a team of respected experts conducting a series of workshops on topics ranging from Discipline with Anger to Tolerating the Teen Years. Meryl holds a degree in communication from Florida Atlantic University.

E-mail: PARENTG101@aol.com

WENDY HARRIS, after fourteen years in the medical billing field, saw a need to create a support system for medical billing professionals nationwide. In 1998, she launched the National Association of Medical Billers from her home in upstate New York. Today, the association boasts almost 500 members. The company's goal is to assist medical billers with training, information, networking, and support. As the mother of two boys, Wendy believes it is her ability to juggle tasks, together with a great deal of determination, that has spurred the growth of her business. Her goal is to grow a well-respected association that lands her on *Oprah!*

E-mail: NatAsBill@aol.com

TAMMY HARRISON wondered how to utilize her years of business experience on a remote ranch in Utah. In 1996, she decided to establish a virtual company, The Queen of Pizzazz, in her home office. Tammy's marketing and creative company specializes in providing small businesses with Web site design, graphic design, and advertising sales. Presently, she is the independent creative representative for Home-Based Working Moms (www.hbwm.com), one of the leading Web sites for home-based working mothers. She is a veteran business owner who has operated numerous companies from her home, including a legal assistance service and a medical auditing business. Tammy maintains her businesses while juggling her husband and four children.

E-mail: tammyh@jdharrison.com

REBECCA HART has experienced a great deal of success in the public relations industry, having worked with companies like Discover Card, IBM, Merck, AccuStaff, and Blue Cross and Blue Shield of Florida. Before starting her home-based consulting firm, she worked as an account group supervisor at the Robin Shepherd Group in Jacksonville, Florida, where she managed a team of public relations counselors on national and regional accounts. She is a syndicated columnist and has been profiled in such national publications as *Inc.*, *Home Office Computing, Business Start-Ups*, and *USA Today*. She has won numerous public relations awards, including the 1997 Dick Pope All-Florida Golden Image Award for the best public relations campaign in the state of Florida. She is accredited through the Public Relations Society of America (PRSA) and is a member of the International Association of Business Communicators (IABC) and the National Speakers Association (NSA). Rebecca graduated from the University of Florida with a degree in telecommunication and is a proud mother and wife.

E-mail: rebhart@mediaone.net

PRISCILLA HUFF is one of the stars who come to mind when you think of home-based businesses for women. Although she owns Little House Writing and Publishing Company and does business information consulting and research services for small businesses, she is best known as the author of *101 Best Home-Based Businesses for Women*. Her latest book, *HerVenture.com*, features sidebar profiles of fifty-five successful women "Netprenuers." Priscilla has also written for *Woman's World*, iVillage.com, Womensenews.org, and has been quoted in *Forbes* and the *New York Times*. She lives in Texas with her family.

E-mail: pyhuff@mindspring.com

TERESA KIRBY and DARCY LYONS are taking the home party industry by storm! In September of 1999, the first Garden Party took place in a living room in California and has already grown to two party consultants covering Southern California. A Garden Party is a party-based sales company that specializes in high-quality gardening tools, art for the garden, and garden-related collectibles. The two women have been friends for over fifteen years and after becoming mothers decided it was time to build a home-based business together. Darcy was formerly the director of industrial engineering for a large retailer while Teresa brings her experience in business development to the company. Their research of several industries led them to the world of home parties where they saw the need for a new and unique product line. The company has two offices—one in Darcy's home and the other in Teresa's. They have developed a system that allows them to run the company without much face-to-face interaction between them but one that generates lots of phone time and e-mails. Move over, Tupperware!

E-mail: agardenparty@earthlink.net

JULIE MARCHESE is the founder of Twinsadvice.com. As a former U.S. Army surgical nurse, she began demonstrating her will to succeed long before becoming the mother of four boys. Julie's long list of credits includes completing Airborne School, receiving the expert field medical badge, and earning her master's degree in business administration from St. John Fisher College in Rochester, New York. Today, Julie resides outside of Chicago with her husband and four boys, who include a set of twins. She is the author of the handbook, *So You're Having Twins: Boy Are You Going to be Busy! Practical Advice on How to Manage Your Life with Twins the 1st Year.* Her Web site is visited by thousands of parents seeking advice and help raising twins.

E-mail: marchesefamily@earthlink.net

SHERRY MAYSONAVE just wasn't happy in 1992 as a teacher in the school system in her area and began looking for a new career, which she discovered in the communication image industry. Today, Sherry is the founder and president of Empowerment Enterprises, one of America's leading communication-image firms. Her business, which she originally started from her home, provides training in the art of communication, professional dress, and psychology. Her clients include business professionals from a variety of industries, nationally known political figures, writers, university professors, seminar leaders, and entertainers. Sherry is also the author of *Casual Power: How to Power Up Your Nonverbal Communications and Dress Down for Success*. Empowerment Enterprises has grown so large and quickly that Sherry's husband, Steve, now works with her full time.

E-mail: sherry@maysonave.com

LINDA MCWILLIAMS felt battered by her three-hour-a-day commute to her job as an analyst for a Fortune 500 company and decided to explore other business opportunities. Fate helped her out when she purchased a graphic of her child's name and its meaning. She decided to apply her own twist to this concept and founded OnceUponAName.com. The company produces unique lithographed names and meaning keepsakes and other gift items. Linda's sales, generated by direct consumer business as well as the Internet, have tripled over the past year. Linda maintains her family of four children and her company from a small farm in upstate New York.

E-mail: ljmcwilliams@yahoo.com

DARCY VOLDEN MILLER dreamed of owning her own business since she was seven years old. As she grew up, she planned not to have children. "Well," Darcy says, "the Big Man Upstairs had a different plan for me." When her baby came, she gave up her eleven-year career with Motorola. She felt so fortunate to have the luxury to be able to stay at home with her new son that she created a business to help other stay-at-home mothers. Darcy now refers to herself as a M.O.M — that is, a Mother On a Mission. Her business, LittleDidIKnow.com is an online destination for home-based business mothers to sell their products and services in a safe haven void of scams. Together, as one big business, the mothers accomplish what they could not do alone. Darcy and her husband are raising their young son in Austin, Texas.

E-mail: darjo@texas.net

GWEN MORAN is a nationally recognized entrepreneur and writer. Founder of Moran Marketing Associates, a marketing communications and public relations firm based in Ocean, New Jersey, she has worked with clients ranging from Fortune 500 companies to small businesses to develop strategic marketing programs. She is also the creator of Boost-YourBiz.com, a marketing information Web site for small businesses, and frequently writes and teaches about small-business marketing and management issues for national business publications and Web sites. Entrepreneurs can read Gwen's monthly column in *Entrepreneur*. She and her husband live in the Northeast.

E-mail: moranmarketing@erols.com

JORJ MORGAN looked no further than her two favorite hobbies, cooking and writing, when she started her home-based business. She is the author of *At Home in the Kitchen: The Art of Preparing the Foods You Love to Eat* and the manager of the companion Web site, www.Jorj.com. Her husband and three sons benefit directly from her venture into entrepreneurship by acting as in-home samplers. As a business owner, Jorj wears many hats besides that of a home chef. She is also a cooking instructor, director of Lifestyle content for Blue-SuitMom.com, businesswoman, and former owner and manager of a catering and party planning firm in Fort Lauderdale, Florida. Her feature articles and food newsletter, focusing on the unique needs of executive working mothers, appear regularly on various Internet sites.

E-mail: jorjmm@aol.com

KAREN WILKINSON OLTION says there's nothing like a bubble bath! If you ask Karen, she'll tell you the best part of launching her business, eBubbles.com, is testing her products. No stranger to consumer product marketing or entrepreneurship, Karen spent over ten years in consumer marketing positions for a variety of companies before starting her first company, a computer graphic design and publishing firm, in 1993. eBubbles.com is an online bath and body boutique offering a unique selection of specialty soaps, body lotions, bubble baths, and personal care products from around the world. Karen identified a need for these products at an affordable cost and then enticed her husband to launch the company in their garage. The couple resides with their dogs in Laguna Beach, California.

E-mail: Karen@ebubbles.com

HEIDI PERRY is the person to look to as a model when you are feeling overwhelmed with life. She and her husband, Dave, are the parents of eight children as well as the founders of Home Business Online. Heidi's daily challenges include running her home-based business and homeschooling four of her children. Heidi and Dave have founded eight companies, five of which began as home-based businesses. Her e-zine, Homebizbytes, is read by thousands of business owners who seek her unique insights and advice each week. Heidi began her entrepreneurial career while attending Brigham Young University where she ran a floral business from her dorm room to pay her tuition. She is presently working on a book, *The Kitchen Table eBay Millionaire*, about how to make money on online auctions with little or no money upfront.

E-mail: hperry@advantage-online.com

LARA PULLEN, PH.D. built her home-based business around her Ph.D. in microbiology and immunology. Her business, Environmental Health Consulting, Inc., launched in Illinois in 1998, provides word-training manuals, scientific reviews, PowerPoint presentations, and consumer-oriented health stories for pharmaceutical and medical companies and universities. Laura applies her scientific training to the communication of scientific ideas and has carved out a niche business that has almost tripled revenues in the past year. She is a wife and the mother of two daughters.

E-mail: lpullen@mediaone.net

SHANNON RUBIO delivers smiles from her home-based business, TheSmileBox.com. Shannon sells gift boxes that are a combination gift basket and care package filled with food and gift products. The box is bright yellow and carries the logo of "Smilin' Sam," which in itself generates cheer in its recipient. Shannon started the company with her mother. Together, they assemble, package, and ship Smile-Boxes from Shannon's North Texas home. Although she has a degree in social work, she has always opted for working from home. Her first business was a computer parts company that she managed while also working as a post-partum doula, helping new mothers develop their parenting skills. A doula helps a mother with breastfeeding, teaches her how to give babies baths, and other things that take place during the first month of the child's life. While running her business, Shannon also homeschools her three sons.

E-mail: rsr817@email.msn.com

LESLEY SPENCER started her home business HBWM (Home-Based Working Moms; www.hbwm.com) in 1995 after the birth of her first child. Until then, she was the full-time PR coordinator for a golf school. Lesley has discovered a strong need for support, information, and networking among parents who work at home. She felt an organization like HBWM would be the perfect way to allow parents to share ideas and support one another. Lesley graduated summa cum laude with a bachelor's degree in journalism/public relations from Southwest Texas State University. She received a master's degree in public relations from the University of Stirling in Scotland while on a full academic scholarship from Rotary International as an ambassador of goodwill. She operates HBWM.com from her home in Texas where she lives with her husband and two children.

E-mail: lesley@hbwm.com

KIMBERLY STANSELL is an internationally recognized entrepreneurial trainer and author of *Bootstrapper's Success Secrets: 151 Tactics for Building Your Business on a Shoestring Budget* and the forthcoming *Witty Workin' Woman: A Problem-Solving Guide for Professional Women*. A retired corporate personnel director, Stansell launched her first venture with only $328.21. She parlayed her entrepreneurial experience into a second business, Research Done Write!, a Los Angeles-based consulting and training firm that presents workshops, seminars, and keynote addresses to audiences worldwide.

> E-mail: kmberlynla@hotmail.com

ROBIN STERNE is the whiz who comes up with the unique look of collateral pieces for big events such as the Blockbuster Entertainment Awards. With over twenty years experience providing design work for well-known brands such as Blockbuster, Blue Dot, and AutoNation USA, Robin has earned a reputation for exceptional design talents. Her clients look to her to create an image that will project their message to consumers, and she delivers it from her home-based business, Wow! Designs, Inc. Robin has a degree in fine arts from the University of Miami, Florida. She began her career with Canada's largest entertainment company, Astral, the producer of the original *Porky's* movies. Today, Robin resides in South Florida with her husband and daughter, Gerri.

> E-mail: robin.sterne@bluedotmail.com

KAITLAND THORSTENSON is a public accountant with more than thirty years experience in creating and establishing ongoing maintenance of small-business accounting functions. While working as a financial manager for St. Louis County in Duluth, Minnesota, she developed a desire to help struggling small-business owners. Today, she focuses her home-based accounting company on serving small companies that cannot afford the services of large accounting firms. She holds degrees from Lake Superior College and the College of St. Scholastica in accounting and business administration. Kaitland is the mother of grown children.

> E-mail: akaihand@hotmail.com

VICTORIA USHERENKO, after an extensive corporate career with First National Bank of Chicago and Transchem Finance and Trade, decided she had reached the peak of her profession working for someone else. She also had a desire to be at home with her son, so she jumped feet first into creating Liaison IT, a boutique executive search and information technology-staffing firm. She quickly carved out a niche by providing CEOs, COOs, and CTOs with multilingual and international experience to the numerous Internet incubators, venture capital firms, and emerging technology companies in South Florida. Victoria is also the founder and president of the South Florida chapter of Women in Technology International, which helps women develop the core competencies in demand by all levels of technology organizations. Victoria holds a business and finance degree from the University of Michigan and a master's degree in international business from Nova Southeastern University.

E-mail: victoria@liaisonit.com

JANESSA WASSERMAN has an undergraduate degree in English literature, a law degree, and a license to practice law. What did she do with all this? She became a stay-at-home mom and started a company to pay off the enormous student debt she had just spent years incurring! She found the solution to her money problem while attending a baby shower months after giving birth to her first son. Wanting to give the expectant mother something unique, she packed a bag for her impending hospital visit. The bag, filled with a robe, slippers, toiletries, camera, and snacks, was a big hit, and friends began asking her to make them one, too. And so, through the very supportive efforts of her husband, Momma Bag was born! Janessa, now the mother of two, lives in Miami with her husband.

E-mail: danjan18@email.msn.com

BECCA WILLIAMS, after one day on the job as a financial analyst, knew she had to escape the ten-by-ten cubicle where she was working. A year and half later with her baby daughter at her side, she founded Wall-Nutz Paint-By-Number Mural Kits from her home office in Oregon. Becca received her MBA from the University of Arizona where she studied entrepreneurship as part of the program. WallNutz is a proud sponsor of Ronald McDonald Houses and donates mural kits through that organization to ill, homebound children to brighten their rooms. Her business is presently focused on getting the Wall-Nutz product on the shelves of small and medium-size retailers and catalog distributors.

E-mail: becca@wallnutz.com

DEBBIE WILLIAMS, an organizing consultant, an author, and an educator, is the owner of Let's Get It Together. She is the publisher of the Organized Exchange e-zine, editor of OrganizedTimes.com, and is frequently quoted in national women's magazines such as *Woman's World* and *Good Housekeeping*. Her home-based business grew out of a desire to find a career that would allow her to be home with her child. At the suggestion of her husband, she explored the organizational services industry. She has now grown her company to include OrganizedU, an online training and support facility. Debbie is dedicated to helping others balance their lives with organizational techniques. She currently serves as an expert advisor for Home-Based Working Moms and BlueSuitMom.com, and is a member of WebChamber and the Texas Retailers Association.

E-mail: Debbie@organizedtimes.com

MICHELLE ZEITLIN has performed many roles in her career, but the most important one, she learned two years ago, was that of mother to her daughter. In order to spend more time as a mom, Michelle launched More Zap Productions. She glides seamlessly between high-powered corporate environments, the trend-setting world of Hollywood, and the magic of Broadway. Known in the entertainment industry as a "triple threat" (actress, singer, and dancer), Michelle has starred in feature films, sung lead vocals, and danced in world-famous ballets. She has also been featured on Broadway, produced dance casting workshops throughout the world, and choreographed for top recording artists. Michelle is an accomplished writer, having been published in the *Los Angeles Times, Reader's Digest International,* and *Seventeen.* She has also written creative/budget proposals for Universal Studios Hollywood and Paramount. Michelle has lectured to students at

UCLA Extension's writing program and Pepperdine University's business and communications program.

E-mail: ZEITLINZAP@aol.com

ROBIN ZELL left college to marry her husband as he was entering the service. Her intention was to complete her journalism degree as they became settled in their new hometown. Ten years and three children later, Robin graduated. Although she prepared her resume for a corporate career, she paused long enough to contemplate how a profession outside the home would affect her family. As she describes it, "I surrendered to motherhood and sealed my fate as a stay-at-home mom by having a fourth child." In 1999, after purchasing a Bragelet, she inquired about buying the St. Louis-based company. Robin now operates Bragelets by Robin out of her Illinois home while managing her family responsibilities. So what is a Bragelet? Bragelets are custom-made name bracelets with porcelain letters spelling the name of your child and a choice of 4 mm semi-precious stones and 14 karat gold-filled or sterling silver beads. Robin generates sales through her Web site, www.bragelets.com, and direct consumer sales. She is looking forward to expanding the company into catalog distribution.

E-mail: RLZ30@aol.com

CHAPTER ONE

Are You Ready?

A re you ready to take the risks and reap the rewards that our forty female entrepreneurs have experienced? Do you think you are ready to join the eleven million women in America who operate home-based businesses? One warning: Jumping into entrepreneurship isn't for the weak of heart. It's challenging, frightening, and physically exhausting. However, if you are an individual with the right attitude, skills set, personality, and financial ability, then launching your home-based business will be one of the most rewarding experiences of your life. You cannot imagine the incredible feeling of self-worth and accomplishment that will engulf you once your company is up and running.

Let's start our evaluation at the heart of your future business: you. Take a look at your personal traits and ask yourself the following questions:

Am I a leader?

Do I like to make decisions?

Am I competitive?

Do others turn to me for help in making decisions?

Do I plan ahead?

Do I like people?

Do I get along well with others?

Am I a self-motivator?

Am I organized?

Do I have the stamina to work long hours?

Am I prepared to lower my standard of living temporarily?

Am I prepared to dip into my savings?

Does my energy level exceed that of others around me?

Do I have a specific business ability?

Have I invented or created a product that is a solution to a particular market?

If you answered yes to the majority of these questions, you possess the right stuff to succeed at working for yourself in a home-based business.

1

What is the most important quality a woman needs to create a successful home-based business?

TAMMY HARRISON, THE QUEEN OF PIZZAZZ COMPANY

Drive and determination—and work you love! I can do a lot of things from home, but I found something in my business that keeps my mind active learning new things as well as giving me the opportunity to communicate with others. To be successful, you must have the desire to find success and not necessarily only in monetary terms. It is also crucial to be able to sell yourself and your products or service. Perhaps the most important but least recognized characteristic is the willingness to accept your mistakes. I have failed at various things over the years, but I have learned many lessons from those experiences. I make sure I remind myself of my errors so that I don't repeat them. I know I will be successful at running my business. By retaining a positive attitude about experiencing small failures along the way, I will enjoy every minute of the growth of my company and of myself.

MOLLY GOLD, GO MOM !NC.

You must be a master at multitasking, with the ability to manage the stress produced by juggling! Multitasking is probably the key component for successful working mothers, and for this you need structure. High achievers create structure for themselves and thus maximize their opportunities to deliver.

DEE ENNEN, ENNEN COMPUTER SERVICES

A positive attitude is the key to success. You need to be the "glass is half full" type of person. I've seen so many women get started in word processing only to give up as soon as they hit the first obstacle. It's sad to see. But I've seen a lot more who accept the challenge and go right ahead. They made it and love it even more because they overcame the hurdles that their business presented them.

SHERRY MAYSONAVE, EMPOWERMENT ENTERPRISES

I think the most important quality for a home-based entrepreneur is to be a self-starter. It's so easy to go to the refrigerator for a glass of juice or to linger on the couch watching the end of a movie. You have to be able to motivate yourself to make those cold calls or type out another proposal. You also have to cultivate relationships and build a network, and you need a healthy ego. Why, you might ask? Because real relationships involve taking criticism along the way, and you must be confident enough to take criticism and profit from it.

ALEX POWE ALLRED, AUTHOR AND GOLD MEDALIST

You have got to be competitive if you work from home. Most successful businesswomen are athletes whether they know it or not. They compete just as athletes do—the only difference is that business is their sport. I know it sounds funny coming from an athlete, but you need the determination that comes with being competitive, particularly when you work at home. It is so easy to let yourself be distracted.

You also have to have passion. It's an interesting fact that women business owners are more likely than men business owners to turn a personal interest or passion into a business pursuit. In my case, I had a great deal of passion about female athletes entering a male-dominated arena when I wrote my first book. I think that's what made it so easy. I believe you can build passion in many ways. Some people have a passion for the quest of whatever they are trying to do. Others have personal passions that are fueled by the need to find a solution to a problem, like a mother's passion to find work and family balance. Debbie Fields, the famous cookie maker, got her passion from going to her husband's office with cookies and having people roll their eyes when she said she was a homemaker. She found her passion in the need to do work others would validate.

Going Out on Your Own

I think the most essential quality for success is a combination of those mentioned above by our contributors plus the willingness to take risks. I have met many very talented women in my twenty years of business. Many of them hold high-level positions within Fortune 100 companies. They are self-motivated, talented, and possess a skill that is marketable. The question that these women most often ask me regarding my various home businesses is "I wish I could do what you are doing. How do you do it?" These women are missing just one thing: courage. Just like the lion in *The Wizard of Oz!* However, the lion was smart enough to see he needed courage to help him reach his goals. Unfortunately, many smart women have yet to find their courage. You need to be aware that there will be many times during this adventure when you will have to draw on your personal fortitude. You may need courage to quit your present job or the courage to hire another person as your company starts to grow.

I believe that the brave spirit of an entrepreneur can be found in just about every woman who possesses the right personality traits, intelligence, and financial ability. Yet it often requires an outside influence to give you the final push to start a home-based business.

These influences can be as numerous as the people who launch their own businesses.

At the time I began my first business, I was the mother of three children under the age of twenty months. I was in a dilemma. I was working as the community relations manager for the *Miami Herald*. After a decade of working on the paper, I had climbed up the corporate ladder and had a Rolodex full of important names and good contacts. For years, colleagues and professional peers encouraged me to go out on my own, but I held back, afraid to walk away from the security of a paycheck. I knew they were right and that the only way I could gain a large income and success was to work for myself, but I couldn't find the courage to actually do it.

Life has a funny way of helping you make decisions. Three months after giving birth to my third child, I realized it was time to ignite the fire. So I created Bailey Innovative Marketing, a full-service marketing and public relations agency focusing on women and parenting products. Owning my own business gave me the flexibility I needed as the mother of three babies and the opportunity to pursue my personal dream. The desire to balance work and family and the growing urge to create my own niche in the business world were powerful motivators.

2

What was the most compelling factor in starting your home-based business?

DIANE DESA, A VIRTUAL ASSISTANT

The flexibility factor ranks high on my list of reasons for starting A Virtual Assistant. I had more than fifteen years experience as a high-level executive assistant in law, corporations, the government, and medicine. I worked for seven years as a paralegal and department manager at an injury causation analysis consulting firm. Earlier, I had served in the Air Force, where I held many managerial positions. When my twin boys entered their teens, I realized that I desired to spend more time with them. I wanted the flexibility that comes with self-employment. Another contributing factor to my decision was the travel schedule of my long-time companion. I wanted to have the flexibility to travel with him to out-of-town seminars and conferences. Operating my own home-based business allows me to do this and not be tied to a desk forty hours a week.

JULIE AIGNER-CLARK, BABY EINSTEIN

The birth of my daughter in 1995 was the reason I started Baby Einstein. I loved spending time with her and wanted to expose her to the beauty of the arts, the things I love. As a former English literature and art teacher, I knew the power of the arts in teaching children, and I went looking for educational tools to introduce classical music, art, and languages to my baby. I found none. Then, in February 1996, *Newsweek* published a cover story on the benefits to children of early interaction with the arts. The research basically said that children who were exposed to classical music and poetry showed increased brain activity and development compared with children who did not receive this type of stimulation. What made the article so important was that it made the scientific theory understandable for the average mom like me. Here was research to support my intuition. The timing could not have been better for me. It was clear to me that there was an untapped niche in the baby market for art-related products.

I immediately started work on my first Baby Einstein video. I sent samples to various catalog companies, asking them to carry my product. After months with no responses, I went to the Toy Fair in New York, determined to find a representative of Smart Right. To my astonishment, the Toy Fair occupied three floors and featured hundreds of vendors and retailers. Overwhelmed but determined, I walked up and down the showroom floors, and, finally, on the second day, I saw three women walking together wearing Smart Right name tags. I approached one woman and forcefully placed my video in her hand. I pleaded with her to take it back to her office and watch it. I think she was so astonished that she did in fact do it. She called the next week and agreed to test-market the video in one of the Smart Right stores. The first batch flew off the shelves. That first year, I sold 100,000 videos.

JEANNINE CLONTZ, ACCURATE BUSINESS SERVICES

The desire to better my family financially and emotionally was the most influential factor in my decision to start my own home-based business. If someone were to write a book about my journey into becoming a business owner, it might be called *From Fish to Fun and Fulfillment!* For years, I worked with a fresh and frozen seafood distribution company. My career in the business included purchasing and sales, but it was my administrative skills that continuously expanded. If there was a company newsletter to be written, I was the first one to volunteer. When the business needed a new letterhead, I was the one managers came to see. I seemed to have talent in these areas, and I enjoyed all the tasks. Time and time again, my bosses told me my abilities could open doors if I chose to explore going on my own.

The death of a close aunt and a small inheritance presented my husband and me with the opportunity to explore entrepreneurship. I intended to use the money to help my husband become his own boss by starting his own business, and I enthusiastically began researching opportunities. I looked at video stores and other retail operations and finally suggested that we open a restaurant. My plan was to utilize my administrative skills to run the front operations while my husband applied his restaurant experience to the back end. Although I had my reservations about the restaurant, I was willing to pursue it in order to create a positive change for our family. My husband was even less enthusiastic. So, with his support, I turned my research around to find a new career for myself. I thought that a business in the area of administrative support would best tap into my skills and provide the most personal fulfillment. When I received my first project before I even formally launched my company, I knew the decision was the right one for me.

ALEX POWE ALLRED, AUTHOR AND GOLD MEDALIST

As a gold medalist on the U.S. bobsled team, I was four months pregnant and thought my life was at the pinnacle of fulfillment. But life's unpredictable outcomes took me from the road to the 1994 winter Olympics to a career as a home-based author. My Olympic training allowed me to live in the training facility in Lake Placid, New

York. There, I trained and lived among male and female athletes who were also training for the Olympics. Unfortunately, the International Olympic Committee decided that bobsledding was too dangerous for females and declined to allow us into the games. It was an incredible disappointment not only to the U.S. team but to female athletes around the world. Here was a group of women training as hard as the men, breaking the same bones, and even in some cases traveling to competitions with male teams, yet we couldn't compete in the Olympics.

The decision spawned a heated argument among female bob-sledders, the IOC, male team members, and other groups. My motivations to get involved were initially self-centered, but as the debates grew and a writing campaign commenced, I realized that my writing skills could be as effective as my physical ability. I had come to know women around the globe who were fighting for equality in the world of male-dominated athletics, and I soon learned that I was able to chronicle their challenges in a very persuasive manner. I spent months writing letters, filing appeals, and handling the business matters of our group. I came to the conclusion that I could be more effective doing the business stuff. If I could keep women united in communication, I knew we would be more powerful as a group. I began writing an international newsletter and soon learned that women athletes shared the same challenges around the world. The relationships I cultivated through the newsletter gave rise to my first book, *The Quiet Storm: A Celebration of Women in Sports.*

SHERRY MAYSONAVE, EMPOWERMENT ENTERPRISES

No one likes to be unhappy in a career, but often it's unhappiness that leads women to start their own businesses. I was a schoolteacher and loved the act of teaching, but I wasn't happy in the *system* of teaching. I looked at many different careers seeking a remedy for my professional frustration. I worked briefly at interior designing because I have a flair for color and had also designed jewelry in a past life. I had some success but it was not a profession that ignited my passion to help people reach their goals. During this time, the communication image industry was evolving. A friend invited me to go to San

Attacking Your Fears

It's fair to say that no matter what factors influence your decision to go out on your own, you always have some reservations and fears. All too often, women are reluctant to start their own businesses for fear of failure. We women have a tendency to like security. Just look at how safety-conscious women are managing their stock portfolios compared with men. While men are more likely to invest in high-risk securities, women tend to invest in blue chips and other conservative stocks. The fear of losing their money on investments often prevents females from taking advantage of short-term gains and thus prolongs their attainment of financial goals. Female aversion to risk may also be a contributing factor to the inequality of wages between men and women. When asked why they don't push hard for higher salaries during negotiations, women often cite reasons such as "I didn't want to risk my boss going to someone else to get the job done" or "I was afraid I'd lose my job if I asked for more." Too often, fear governs our decisions and makes us tolerate an unhappy situation. Quite often, fear prevents pursuit of our dreams.

Fear comes in many shapes and colors. When a woman begins considering a home-based business, she may experience fears of no income, no clients, and, most prominently, the fear of failure. Prior to taking your first steps into self-employment, it is important to be honest with yourself about what frightens you about starting a home-based business. If you have been contemplating starting your company for a long time, you probably can identify the fears that have held you back thus far.

To attack your fears, try this exercise:

1. Ask yourself what are your biggest fears about starting a home-based business.

2. Write each fear down on the left side of a blank piece of paper.

3. In a column down the center of the paper, list the worst-case outcome you will experience should your fears come true.

Francisco and hear the image consultant Joan Collins. Sitting in the audience that day, I realized that building a personal image consulting business was the career for me. I must say I am happy in my new profession. Now I combine the communications skills I once used in the classroom with my desire to help individuals reach their goals through nonverbal communication. I felt suddenly a passion was ignited inside me.

SANDI EPSTEIN, WORK/LIFE COACH

I went from a career in marketing strategy to life strategy work because of the following values and desires I have for what I want from my life. I want to:

- Be uncompartmentalized in my work and personal life. Who I am at work is who I am personally. My work is an expression of myself.
- Work independently with the people I choose.
- Make good money to support travel, home, and my sense of values.
- Be the primary caretaker of my children.
- Suit my diverse interests and curiosities.
- Do what I enjoy, help others, learn constantly, stretch myself.
- Be in the zone.

What does being in the zone mean? Michael Jordan talks about this. It is when somehow all your training, skills, and knowledge come together in a moment of effortlessness, and your performance is so outstanding that you break records and score seemingly impossible points.

For me, to be in the zone is, first, to get my needs met so I'm not wasting time and energy on neurotic or trivial pursuits. Next, it's to orient my life around the things that are important to me. Last, I step back and let it all come together. As a result of being in the zone, I find business comes to me—I don't have to go to it. I do higher quality work, I feel fulfilled, and I am amazed at what is possible.

4. On the right side of the paper, list a skill or experience you have that can help you to overcome the potential nightmare you fear.

If you find yourself overwhelmed by one particular fear, try the same exercise and work only on that fear. In the column of reactionary skills, list all the ways you might react to the negative outcome of your fear. Remember to draw on prior similar experiences. Was there a time in your career when you feared you would lose a client or be passed over for promotion? Think for a minute about how you reacted and how you overcame the obstacles presented to you at that time. I am sure you will agree that a new situation is always more intimidating because it includes unknown outcomes. If you look back on fears you have conquered, you probably see them as less frightening now. Another bit of advice I offer you is to practice looking at your fears in the past tense. I always imagine how I will look back on today's fears at this time next year. Often, they don't look as scary.

Let's pretend for a minute that you want to start a company that writes press releases. Your greatest fear might be having no clients and thus no income. The first items to put on your solution list should be potential customers. Second, include people you know who might become your clients or who have access to others who might become the customers for your company. Do you know a local accountant who does tax returns for small-business owners? Small-business owners are perfect targets for your press release writing business. Don't forget to list any groups or associations you belong to that can help you network to potential clients. At this point, your solutions list is probably getting much longer. Hopefully, this exercise will reveal to you that there are more solutions to your fears than you initially imagined.

If you can produce at least one good solution to each worst-case scenario, you should feel comfortable tackling your list of fears. Most fears become relatively small when broken down into a short list and laid out next to a long list of solutions.

Visualization is another good way to overcome your fears. Close your eyes and put yourself in your new role as a business owner. Watch yourself doing the tasks of your new job. Now switch the scene to one of your worst-case scenarios. How do you handle it? Do you apply a solution you've already listed or do you create a new solution? As you watch yourself solve the problems presented to you, you will realize and appreciate the scope of your experiences and skills. The most important part of this exercise is to allow yourself to feel the triumph you will experience once you have overcome the challenges of your most dreaded fear. Take a minute to feel success; it's truly contagious and addictive.

3

What was your greatest fear before you started your business?

DEBBIE WILLIAMS, LET'S GET IT TOGETHER

My greatest fear centered on how to set my fees or rate the services I was providing to my customers. I was afraid if I overcharged for my services, I would drive away potential customers. On the other hand, if I undercharged, I would lower the perceived value of my service and risk not building a profitable business. In the end, I decided that undercharging was far more damaging to the growth of my business. I could always lower prices that were too high, but the perceived value of my services must be established from the start. I really worried about the fee structure, because I was entering an industry that was fairly new to me, and I had no formal training. I couldn't get advice from people in the industry because they were afraid of price fixing. I would suggest to those entering new fields that they consider testing various price levels prior to setting a fixed fee structure.

DARCY LYONS, A GARDEN PARTY

Fear of failure. In some ways I think it was also the fear of success even though I had a strong desire to do well on my own. I had worked for many different employers, and I knew I was missing out on the satisfaction of creating something from ground zero and the excitement of building something really big. I finally decided to put the fear aside. I told myself to take the advice of Nike and "Just do it!" In my case, it helped to have a partner who was a good friend to share my feelings of uncertainty with. Partnership is a good way to cut your fears in half. Fortunately, I also have her to share our success with. Now that I've gotten over my initial fears, I look back and am amazed at how far our company has come.

BECCA WILLIAMS, WALLNUTZ, INC.

In creating WallNutz, I thought, here I am investing so much time and money and what if the business ultimately fails? I've always had things that were important to me work out. I still find it difficult when my MBA classmates ask me how my business is going. I'd like to tell them it's been wildly successful and we are making tons of money, but that would be far from the truth. However, I was recently very proud when I saw myself listed as "President and Founder of WallNutz" in our alumni magazine. I manage my fears by seeing failure in a different way. I know that even if WallNutz isn't as successful as I'd hoped, the experience has taught me a great deal and given me new ideas and led me to people with whom I may start more successful future ventures.

TAMMY HARRISON, THE QUEEN OF PIZZAZZ COMPANY

Although I am a very confident person, I was fearful of how I would manage the emotional and physical demands of a business as well as being a mother and wife. Being a mom is difficult in and of itself. Trying to run a business is difficult. Trying to combine the two without a clear line between them takes a lot of energy. My husband started his own business when I was pregnant with our first child. I handled the office duties while he handled the customers and product. I got a good sense then of what types of duties and paperwork were necessary to keep afloat, work toward success, and take care of our family and myself. Then, after having my first child, I telecommuted at my regular job, and all I had to worry about was the work I was assigned. I started my own business over a year ago. I am the sole proprietor and handle everything from billing to marketing to doing the work. This takes a lot of emotional and physical energy.

Combine that with taking care of my children during the day, and I am beat by bedtime!

Taking Risks

Behind every fear is our unwillingness to take risks and follow our dreams. As with most things in life, the level of risk increases with the degree of fear we experience. The more we fear something, the less likely we are to risk it. The reluctance to take risks is something we all share in varying degrees. From the time we are infants, all of us establish comfort zones where we are safe from adversity. This desire to be comfortable continues as we grow into our teens. It is shaped by personal relationships and experiences we have throughout those years.

So what does this have to do with starting a home-based business? Let's look at two fictitious children, Karen and Susan. Karen's mother has been a manager at a local retailer for twenty years. She has earned a few middle manager promotions, but she knows she will never reach a position that will satisfy her personal goals. Every evening, within Karen's earshot, her mother voices her frustration to Karen's father. She complains that she wishes she could leave to do her own thing, but she just can't say goodbye to the benefits and the regular paycheck. She admits that she will keep being miserable, unless something better and risk-free comes along. Now look at the other child, Susan. Her mother ran an invitation business out of her home while Susan was a toddler. Sales slipped and her mother closed up shop as Susan became involved in sports and other after-school activities where her mother had to drive her. Then, when Susan started middle school and the school bus took the kids to games, her mother started a soap company in the basement. It took off, and two major retailers now carry her products. Which child do you think will have a healthier attitude toward risk when she grows up? Susan, of course. She has witnessed firsthand her mother's failure and success. She has watched her mother exhibit a high level of self-confidence, a quality that grows with the willingness to take risks.

By the time we reach adulthood, we not only have developed our level of tolerance for risk but have applied it numerous times to the decision-making process. A high school graduate with a low level of self-confidence and high level of risk aversion may follow her high school sweetheart to a big out-of-state college rather than risk losing the relationship to distance or may select a smaller, less academic university to avoid the risk of failing scholastically. In life and particularly in business, the more dangerous the risk we take, the greater fear it generates. But, the greatest risks also yield the most satisfying outcomes. As the old saying goes, "The greater the joy, the greater the pain that precedes it."

4

What was the greatest risk you took to start your business?

LESLEY SPENCER, HBWM.COM

I risked my home to start my business. My husband and I started building a modest home when I was about four months pregnant. I was working full time as a PR/tour coordinator for a golf school and had every intention of returning to my job. We moved into our home when I was seven months pregnant and had just enough time to unpack, get settled, and decorate the baby's room when my due date rolled around. All seemed well. However, my world did a complete 360 when our baby was born. When I saw her, my heart overflowed with joy, and I immediately fell in love with her.

During my maternity leave, I slowly but painfully came to the realization that I could not leave my baby for nine to ten hours a day. After much consideration and with a wonderfully supportive husband, I explained to my employer that I could not continue working full time. Since we depended on my salary for our month-to-month expenses, I decided that I would try to find freelance work.

I went out soliciting work (something I was too afraid and too proud to do in the past), but I was determined to find something, and I had the best motivator in the world. We knew if I failed, we faced having to put our new home on the market. Nevertheless, it was a chance we wanted to take. We cut our bills by canceling cable television, call-waiting, and eating out. My husband took twenty-cent packs of noodles to work every day for lunch. We got lower quotes on insurance and changed carriers to save some money. We used coupons for groceries and installed ceiling fans to reduce our electric bills. When one of our cars died, I took my husband to the bus stop so he could get to work. We were scraping by on very little, but we were happy. I did make just enough, almost to the penny, to help pay our bills. We did not have to sell our home.

DEBBIE GIOQUINDO, PERSONAL TOUCH TRAVEL

The greatest risk I took in starting my home-based business was investing my personal savings to get the company off the ground. My fear was that if I failed, I would lose my investment. My fears were compounded by the realization that failure could open me up to lawsuits by angry travelers.

Another risk I took was hiring independent contractors to work for me when I needed to expand my support system. These employees represent the agency, and I need to be certain they uphold the same business values I do.

ALEX POWE ALLRED, AUTHOR AND GOLD MEDALIST

Money always seems to be the major risk when launching a business. When I decided to become a full-time author, the costs were mammoth. For my first book, I needed to conduct lengthy phone interviews and, unfortunately for my budget, the majority of them were long distance. In addition, I had to travel. During this time, my husband and I were really struggling personally, so it was hard to justify to him that I was doing the right thing for us. But I knew this was right, I knew I could make it work, I had this undeniable feeling of success. Still, my husband and I fought about telephone bills and other expenses. We were under great strain, but finally the gamble has paid off.

KAITLAND THORSTENSON, CERTIFIED PUBLIC ACCOUNTANT

The greatest risk I took in launching my home-based accounting company was doing it in a city new to me, with no clients and no customer base. I had just moved to Minneapolis with my former husband and children and wanted to find a way to use my skills in accounting. Before then, I had worked with families of lesser means who were trying to run small businesses. I sought to recreate the personal fulfillment this gave me by going into business for myself. To my delight, I acquired my first client by being in the right place at the right time. I was in a computer store purchasing updates for my accounting software to launch my business. A gentleman was in the same aisle. He was not sure what he was looking for, and I helped him pick out an accounting program he could use to keep his books. It turned out he had hired an accountant who had made mistakes and created errors in his records. My short talk with him led to weekend work restoring his records. That gave me the confidence to go after additional work. My home office allows me to help small-business owners by giving them an alternative to the costly services of a full-service accounting firm.

The Loneliness Factor

One risk that is important to consider before you decide to launch a home-based business is the feeling of isolation that can develop from working alone. If you become one of the millions of women making the transition from traditional office to home office, you may find the lack of human interaction will be startling. If you enjoyed lunching with coworkers, gathering around the coffeemaker to discuss the latest episode of *Ally McBeal*, or brainstorming with your peers on a new marketing idea, the isolation from others may take some getting used to. Mothers in particular describe the feeling as a desire for adult conversation and human interaction. Even if your business involves visiting clients or speaking to people on the phone, there will be times when you feel alone. There will be a day when you look at your computer screen and realize that there is only one person in the world who wholly believes in what you are doing and how you are pulling it off. Fatigue from working long hours may contribute to your despair. If you are aware this can happen, you will be on the alert to create opportunities to interact with others and keep your creative juices flowing.

5

How do you control the loneliness of working from home?

LESLEY SPENCER, HBWM.COM

Working alone doesn't have to be lonely. Working from home certainly has its advantages, but most home-based workers will admit to a few disadvantages, including working alone. You may not miss the office politics, but what about the daily interactions with other adults? It takes time to adjust to not having coworkers to chat with or bounce ideas off. Our coworkers serve as a form of support when we work in a regular office. Without them, we have to learn to turn to others for support.

Organizations serve a vital role in keeping home-based business owners connected to the outside world. Many times fellow professionals can become the outlet you need to bounce ideas off or to get new and fresh ideas. Home-Based Working Moms (www.HBWM.com) does just that through various channels offered through their membership, including the members' listserv. Members can post messages and instantly have five or ten helpful responses. Associations often offer weekly e-newsletters, print newsletters, message boards, informational Web sites, and many other opportunities to connect members for support and networking.

In addition to associations, here are other ways to connect with people to help keep your life balanced and enjoyable.

Get Involved

- Take a course in a business subject or a subject you've always been interested in.
- Schedule an occasional lunch with friends or ex-coworkers.
- Find other home-based workers in your area to meet with.
- Get involved in a neighborhood group or play group.
- Find a new hobby involving others.
- Use the Internet to connect with others via e-mail, bulletin boards, and chat rooms.
- Join your local Chamber of Commerce or other organizations and attend the meetings.
- Volunteer for community activities (that's networking too).

Get Away

- Plan time for yourself and your family. Don't let work interfere with your happiness and health.
- Plan a weekend getaway once a month, if possible. It doesn't have to be an expensive trip. Visit family or friends, go camping, rent a cabin.
- Make a date with your spouse at least once a month so that you can stay connected as a couple.
- Set aside a few minutes every morning or evening to revitalize yourself.
- Read a book, say a prayer, meditate, listen to soothing music.
- Talk a walk. Walking is good not only for your body but also for your mind.

Find Help

- Hire part-time help to do some of the work that is bogging you down.

- If you have children, look into part-time childcare options.
- Consider a Mother's Day Out program, part-time preschool, or hiring a baby-sitter to come in when needed.
- Contact your local high schools or colleges to see if they have an early childhood development program where you can get names of potential baby-sitters.

A Word About the Neighbors

Another risk you may need to consider is the attitude of your neighbors. Operating a home-based business can affect neighbors if your type of operation requires clients to visit your office, employees to park in your yard each day, or frequent deliveries to your home. It's always good to get the reaction of neighbors in case they have negative opinions about you running a business from your home. Take the time to help them understand any traffic, noise, or sanitation effects your endeavor will have on them and their property. A little consideration can go a long way to gaining the support of potentially angry neighbors.

Gathering Resources

So, do you think you are ready to take the risks, confront your fears, cope with the loneliness, deal with the neighbors, and pursue a career as a home-based business owner? Well, then, it's time to start doing your homework and gathering your resources. Careful preparation from the beginning of building your business will save you time, aggravation, and possibly money later on. In fact, the Small Business Administration cites lack of good preparation as one of the top reasons why so many small businesses fail. You deserve congratulations, though, because you are taking the first step in preparing yourself by reading a book like this one. Fortunately for you, the rapid growth of home-based business owners has spawned an equal growth of available resources.

RECOMMENDED READING

Edwards, Paul and Sarah. *Home-Based Business for Dummies* (IGD Books Worldwide, 2000) and *Working from Home: Everything You Need to Know About Living and Working Under the Same Roof* (Putnam Publishing, 1999)

Ennen, Dee. *Success from Home: The Word Processing Business* (Adams-Blake Publishing, 2000)

Huff, Priscilla Y. *101 Best Home-Based Businesses for Women: Everything You Need to Know About Getting Started on the Road to Success* (Prima Publishing, 1998)

Parlapiano, Ellen H. and Patricia Cobe. *Mompreneurs: A Mother's Step-by-Step Guide to Work-at-Home Success* (Berkeley Publishing, 1996)

Stansell, Kimberly. *Bootstrapper's Success Secrets: 151 Tactics for Building Your Business on a Shoestring Budget* (Career Press, 1997)

Weltman, Barbara. *The Complete Idiot's Guide to Starting Your Own Home-Based Business* (Macmillan Publishing Company, 2000)

Your local bookstore or library carries a number of great titles devoted to home-based business. The most popular authors who write on home-based business are listed in the box.

The Internet serves as another great resource for future entrepreneurs. There are literally hundreds of sites designed for home-based working women and the issues of small-business owners. The combination of information from several sites could keep you reading for weeks. One of my favorite sites is Home-Based Working Moms (www.HBWM.com) which provides information, a newsletter, and advice. HBWM.com also has a strong and supportive community of working mothers who are in all stages of their businesses.

Among other informational sites not exclusively for home-based working women but offering useful information are IBM's small-business center (www-1.ibm.com/businesscenter), which offers useful tools for small businesses and Smartmoney.com (www.smartmoney.com/ask/index), which contains advice and a business plan template. At the risk of demonstrating the self-assertiveness that you must demonstrate as a small-business owner, I invite you to visit our site (www.bluesuitmom.com). It contains a women-owned directory, together with useful work and family-balance information that you'll find helpful once your company is up and running.

Networking with other home-based and small-business owners is a way to learn quickly and avoid mistakes made by others. To find support groups in your area, consult your local Chamber of Commerce, the economic development committee in your city, and area colleges and universities. Many government agencies sponsor educational meetings for small-business owners. If there is a government center in your city, inquire at the special events office.

Membership in a business association provides you with the opportunity to network with weathered business owners. The National Foundation for Women Business Owners (NFWBO), a nonprofit research and leadership development foundation, is recognized as the premier source of information on women business owners and their enterprises worldwide. You can visit their Web site (www.nfwbo.org) to find the nearest chapter in your area. Another association to consider is the American Association of Home-Based Businesses, Inc. (www.ahbb.org).

My final suggestion for finding resources is to look at the people around you. As you think about your new career, reevaluate the relationships you have with professional acquaintances or vendors. Suddenly, the freelance graphic designer who created your ads while you were a big company manager can be a wealth of information on the dos and don'ts of building a service business. I bet she knows which tax forms need to be filed or how to collect delinquent accounts payable from your former employer. Take a good look around and see who you know that is already running a small business. They can provide you with a wealth of firsthand information.

6

What resources did you use to help you build your home-based business?

WENDY HARRIS, NATIONAL ASSOCIATION OF MEDICAL BILLERS

I sought out a number of resources. The most worthwhile was an entrepreneurial class offered by our Chamber of Commerce. It was a fifteen-week class that taught topics such as money management, marketing, building a business on the Web, legal issues, loan preparation, networking, business plans, and keeping track of accounts receivable. The entire program was well-rounded, and I received a lot of very useful information. The best part of the class was I became a member of the Chamber and had access to free business advice through the Service Corps of Retired Executives (SCORE). This is a group of retired businessmen who give their time to help new business owners. Luck seemed to go in my direction. The person who helped me was actually a young gentleman, Peter Desmond, who happened to be a CPA! His skills and insights helped me more than I can describe.

MOLLY GOLD, GO MOM !NC.

Truthfully? I didn't use that many resources. My start was more like flying by the seat of my pants. I used momentum and enthusiasm as much as anything else. Foolish giddiness! I have a few family members who are self-employed, so they got us going with the basics for county licenses, state incorporation, and other legal matters. Beyond that, I used BusPro software to create my business plan. My biggest business resource is my father, who is also my COO. Now that we are

RECOMMENDED WEB SITES

Following are Internet resources to get you started with your own home-based business:

BlueSuitMom.com: www.bluesuitmom.com

Catalyst: www.catalystwomen.org/home.html

*Entrepreneur/*Entreprenuer.com:
   www.entrepreneur.com

Federal Trade Commission: www.ftc.gov

Forum for Women Entrepreneurs: www.fwe.org

Home-Based Working Moms.com: www.hbwm.com

Inc.com: www.inc.com

Mothers' Home Business Network: www.mhbn.com

National Foundation for Women Business Owners:
   www.nfwbo.org

Small Business Association: www.sbaonline.com

up and running, I use my customers and potential customers as resources for learning what my market wants in our product. I now have a database of lifestyle features my customers would like to see in our calendars. This is my most useful resource today.

DIANNE DESA, A VIRTUAL ASSISTANT

I enrolled in and successfully completed the virtual training program (VTP) at AssistUniversity (www.assistu.com). I am confident that the training and access to resources I received enabled me to build my successful virtual assistant practice. I also learned a lot through the

FINDING RESOURCES FOR YOUR
HOME-BASED BUSINESS ENDEAVOR

- Subscribe to *Entrepreneur* and other periodicals written for small-business owners.
- Visit your local library or bookstore for books on home-based businesses.
- Call your local Chamber of Commerce to find programs and lectures.
- Join a local chapter of the National Foundation for Women Business Owners
- Surf the Internet
- Visit message boards and chat rooms on HBWM.com or MHBN.com
- Tune in to *Working from Home* with Paul and Sarah Edwards on the Home & Garden Television Network
- Talk to people you know who are home-based business owners.

International Virtual Assistants Association (www.ivaa.org). This organization is a wonderful resource for both novices and experienced virtual assistants to meet, exchange ideas and resources, and make valuable contacts with colleagues and friends.

BECCA WILLIAMS, WALLNUTZ, INC.

My father-in-law is a successful entrepreneur and has many contacts from whom I've asked advice. I've worked with the Berger Entrepreneurships program at the University of Arizona and, although it didn't actually work out, they were willing to sponsor a summer intern for WallNutz. Friends from the MBA program at the U of A have been helpful in brainstorming, reading through drafts of various business plans, researching and setting up an accounting, inventory, and invoicing system, and even helping operate booths at trade shows. SCORE provided me with a fantastic advisor in the toy industry who taught me standard retail practices that I needed to know in order to speak to buyers. Finally, the Internet has been an incredible resource. In the first few months, I've found good information on HBWM.com, WAHM.com, and bluesuitmom.com. I also joined two e-groups of female business owners that network and share information. Both groups have been valuable from a business standpoint, and, in addition, I've found women friends with interests and challenges similar to my own.

Teresa Kirby and Darcy Lyons, A Garden Party

We consulted almost anything we could get our hands on. We subscribed to garden-related magazines and garden retail catalogs. Our travels took us to every garden boutique and mass retailer in California, or so it seemed. Of course, we also surfed any and all garden-related Web sites. Our friends also gave us a stream of information and guidance. Finally, we talked to consultants for other party-based sales companies such as the Pampered Chef, Party Lights, and Country Peddler.

CHAPTER TWO

Effects on Your Family

The launch of your home-based business will greatly affect you and your family. Hence, the first people you should discuss your ideas about self-employment and your home-based business with are your family members. The discussion might be between your spouse or significant other but in many cases may involve older children. If your plans involve the support of your extended family, whether they live in your home or not, they should also be included in your initial discussions. Together, you will want to discuss your personal goals, your professional expectations, the financial effect on your family, and how you expect to succeed in business.

To open the channels of communication ask your family the following questions:

1. Is my home-based business going to be the primary source of income for the family?
2. Who will be the primary childcare giver?
3. Will you invest personal money into my company?
4. Will I work full time or part time?
5. How long are you willing to wait until my company is profitable?

6. How much time away from my home responsibilities are you willing for me to devote to my company?
7. Are you willing for me to travel for business, if necessary?
8. How much money do you hope I will make per month or year?

The answers to these questions will help clarify expectations among all members of your family as well as help you write your business plan (see chapter 4). It is imperative to the success of your home-based business that you meet both your personal and professional goals. You want to feel good about what you are creating from the beginning because, when times get difficult, you will need to draw on these emotions to keep you going.

Keep in mind your goals as you move forward in determining the type of business you seek to build. I often hear women say that they want to start their own home-based business so that they can have greater flexibility and work fewer hours. I always cringe at this statement because, although they may be able to enjoy greater flexibility, they will be surprised at the long hours involved in owning a business. Once you have begun to set up your business, you may find that you have never worked harder or put in longer hours. It's hard to describe how hard you can work when your determination to get your business off the ground kicks in. If this is the first time you are putting your passion to work, your energy may surprise you!

Consider Debbi, a communication specialist working for a large company in a traditional office. If she needs to send a press kit overnight to a magazine, she asks an administrative assistant to take care of it. The assistant will fill out the packaging slip, find the right size box, and take it to the FedEx center. If, later, Debbi is self-employed running a public relations business from home, she will have to do all this herself, including driving to the FedEx drop-off center. What once took her five minutes, now will take twenty minutes or more. If you were working forty hours a week managing a communications department, chances are it will take you sixty hours to do the same job working for yourself. The time you actually work on providing your service to your clients is diminished greatly, due to administrative tasks. You may gain a whole new appreciation for the accounting, human resources, and marketing functions that go on behind the scenes in your current job!

A good way to imagine the scope of your new responsibilities is to look at the corporate organizational chart of your present employer. Each department listed on the chart represents a set of tasks you will have to perform in some way while setting up and running your own company. I remember the first time I called the phone company to hook up business lines for my office. As a marketing and business development executive, I never knew there were so many variations of phone service. Today, I know way too much!

Most women will tell you that the time and commitment required to operate a home-based business are enormous, but so is the benefit to their families. In my case, running my own business enables me to attend school plays, eliminate out-of-town business travel, and remove the salary cap imposed by my former employer. There are days when I speak on the phone to CEOs of large corporations and minutes later I am in the classroom of my daughter, Madison. I schedule meetings around field trips and take long runs in the morning to keep up my marathon training. My children enjoy the fact that Mommy is not rushing out the door every morning to go to the office, and my husband appreciates an increase in the number of home-cooked meals. I gain personal fulfillment in having a professional career and at the same time controling my daily schedule.

7

What effect does your home-based business have on your family?

WENDY HARRIS, NATIONAL ASSOCIATION OF MEDICAL BILLERS

My husband loves me being home because I can work on my business and do laundry at the same time! My boys like having me there when they get home from school. I can be Mom first and Mrs. Businesswoman second. I can work my business at night and when the boys are at school. I get to attend school functions that I never could when I worked full time. I can be at home when the boys are sick. Recently, my son, who is fourteen years old, five-feet-eight, 210 pounds and very athletic and also very clumsy, was playing a ball game at school and took a shot directly to the bridge of his nose. It bled, and X rays revealed it was broken. I was able to be there the entire time, tending him through the night so that he didn't roll onto his back while he was sleeping. If I worked outside my home, I would have been too tired to go to work and had to deal with an angry boss the next day. I never need to schedule appointments to accommodate someone else's schedule. My schedule is my own.

DIANE BALLARD, DKB ASSOCIATES

The experience of owning a home-based business has been positive for my children, my husband, and me. It's a win-win situation for everyone. The kids benefit because they see me more often. Even though I may be in the office working some nights, they are happy to be in the same room with me. They usually color, do homework, or play games beside me. Also, I don't miss the long commute. I cook a decent supper, and we can eat as a family because I do not arrive home late every day.

DIANE DESA, A VIRTUAL ASSISTANT

Our life is much more relaxed and stress-free now that I have a home office. I see more of my boys, I'm able to keep closer tabs on them, and I am much more a part of their lives. My companion also enjoys my working at home. I am happier, and he sees the results of that. I'm also able to cook tastier and healthier meals. I love to cook, and working at home has made it easier for me to indulge this passion. When I was in the early stages of my business, the only thing I did was work and try to keep my family afloat. However, my family remained extremely supportive of my efforts because they knew my building a successful home-based business would make me a very happy, fulfilled person. We all know that when Mom is happy, everybody is happy! Now that I am successfully working at home, life is not so stressed or hectic. It has had a calming effect on us all.

Shannon Rubio, TheSmileBox.com

Ugh! It has been pretty stressful, to be totally honest. I think I am setting a good example for my children as far as working and entrepreneurship, but it has been really difficult. I work long hours and get very tired. I always feel like I could be a better parent when I am in the middle of working. My husband is very supportive, but that does not lessen the guilt. There is also inventory all over my house, as well as gold glitter from the boxes everywhere, which we cannot seem to get rid of! Our garage is full of inventory and supplies for the business. We have all had to rearrange our lives to squish this business into our home.

Lara Pullen, Environmental Health Consulting, Inc.

Owning my home-based business has been incredible! I am at home, I am doing something that I enjoy, and I am earning more than I did with my employer. I am happiest with the balance of working and taking care of my family. That happiness translates into a happier family and a happier me.

Debbie Williams, Let's Get It Together

I think the most positive effect my business has had on our entire family is that Mama is happy and fulfilled. Happiness is contagious, and using my education and work experience stimulates me and helps me grow as a person. I really think I'm a better mother and wife for it, looking for other outlets for communication, creativity, and sharing of ideas with others besides my family.

I've grown as a businesswoman, which has developed my tolerance for others and improved my negotiation skills. That's crucial when you're a wife and mother!

Positive Impact on Children

One of the greatest positive impacts of a parent owning a home-based business can be on your children. For mothers, being an entrepreneur gives you the opportunity to set examples of commitment, dedication, and overall high work ethics to your children. You can tell children a hundred times that hard work and devotion pay off, but if they actually watch how hard you work to accomplish things, they learn the lesson. My husband, Tim, has a favorite saying about parenting he read somewhere, "If you tell a child, he will remember. If you show a child, he will repeat. If you involve a child, he will learn."

If you ask my six-year-old son, Owen, what his mother does for work, he will tell you that she is writing a book about hard-working moms and she is on the Internet. It's not exactly right, but almost. Just the other night his friend Hunter slept over. As I was tucking them into bed, I heard the following conversation:

"After my mom tucks us in, she goes into her office to work," said Owen.

"What kind of work does your mom do?" Hunter asked.

"She is writing a book with lots of chapters. Sometimes she uses the wrong words or doesn't spell them right, but it's okay because she has a person who tells her that she did it wrong, and she corrects her mistakes," replied Owen.

As I kissed them both good night, Hunter asked me, "Will you put me in your book, too, Mrs. Bailey?"

"Sure," I answered.

Well, here it is, Hunter. You are in my book.

The point to this is that through my actions Owen was learning about the world of publishing, learning that even his mom makes mistakes, and it's okay to recognize your mistakes and fix them. I left his bedroom that night with a sense of pride that my children were benefiting in more ways than I truly knew.

Teach your children your business and get them involved early in helping you. Remember, though, treat them as you would employees. You would never yell at an employee, so extend the same professional courtesy to your children.

Pay your children for the jobs they do for your business, and they will gain an appreciation for the work/reward concept. I pay my first graders a dollar an hour to put labels correctly on postcards. If they do a good job, they get paid and come back and ask me to do the job again. This simple lesson goes a long way in instilling good work ethics in our children.

Another important lesson I am teaching my children is to love their work. I truly love what I do, and my children know it. They witness my excitement when I get an e-mail from a working mom expressing her appreciation for advice found on BlueSuitMom.com or when a newspaper features my site in a positive story. I feel confident that my four children will grow up to follow professions that they enjoy because my husband and I have set that benchmark for them.

Perhaps the most important lesson children of entrepreneurs learn is the willingness to take risks. As you demonstrate your high tolerance for taking risks and the self-confidence associated with it, you are saying to your child that it's okay to try, even if it means the possibility of failing. Imagine the sense of relief for a teenager to know it's okay to pursue dreams.

I was reminded recently of the effect my work has on my children. My daughter Madison came home from school and proceeded to tell me about her day. She described how she gave her oral book report to the class. "Mommy, almost everyone in the class did their research on the Internet like I did," she explained. "Yep, but I knew my report was going to be the best, because I was the only one whose mom owns the Internet." Her expression of pride reassured me that my work was having a positive effect on my family.

8

How has your business rubbed off on your children?

ALEX POWE ALLRED, AUTHOR AND GOLD MEDALIST

I love to see that my five- and seven-year-old are grasping what I do more and more each day. I see my daughter developing a great interest in books and computers. Just the other day, as she was selecting a *Little House on the Prairie* book at the library, she looked up at me and asked, "Mom, is this one of the books you wrote?" It's a great feeling when you know you are setting a good example for your children.

DARCY LYONS, A GARDEN PARTY

It's been a fun learning experience for all of us. My four-year-old has been developing his mathematical skills by counting inventory. My two-year-old helps, too. He picks up stray packing peanuts and places them in the trash.

Maintaining Work and Family Balance

But how do you manage a business while meeting the demands of a family? You'll soon see that there are about as many solutions as there are Cheerios down my sofa. This is where your family goals and lifestyle most influence your business plans.

I maintain my work and family through careful planning and by establishing processes within the family. As the oldest of nine children, I learned at an early age that you have to delegate to manage a household. Growing up, it was my job to vacuum the upstairs bedrooms before going to school. To me, managing work and family is all about time. I try to limit the amount of unproductive time in my day. In our house, we have created processes and systems for almost everything. We have a system for showers, laundry, homework, business travel, extracurricular activities, and household chores. We still rush from one task to the next, but by having a process in place, we control time-wasters like looking for lost shoes. I have a rule that no one should ever walk in from the car with empty hands. This way, shoes, homework, and half-eaten snacks make it into the house and save time finding them later. I apply the same rule when walking from one side of the house to the other. Also, the entire family knows that if there is something at the foot of the stairs, it's your job to take it with you and put it where it belongs upstairs. Every saved minute adds up by the end of the day!

I learned early on in trying to maintain balance that I must lower my standards when it comes to unimportant tasks. I remember the day when that lightbulb went off in my head. I was stressing over towels that weren't folded according to my standards, and two toddlers were tugging on my leg as I tried to refold them. I suddenly realized I was driving myself crazy worrying about towels. Now, I direct my efforts to more essential tasks, like reading to my children, earning a living, and exercising once in a while.

One thing that helps me balance work and family is my approach to cooking. Although my friends make fun of me, I know they secretly envy my strategy. My rule: Never cook without doubling the recipe. If I am making pasta sauce, I double the recipe and freeze half. I also cook all the week's meals on Sunday afternoon. My mother always said, "Never turn on the oven for one item." When I come back from the grocery store on Sunday afternoon, instead of shelving all the food, I unpack directly into the oven, casserole pan, or Crock-Pot. Sunday dinner is normally meat and potatoes but, while the oven is on, a chicken or turkey breast is roasting. I always keep a pasta sauce brewing on the stove. Having homemade sauce means I only have to boil noodles during the week. Monday night is always a Crock-Pot dinner with vegetables and meat. On a busy day, all I have to do in the morning is plug in dinner for that night. Planning my meals on Sunday when I'm rested allows me to avoid stress at the end of each workday when I'm tired.

9

How do you manage both business and family?

ALEX POWE ALLRED, AUTHOR AND GOLD MEDALIST

It's sometimes tricky to work and balance children. I have a sixteen-month-old at home with me during the day when my other two children are at school. He is a real handful. I think I'm going to be an Olympic hurler by the time he is five. Sometimes the children get in the way of my work. While I was working on my second book,

Entering the Mother Zone, I was tracking down model Kathy Ireland. She is so busy with her clothing line, special appearances, and work-out videos that I needed to assure her agent that I was organized and together, but, in the midst of this negotiation, I suddenly realized why my house was so suspiciously quiet. My three-year-old daughter had figured out how to trip the special lock on the front door and had taken my one-year-old daughter for a walk down the street. Thank God for mobile phones (invented by a woman, by the way). I was able to walk around the house searching for my little people and happened to look out a window and spot my babies. Gasp! I hung up and sprinted out of the house. While I was able to capitalize on the "catching her in the act" moment and punish my daughter, I never heard from Kathy Ireland's people again. I always tell my daughter that she cost me a supermodel. All kidding aside, unexpected moments like these are part of the parental balancing act.

Today, there is no school, and it would be a waste of time for me to try to do computer work with the children at home. So, we did all kinds of errands together. Last stop was Blockbuster. I've timed it so that while the baby sleeps, the older ones can watch their movie and I can get two good hours work done. Tonight, when everyone is asleep, I will put in another two hours. I'd like to get more than four hours today, but this is the reality. I know a lot of people who are determined to get a certain amount done each day but at what expense? I'd love eight hours, but I'll take four, knowing that no one feels neglected. To me, working from home is about meeting my family's needs.

For years, I would get mad because no one seemed to care about what I accomplished. After taking the attitude that the home is my office and all these other "duties" are part of managing the office, I was able to focus more, get less frustrated, and give more quality time to everything and everyone.

JULIE AIGNER-CLARK, BABY EINSTEIN

I try to separate work from family time. I feel like when I am with the kids, I want to be with kids, so I try not to dilute my attention when we are together. Once the lights are out, I work until midnight.

TAMMY HARRISON, THE QUEEN OF PIZZAZZ COMPANY

I could sit and work all day long and just ignore the kids or vice versa, but I constantly remind myself why I want to work from home! I do not work on Tuesday and Thursday afternoons as that is kid time, and we plan and play on those days. I also do not work very much on the weekends, only checking my mail but not doing much else unless I have a deadline looming.

Most days, I spend four morning hours working with and around the kids. After lunch I check my mail one more time before going to town to pick up our daughter from school. Then we return home and all lay down for naptime—a very important part of my day! After nap, it is usually time to read with the kids or get dinner started and start the evening duties of playing as a family, reading, bathing, and getting the kids in bed. I then spend about four or more hours at the computer doing work that requires concentration. This is very precious time to me as this is when I am doing work that will make or break my business.

MOLLY GOLD, GO MOM !NC.

My tips to keep work and family in balance are pretty basic:

1. Have a dedicated workspace that is entirely separate from your family world. By having a separate space, you force yourself to have your head in the game when you are with your family and in the game when you are at work. I know this, because my desk used to be in the kitchen...AAK! I was checking e-mails while making peanut butter sand-wiches, spending more time distracted with work than focused on the kids. In your workspace, make a place for your kids with quiet activities like a Lego table, coloring supplies, blocks, books, and puzzles. There are days when everyone needs to be together, and you should have sup-plies on hand to accommodate company. Let your children know they are welcome when you say so; even make it a regular event. "Every Friday you can play in Mommy's office and do your special work."

2. Set dedicated work hours, even if they are in the middle of the night. This again helps keep you focused on a single task. You also need your work hours to be free from interruptions. I get ten times as much done in half the time if I work in one sitting.

3. Revisit the roles of each spouse and rethink conventional parenting roles. Focus on what needs to be done to run your house and then split things up based on who can do what when. It is that simple. Consistency of one parent is the necessary element. It is a treasure when we can all four be together, and we make a marked effort to do that. It can be easy to get in the habit of tag teaming, the you-take-them-then-I'll-take-them routine. The kids know we both work and that Mommy's first and favorite responsibility is our family, and that helps.

4. Say no and then, at the right time, say yes to family fun. Having two careers at home, we find that work can rule the roost too easily. So we try to restrict work to our set schedules, honor family time, and then choose family first for social times as well. It is far too easy to give away all of your time to things that don't matter. We love to play with the boys in the park, go on bike rides, out to lunch or whatever on the weekend. This gives us family time that's relaxing for all of us. My husband, Loren, opts out of week-night business functions unless they are critical, so we can each take a child for bedtime, letting them know at the end of every day they have our full attention and love.

5. Play and laugh. I do best when I get my runs in four or five times a week, and the kids are happiest when they are outside riding their bikes and playing hard. If I sprinkle the week with a play date or two, we are all much happier. We all need to have our creative needs met and this helps do this. We laugh, see friends, have adventures, and everyone's needs get met on a certain level. If I make sure we all play and laugh, it is easier to work at night because I feel like I

have a life. I'm pretty social, so calming the chatter bug for pure ambition has been a radical change. My good friends know I don't have a life outside my family unit and work. But think about that. What really matters when you die is the kind of mother, wife, daughter, and then friend you were. So we do have quite a life, very focused and very full.

HEIDI PERRY, HOME BUSINESS ONLINE

My husband and I are both very entrepreneurial. Even when my husband had a full-time job, we had another business going on the side. It's in our blood, something we need to do. We also feel strongly about being home with our children and love the idea of homeschooling them. So, being home-based is a natural for us. Add to this church responsibilities, being on a children's theatre/music committee, lots of service projects, baseball and basketball games, ballet, and numerous music lessons, and we are, well, the all-American, active family.

People ask how we do it. That seems funny to me because, to be quite frank with you, I wonder how everyone else does it. Admittedly, there are days when I feel like I've completely lost my marbles. However, I will tell you that, in some ways, homeschooling actually helps me to keep my business and my life organized.

When homeschool is a problem, I find that my business has problems also. When homeschool goes smoothly, my business accomplishments soar. They are intertwined. Don't get the wrong impression here. I'm not one of those super-organized women who has her whole life planned out and goes about accomplishing every task with a very calm exterior. Yikes, that doesn't describe me at all.

I don't do all these things because I'm organized. Rather, I organize because I've chosen to put all of these things into my life. I organize purely out of necessity.

I'll share with you some things I've learned over the years of what has and hasn't worked for me in homeschooling and running a home-based business at the same time.

1. First and foremost, I had to know why I wanted to home-school, just as I did when I wanted to be self-employed. I

had to know that I really wanted to do it so that I could be committed and stay focused.

2. I've just had to accept that my house will never look like something out of *Better Homes and Gardens*. I have children home all day, and I work much of the day in our home office. My house doesn't have a chance to be a showcase. It's one of the things I've learned to let go of.

3. Our children take more responsibility for household chores. We have started them at age four folding and putting away their own laundry along with other household chores. There are things expected of them and they understand why.

4. My office hours are not from 9:00 A.M. to 5:00 P.M. They're in two-hour parcels from dawn to midnight, Monday through Thursday. I work fewer hours on Fridays and Saturdays and don't work at all on Sundays. During deadlines, I'm known to stay up till 2:00 in the morning. I don't like it and try very hard not to, but sometimes it just has to be done. I've found taking smaller, two-hour chunks of time in the office during the day is far more realistic and productive than trying to fit in large amounts of time. The children can't handle Mom being in the office for long periods of time, and I can't handle the constant interruptions long office stints bring.

5. Sometimes I just have to get away. When I have a lot of writing to do or something that requires a good amount of focused time, my husband takes time off to watch the children one afternoon while I take the laptop and go hide myself in a study room at the local library. I do this once a week or so, often on Fridays. We tried to schedule a regular time for this, but events kept getting in the way, so we've both learned to compromise and take it as it comes. I cherish these times when my thoughts and I are alone in a quiet room. At times I don't know what to do with the silence!

BALANCE TIPS

- Plan each night for the next day. Pack backpacks and lunches, lay out your clothes.

- Keep a family "in-box" for homework and other papers that need attention.

- Create a communication center for your household. A large corkboard works well. Post individual schedules, family reminders, and your child's artwork where everyone will know to look.

- Double your recipes and freeze half.

- Assign household chores to every family member. Even toddlers can do small tasks like sorting toys.

- Lower your standards when possible.

- Create a "remember" corner in your house for library books, book bags, and gym clothes that have to go somewhere soon.

- Set hours in your day when you do not work. Take at least one night a week off from everything. Do something that takes no brainpower: Sit on the couch with the remote, read a magazine, take a bath.

6. Running a fairly relaxed homeschool has been easier for us. When I first started homeschooling, I had these visions in my mind of what our schedule would be like and how smoothly it would all run. It didn't take long to realize that

wasn't realistic. Our business and whole family suffered when I found myself running back and forth to the office trying to juggle both. Over time, our homeschool has become more relaxed. Our older children do their school-work in the mornings and are done with formal work by around 10:30 A.M. The rest of our children's day is spent doing chores and pursuing their own interests.

7. To encourage constant learning when Mom isn't available, we've filled our home with educational games, software, magazines, books, videos, and toys. This has stimulated the children to learn on their own after formal school hours, and it takes tremendous pressure off me. It's interesting that since we've taken this approach, our children are actually reading and writing more.

8. One of the keys to juggling a business and home schooling is flexibility. That's part of the process—evaluating and then reevaluating and being flexible enough to make changes where they are necessary.

Finding Childcare Solutions

Balancing your business with taking care of your children in the home can work very well if you create a support system. Some women find it helpful to have regularly scheduled help such as a nanny or housekeeper so that they can clearly define their roles as caretaker and business owner. Others choose to squeeze their business work in between household chores and family activities. There is no right or wrong choice in selecting a childcare solution. Just as you must choose a profession that fits your skills and interests, you must choose a childcare solution that fits your personal expectations and financial limitations. If you are planning to make only $500 a month, it makes little sense to employ a nanny who costs you $800. Go back to the list of questions at the beginning of this chapter and decide whether a full-time nanny or a part-time housekeeper will help you reach your goals.

10

What's your solution for childcare?

VICTORIA USHERENKO, LIAISON IT
I set up the office in the baby's bedroom and for the first six months juggled taking care of the baby while conducting research, phone interviews, etc. I tried to make telephone calls while the baby slept and would also schedule meetings around the baby's nap times. My husband is very helpful and took care of the baby when I had to go on appointments. However, when he wasn't available, I took the baby with me.I finally got a nanny after the baby turned six months. She comes to my house from 10:00 to 4:00, Monday through Friday. I still work out of the baby's bedroom and get to interact with my son throughout the day.

LARA PULLEN, ENVIRONMENTAL HEALTH CONSULTING, INC.
Although my daughter has just started attending Montessori school in the mornings, I have a baby-sitter who comes to my house every afternoon from 2:00 to 5:00. She plays and cares for my daughter so that I can work.

MOLLY GOLD, GO MOM !NC.
Although I am my children's primary caregiver, family members often step in as baby-sitters to give me a window of time to work. My father not only acts as the COO of Go Mom !nc. but from time to time also wears the hat of child entertainer.

ROBIN ZELL, BRAGELETS
I started off by making a huge mistake. I put my two little ones in day care two days a week so I could work. That decision had my

bottom line seeing red. Now I just use a co-op program at a local church two days a week, and my three-year-old goes to preschool. This alternative is far more in line with the financial goals of my company, but it means I have to work mostly at night and during naptime.

11

How do you balance work and family?

SANDI EPSTEIN, WORK/LIFE COACH

I think balance is different for everyone. I identify it by the following feelings:

- I have enough time for family and work.
- Life "flows" and feels relatively effortless.
- When something in my life goes awry and the baby-sitter gets sick or the car breaks down, I have the resources to cope.
- I am on the path I want to be on personally and professionally.

Balance has these characteristics:

- It is not a constant; it comes and goes as things change in life.
- It has to be worked at.
- Seeking balance is stimulating and can become a true learning experience.

There are many components to finding balance, some that we know consciously and others subconsciously. Here are my "top ten" components to finding balance:

- Recognize that balancing roles as mother and business person is a job in itself and requires a pat on the back every so often.

- Take time to think how you will achieve balance this week.

- Apply your best analytical and creative thinking to problem-solve this task.

- Remember yourself, your needs, your wants, your happiness—they are the ultimate barometers of balance.

- Have faith that there is a way. Don't put barriers in front of possibilities—you can make it work.

- Know that what works this week may be out of whack next week. Stay flexible and open to new solutions.

- Know the signs of imbalance, including resentment, fatigue, feeling overwhelmed, depression, unhappy family members, dissatisfaction with your work.

- Revisit your core values and live them. Know what is most important to you today.

- Delegate the things that interfere with the important stuff.

- Find joy in the process.

DEE ENNEN, ENNEN COMPUTER SERVICES

I stay in balance by keeping focused. When I'm working, I concentrate on that and don't feel guilty. When I'm with the kids, I enjoy them! My advice is to shut the door to your office and keep it shut. Use caller ID and screen your calls during the evening. Learn to say no. Some clients can take advantage of your services and always have a tale of woe to go along with rush jobs. Mostly, this is because they haven't composed their letters on time. I don't want my family to suffer because of this.

I'd say, know your limits. Often during the process of getting started, you can get so wrapped up in your business that you lose sight of why you started it in the first place: to be home with your kids. Also, allow plenty of turnaround time. Even though your child normally takes a two-hour nap, don't count on that. Allow yourself more than enough time to do a good job.

HOW TO FIND A BABY-SITTER

Use word of mouth: Speak to other parents at the park or school events. Most parents protect their best sitters, but their sitter may have brothers or sisters who are available.

Look at churches or synagogues: Older women like to be around children and may welcome the chance to read to a child for a few hours a week.

Call the local high school: Contact the guidance counselor for recommendations on students. Also, ask the principal if you may post a notice in the teachers' room—sometimes young teachers like to supplement their incomes by watching children in the afternoon or during the evening.

Talk to the neighbors: Older neighbors or other moms might be able to identify teenagers or retirees in your neighborhood who might like to work a few hours a day. Ask around.

Post flyers: Go to local libraries, day care centers, and youth centers. Post your telephone number, but for security purposes omit your name.

All through my business I've kept my kids involved. They know most of my clients, several of whom have been with me from the beginning fourteen years ago and have seen my kids grow. During the holidays and on special occasions, my kids get involved in the fun stuff like dropping off goodies to clients. We always take

Call the agencies: Licensed childcare agencies are listed in your local Yellow Pages.

Seek domestic help: Put out the word among the domestic helpers who frequent your neighborhood. Everyone has a sister, and you never know.

Ask your pediatrician: Sometimes your doctor may know of other mothers who will watch children for extra spending money. If it's a mother of a child your doctor is familiar with, you'll know firsthand the kind of care she provides her own children.

Take a classified ad: The response to an ad can sometimes be overwhelming. Look in your local paper for an ad soliciting a similar baby-sitting situation. Try calling the person whose ad you see in the paper and see if they had an excess of good respondents. Offer to split the cost of their ad to obtain the name and phone number of a possible sitter.

Whatever channels you choose, you should always carefully screen prospective candidates. Make certain they are experienced and come with good references. Most of all, remember that a mother's instinct is always a strong indicator of safety and success.

---

cookies and candies or popcorn tins to all my regular clients to celebrate the holidays. My kids love doing this, and my clients look forward it to as well.

I also have lots and lots of crafts at home. Throughout the year I'll buy things on sale; then if I have to work while the kids are

THE BEST OF WORK AND FAMILY: TIPS FROM BLUESUITMOM.COM

- For those nights when dinner and cleanup need to be quick and easy, serve the food straight from storage containers. There will be fewer dishes to wash, and leftovers can go straight from the table to the refrigerator.

- Evaluate your productivity on a regular basis. If it seems you never get to the bottom of your in-box, look at the way you spend your day. Are you touching the same piece of paper twice? Do you shuffle work around your desk? Change one habit a month until you find your productivity increasing.

- Choose a distinctive color of sticky-notes. Whenever a coworker does something commendable, write a quick note of praise and leave it on his or her desk. The unusual color will stand out.

- Set up an in-box for yourself. Have your children put completed homework, lunch money requests, and permission slips in an assigned slot so when you come home from the office you can find all the papers that need your attention before bedtime. If the system works in the office, it might also work at home.

- Don't get caught without rainy day diversions on hand. Visit toy manufacturers' Web sites, like Lego, Fisher-Price, and Playmobile, and print out coloring and activity sheets. Keep them tucked away in a folder for the next time you're stuck inside all day.

- For quick trips when you don't need to pack a big diaper bag, keep a smaller "to-go" bag. This can be as simple as a large Ziploc filled with the essentials: one diaper, small package of wipes, flat toy or book, disposable bib, and snack-size Ziploc filled with Cheerios. If you carry an oversized purse, your "to-go" bag should fit right inside.

- The kids are back in school, and that means a constant flow of paper into your house. What do you do with all the cherished artwork, superior spelling tests, and original stories written by your child? Grab a three-ring binder. Hole-punch your favorite pieces and file neatly as a durable keepsake of the school year.

- Assemble a tagalong kit containing all the little things your baby might need as you move through the house completing daily chores. Include a spare diaper, wipes, pacifier, ointment, and favorite hand-size toys. If you tote your kit outside to the garden with you or upstairs to your office, you may gain a few minutes in your day.

- Always keep a container of cooked rice or noodles on hand in the refrigerator for quick and easy dinners during the week. They can be added to a can of soup for a speedy casserole or topped with a ready-to-eat sauce. Toss noodles with crisp vegetables and a bottle of vinaigrette for a fast pasta salad.

- During the holidays, hire a neighborhood teenager or retiree to help you do small jobs that don't need your personal touch, such as addressing holiday envelopes or wrapping gifts. Teenagers love to make $5.00 an hour for jobs they can do while watching television.

here, I'll get them started on a fun project. I buy videos that my kids enjoy. That helps when I need to work.

I recently had to type a manuscript for someone who was behind schedule and needed to get it to the publisher quickly. I had to work several evenings and into the weekend. I rented my kids' favorite videos, and this allowed me to work pretty much uninterrupted. They also made several paint-by-number pictures and created some Christmas tree ornaments. When I was done, we all went to our favorite restaurant and had a mini-celebration.

12

What family issues did you face when starting your business?

ROBIN ZELL, BRAGELETS

Telephones! When we started Bragelets, we only had one phone in the house. I soon realized that with children who are fourteen, eleven, four, and two, that wasn't going to be enough. We now have two phone lines, and there are fewer fights over who gets to use the phone.

MOLLY GOLD, GO MOM !NC.

Frankly, our family issues arose because my husband also works from home, having owned his company for six years. It's been a delicate art for both of us to learn to respect the other's priorities. He's had to become as creative as I am with his workdays. Sometimes one of us races to the office in the morning while the other handles the children's routine. We play tag team through lunch hour, kindergarten drop-off, nap time, and kindergarten pick-up until dinner at 6:00. The one who stayed up latest the night before is excused from helping on the home front the next morning. Often, I have to decide either to go to bed or surrender to an all-nighter. It all depends if my husband is home, downtown, or traveling if I put myself through the thirty-six-hour test.

DARCY VOLDEN MILLER, LITTLEDIDIKNOW.COM

Prior to starting my business, I thought I could do it all and find balance with everything in my life: running a business, a home, my family, and my personal life. I couldn't. Some things had to be sacrificed, and this threw off the balance of "the wheel." I couldn't do everything around the house, and my husband and perhaps even my son suffered from it. I found that my husband, until then my biggest supporter, was soon becoming my biggest saboteur, because I wasn't taking care of the house and our family as I once did. I know that eventually I will find that perfect harmony. In the meantime, I'm still looking.

JEANNINE CLONTZ, ACCURATE BUSINESS SERVICES

First and foremost, I didn't want my family to think I was home eating bonbons and watching soap operas! In the beginning, I think they thought I was their personal assistant just because I was home. They'd hit me with their errands and requests, and I felt obliged to do them. Then I found myself cleaning the house instead of making the dreaded cold call to try and generate some business. Finally, I sat the family down and told them that I needed to put in full-time hours to get the job going, and they needed to remember that before they asked me to handle their personal jobs. I also talked my hubby into letting me hire a cleaning lady to come in twice a month.

BECCA WILLIAMS, WALLNUTZ, INC.

Figuring out the budget was a big concern. We spent evenings poring over spreadsheets, running numbers on how big a house payment we could afford, what did the food budget need to be, and how much could we spend on Christmas each year. After starting the business and having the baby, we had to work through some "housework equity" issues. My husband's mom always stayed home and took care of children and household business, so he assumed that was the way our family would operate once our daughter came along. He has since realized that I can't handle all that needs to be done around the house as well as work full time at my business.

13

How has your relationship with your husband or significant other been affected by your home-based business?

JULIE AIGNER-CLARK, BABY EINSTEIN

My husband fully understood the work involved in being an entrepreneur when I started Baby Einstein, because he had recently been an entrepreneur himself. In 1980, he started a company that put together science curricula with laser disk technology. We met when I went to work with him before he sold the company. He's a good person for me to be around because he has the entrepreneurial spirit. He was working for a foundation when I started Baby Einstein, but he eventually quit to work with me. My relationship with my husband is so much better than with anyone else. If I had to work with anyone else, I don't think I could. Some men feel threatened and don't like it if their wives are successful, but my husband isn't like that. The biggest adjustment for us working together was that we had to learn to step from our marriage into a working relationship. When we don't agree on something, I have to remember to speak to him like one of my sales guys rather than my husband. I would never say things like "Shut up" to an employee like I might to my husband on occasion. It's critical that you treat a spouse as you would an employee. Leave outside the office the things you would say to someone you know as well as your husband.

ROBIN ZELL, BRAGELETS

My husband and I have been married for fifteen years. Throughout that time, I have worked or gone to school off and on, but I did so around his schedule. Owning a home-based business is more intrusive on our relationship. One of our biggest problems is that my husband wants me to make a profit right away. Luckily, I know better. He wants to look at the numbers all the time, while I am still trying to figure out my business plan!

WENDY HARRIS, NATIONAL ASSOCIATION OF MEDICAL BILLERS

When I first thought of the idea for my company, my husband had his doubts. I think he thought I was getting in over my head. He suggested I start a consulting business. I think sometimes he has such high hopes and dreams for me that he doesn't stop to look at the big picture. After a while, I convinced him that my idea would be better for us all, and eventually he came around.

It's been our goal from the beginning that he would become a partner in the business as soon as I'd grown it large enough. He now does all the bookkeeping and marketing of the company. The only problem is that I have all the experience in the medical field, and he doesn't. Sometimes it becomes a problem when he doesn't understand different aspects of the business.

JEANNINE CLONTZ, ACCURATE BUSINESS SERVICES

I think we communicate much better now that I'm home. I was so rushed working a sixty-hour week and driving two hours a day back and forth to work that we didn't seem to have much time to share and listen to each other. That's been a dramatic change. We actually laugh together—something we hadn't done for a few years.

DEE ENNEN, ENNEN COMPUTER SERVICES

Back when I started my business in 1985, home-based businesses were not as popular as they are today. My husband and I were used to the luxury of a second income, and he was skeptical at first about giving up that security. As with many couples, we barely made it, and with a new baby it was even more frightening. I truly believe that once he saw my determination and how much I believed in the business, he started to lose some of his doubts. I also took the time to write up a good business plan. It wasn't anything technical like you'd need for a bank loan, but it outlined how I was going to operate the business and make it a success. Also, I targeted local businesses and clients who would provide steady work. This ensured me a regular paycheck, and once the money started coming in, my husband was fine with my decision. Today I don't think he'd want it any other way.

DEBBIE GIOQUINDO, PERSONAL TOUCH TRAVEL

When you operate a small business, especially from home, there are times when your spouse will go through periods of resentment as you devote time and energy to your business. I can honestly say my husband and I have not yet worked through resentment issues created by my career. Most of the time, it is my resentment of the freedom he has to work without the inconveniences of balancing a family at the same time. He can get up and leave for work every morning on time. Because I work from home, I have to squeeze my workday into the schedules of my children and housework that needs to be done. It is exhausting at times.

As much as men want you to succeed, they also want you to be there in the capacity you were before your business. You may have arguments about your new role, and it is important that your family knows that this is a part of who you are and that you are doing this not only for yourself but also for the family.

Another tip for women just starting a home-based business is to find a friend to travel this road with. A buddy is a great sounding board and can pick you up when the going gets tough. The reality of being a home-based working mother is that it is a very lonely world. Your issues fall between a nonworking stay-at-home mother and an out-of-the-home working mother.

WENDY HARRIS, NATIONAL ASSOCIATION OF MEDICAL BILLERS

My husband sends me e-mails every day from work telling me how proud he is of my success. We have the time and money to do a lot more things together now than we used to, such as dinners out, shopping trips, vacations. Oh yeah, he loves having dinner on the table when he gets home and clean socks in his dresser drawer when he needs them.

SHERRY MAYSONAVE, EMPOWERMENT ENTERPRISES

When and if your husband comes to work with you as my husband did, it's important to find quality time away from business. I suggest that you have a date night and make a rule not to talk about business. Our partnership in the business evolved as my company rapidly grew. I needed his help, and he stepped in. It is important for us to recognize each person's area of expertise. We aren't all wired in the same way. I have a need for downtime and creativity. We have different sleep patterns and different ways to cope. His skills are in marketing, and he's a good managing partner.

14

How were you affected by becoming a home-based business owner?

JULIE AIGNER-CLARK, BABY EINSTEIN

I was always a pleaser. If I disagreed with you, I would say okay and go on. Yet when we had a meeting about sales the other day with a major partner, I said to myself, "It's your company and you can say whatever you want." I now psych myself up to say what I really want to say, and I feel so empowered when I do. It feels so good. This business has made me a much more straightforward and honest person. There was a point when I was agreeing, agreeing, and agreeing. But one day I realized that I can agree until someone throws my company down the tubes, or I can speak up. When you apply the same feeling you have for your child to your business, you take control. You wouldn't want your child hanging out with the wrong group of people, so why would I allow a bad group of people to get anywhere near my business? It's a sense of true love and feelings of protection.

DEBBIE WILLIAMS, LET'S GET IT TOGETHER

I had to develop a serious attitude about my business. Initially, it's a passion and eventually it becomes a business. Once you start setting fees, it's no longer a hobby—it's a career. I sometime use child psychology to remind myself that I am running a real business. To do this I use the door to my office. At 4:00 each afternoon, I close the door to my shop. It helps me to transition from corporate mom to mom and wife. Closing the door is the key. When I started, my son was a toddler. I used tricks that I had used while teaching. I set up centers in my office with goody bags and activities. Although you say you are going to work at home, you have to realize that children are little people with rights. There are times when you have to conform to their schedules.

A home-based business should be based on your work style and lifestyle. With an only child I find it's easy to redirect his attention when I need to work. Instead of being a slave to technology, I've learned to use technology to find work and family balance. I use voice mail as well as e-mail to help me respond to my customers on my schedule.

Making the Transition into Entrepreneurship

Taking the step into entrepreneurship will have a huge impact on you and your family. It is a big endeavor requiring proper preparation to produce positive effects for everyone.

If you already know the type of business you plan to establish, you are ahead of the game. You will be able to devote more of the incubation period to writing your business plan, building the infrastructure, and establishing your network of potential customers. If you are indeed one of the lucky ones who knows the type of company you will be starting, there are a number of things you can do to leverage that advantage.

If you are presently employed, begin to prepare yourself now while you have a steady paycheck. Begin to increase the networking opportunities your present position offers you. If it's been a few months since you've been to the Chamber of Commerce breakfast, start going again. You'll need those contacts once you are out on your own. Call old clients to reestablish a relationship, particularly if they represent a company you might want to work with in the future.

Make sure you are on the best terms possible with anyone who can be a future client. Think about your present employer becoming your first customer. Perhaps there is a project you know of that has been passed around for years because the company just doesn't seem to have the person to do it. Prepare a plan that outlines how you can effectively help your employer or company meet their goals. If you explain that you are leaving your position to reach your personal goals and express your willingness to still be a part of the team on your terms, you might be pleasantly surprised at their reaction. Never bad-mouth your former employer, either before you leave or after, because no matter what your initial business may be, you may one day decide to create another business where your former employer could become a prospective customer.

When I was leaving my position with the *Miami Herald* in 1996, it came as little surprise to my boss. I had three children under two years old, I had expressed my desire to build my own company for quite some time, and the stars seemed aligned for me to give it a try. During my tenure, I had created and produced the South Florida Parenting Conference, a program I knew the *Herald* wanted to continue. I also knew there was no one except me who knew how to do it. I saw it as the perfect opportunity to turn my employer into a client. So, along with my resignation, I presented a plan that outlined the work I could still do for them and the money they would save by not having me on the payroll. It was a win-win situation for the *Herald*, because they got the benefit of my work without the cost of retaining a full-time employee. Can you imagine what I was costing them in health insurance as a woman with a husband and three children? It made it a lot easier to start my company knowing I had my first paying customer.

Some experts suggest six months to a year of preparation before going out on your own. During this time, try to take on project work with prospective clients but be careful not to let your moonlighting get in the way of your performance in the office. You need also to be aware of your legal obligations to any noncompete agreements you might have signed with your present employer. If there is no conflict, you might tell trusted clients that you are considering going out on your own and gauge their level of interest in sending you business and larger projects on a consistent basis. Knowing the amount of business you have lined up prior to launching your company will help you build your business plan and formulate financial projections.

CHAPTER THREE

Finding the Winning Concept

How many times have you heard the story of Sheryl Leach, the creator of Barney the big purple dinosaur? If you have a child who loves the "I love you" song, you probably know who Sheryl is. I bet you've asked yourself more than once why you weren't the one to come up with the idea for Barney. Here's another thought to ponder. What motivated the creator of the Razor Scooter to do the obvious and attach roller blade wheels to a scooter? I know these are extreme cases of what a good idea can produce for you, and perhaps your expectations are not to hit it that big, but what if you do have the next big idea? It's certainly possible!

In order to build a successful business, you have to find the right concept. In this case, the word "right" means a business idea that fits into your lifestyle, career expectations, and goals. So where do you find it? In this chapter, we'll begin the search.

You might already have a specific business in mind or an idea to produce a product. If so, congratulate yourself, because you can leap ahead and follow the steps to prepare yourself for business. If you are among the numerous individuals who have the desire to own their own businesses but don't know what type of business to pursue, it's time for a self-evaluation of your personality, skills set, education, professional experience, and contacts. By identifying your strengths, talents, and strong relationships and matching them with your expectations, you will uncover where your opportunities lie.

What are your interests? Do you have a passion you can turn into a business? Do you want to do the same type of work you've done in the past or do you want to get into something very different? Will you have a product-based business or will you be a service provider? Will you serve local markets or go global? Online or offline? Do you want to work full time or part time? Will your income be your household's primary or secondary source of money? All of these questions address the issues you must clarify to find the right concept for you and your family.

First, determine why you want to own a home-based business. Although you might think you know the answer, other reasons may surface with more thorough evaluation. Check the statements below that relate to your motivations and keep them handy while you continue to read this chapter.

- I see greater flexibility and freedom if I work at home.
- I've always wanted to be my own boss.
- I want to be valued for the work I produce.
- I want to do what I want to do when I want to do it.
- I want to improve my standard of living.
- I am bored with my present job and need a challenge.
- I have a product or service that is in demand.
- I want to be at home with my children.
- I am tired of the travel associated with my present job.
- I have an idea for a product or service that does not presently exist.
- I can provide a service better than anyone now in the market.

Now, set your answers aside while you take an inventory of yourself. Remember to be honest and practical when answering the set of questions. If you are the mother of four children and want to be the primary caregiver, then, even if you are willing to work eighty hours a week, it's probably not practical to own a business. The more honest you are now, the less likely that you will hit obstacles in your road to success. Write down the answers to the following questions:

- What are my strengths?
- What are my weaknesses?
- Am I willing to delegate to individuals who possess strengths in areas of my weaknesses?
- How much of my time am I willing to invest?
- Do I like to work with people or by myself?
- How much of my own money am I willing to invest?
- How long can I afford to be without income?
- Am I willing to compete for business?

Take a minute to compare the list of your business motivations with the self-evaluation. If your desire to work from home is to be home with your children and you are only willing to work ten hours a week, then a less labor intensive business would be the right fit for you. But if you are willing to work fifty hours a week and have a desire to run a global company, you can start to stretch your business ideas to include fancy Web sites or manufacturing a product.

Be careful that in your quest for finding a solution to one concern you don't create a different problem for yourself. Remember Debbi the communication specialist in chapter 2? Being self-employed allows you the flexibility to work the hours you want to work, but it also means you must be available to your business 24/7. You need to consider all elements of your business idea prior to launching your company. You may decide you are going to set limited hours of operation for your business in order to have family flexibility. However, your customers may live in other time zones, particularly if your business involves the Internet. The problem is that if you are closed when your customers want to do business, they will go to someone who is open.

Before I created the concept for BlueSuitMom.com, I was commuting from South Florida to Denver, Colorado, nearly every week.

The challenges that business travel can add to an already hectic home life are as numerous as the hours spent in airplanes and strange airports. I began searching the Internet and print publications for advice on balancing work and family and found few that addressed my issues. My intuition told me that there were other working mothers who could use the same tools I was seeking. After conducting unofficial research with every working woman I met in airports, grocery stores, or on playgrounds, I knew I had the right idea for a business. I would publish an online magazine for working mothers and deliver work and family balance tools, information, and advice. I also knew that my experience as a working mother of four would serve me well in designing a product, my contacts established when I produced the parenting conference would help me to produce the product, and my marketing experience would help me promote the product to other working mothers. I had found the right concept for me.

15

What led you to your business idea?

BECCA WILLIAMS, WALLNUTZ, INC.

My husband and I were thinking about decorating the nursery. I wanted a mural on the walls but I knew that muralists were expensive. In high school, I had painted a mural in my room so I knew it wasn't hard. I thought it could be a good business idea. I came up with a survey and found that lots of parents were interested in doing murals in their kids' rooms, but lacked the artistic ability. Kits seemed like an obvious way to help people overcome their fear of painting their walls.

I don't know that WallNutz can be defined yet as a "winning concept." I think it will eventually be successful, but it inspired me to look at other businesses that offer increased upside and/or payback sooner. What definitely has been "winning" about WallNutz is that it has taught me a lot about marketing a company and a new product, dealing with logistics of large- and small-scale orders, and introduced me to a network of people that can help me with future business endeavors.

JEANNINE CLONTZ, ACCURATE BUSINESS SERVICES

A great deal of hard work and long hours led me to starting my business. No matter where I've worked the past twenty-seven years—fifteen years of it in direct outside sales—the high level of customer service and my administrative abilities always accounted for my success. I knew that a business based on my experience was the right one for me. The level of service I could provide customers of Accurate Business Services was something I knew my competitors didn't offer.

You have to recognize that building a business isn't easy. I knew it was important to do something I enjoyed. I can't tell you how many phone calls and e-mails I get from people saying, "I can type; I can start my own business, too." It's a lot more than just typing. You have to be skilled and knowledgeable about the software and systems you and your clients use. You have to be creative and innovative to be successful.

ROBIN ZELL, BRAGELETS

My love for the product and a desire to do something for money brought me to owning my business. After the birth of my fourth child, I ordered a Bragelet. I enjoyed the product so much that I began talking to the owners. I always tell everyone, "I loved my Bragelet so much, I bought the company!"

AMILYA ANTONETTI, SOAPWORKS

I created my company after I found a solution to my son's health problems. I was faced with an infant who was gray in color, had difficulty breathing, and would cry until he passed out. The doctors couldn't explain what it was that kept sending my son to the emergency room. I began keeping a journal about his illness. Sometime about his first birthday, I discovered that, every time I cleaned the house, my son had a major attack a couple of hours later. I began asking other mothers if their kids reacted to cleaning products, and I also began doing research. Ultimately, I went to homeopathic doctors who confirmed my hunch that my son was indeed allergic to everyday items in my cabinets. I started asking some of the women in the senior citizen residence near my home what they had used to clean their homes before today's products were around. Based on what they told me, I began mixing vinegar, borax, and baking soda solutions in my kitchen and trying them on my household messes. I just kept mixing until I found solutions that worked and my son could tolerate. Friends began testing the solutions for me, and, surprisingly, they wanted to buy them. That was the birth of SOAPWORKS.

JANESSA WASSERMAN, MOMMA BAG

The idea for my business fell into my lap by accident. A friend was being honored at a first baby shower, and I wanted to give her a unique gift. I remembered that the one thing I procrastinated on preparing was my hospital bag, because the thought of going to the hospital to deliver stressed me out. I thought packing my friend's bag would provide relief from the huge task of running around from store to store in her ninth month of pregnancy assembling all the necessary items. I headed out to the stores in search of the bag I had in my imagination. I was unsuccessful. Although every store sold layettes and bags of items for the baby, none carried a product for the mother. Determined that this was the gift I wanted to give, I assembled the bag myself. At the shower, it was a huge hit. Women began calling me to assemble the gift for other showers they were attending, and I thought there must be a business somewhere in this good idea.

DIANE DESA, A VIRTUAL ASSISTANT

For quite some time, I wanted to find a business that allowed me to work from home. I tried several multilevel marketing businesses, but none were successful. In April 1999, someone introduced me to the concept of virtual assistance, and a lightbulb went off. This was it. This was for me. This was the business I was looking for. I am an experienced executive assistant; I could build a business based on something that I knew, something that was familiar to me. I spent a year and a half studying the business, researching it, and training myself to be a successful virtual assistant.

LARA PULLEN, ENVIRONMENTAL HEALTH CONSULTING, INC.

When I started thinking about launching my home-based business, I asked myself the question "What would people pay me to do while working from home?" I initially assumed that my business would be more environmental consulting, such as writing risk assessments. That didn't work for me. I then thought I would write articles for magazines. The magazine industry proved to be very hard to break into, and the pay was considerably lower than pharmaceutical jobs. I found my niche when I settled on writing training manuals, scientific review articles, and health stories for medical and pharmaceutical companies.

TERESA KIRBY, A GARDEN PARTY

Darcy and I recognized the lack of unique garden products available through mass retailers, online, or via catalog, and we also believed that the customer should have the opportunity to "touch and test" products prior to purchase. With this combination, we felt we had found a potentially successful niche. The concept for A Garden Party also seemed to fit the experience Darcy and I brought to the table. Darcy had worked for various landscape architecture firms, and she had contacts with potential vendors. She had also worked as a retail management consultant for Arthur Andersen, and we knew her time helping young and growing companies manage their cash flow would come in handy. I had worked as a paralegal and helped many start-up businesses find their way through legal documents, and that would be useful, too.

DEBBIE WILLIAMS, LET'S GET IT TOGETHER

My husband suggested it, actually. I had just finished organizing a friend's paper management system, setting up files in her home, and was thrilled to help her out. He suggested I organize people's homes and offices. It made sense to me once he presented me with the idea. I use my sales and educational background to market a skill that I enjoy sharing. He offered to build me a Web site to promote my company. It all developed from there. It's amazing how similar the teaching of organizational and time management skills is to the teaching of reading!

16

What skills and talents did you apply to your home-based business concept?

MOLLY GOLD, GO MOM !NC.

By working as a meeting planner, I honed all of my natural organization skills. Having a sense of order is something that is in my fabric as a person, even as a child. So, creating the product was a natural extension of my own thinking about how to get stuff done! By working in sales and marketing previously, I've been able to develop those much needed writing skills. The process of setting up my home business was more challenging logistically than I anticipated, only because you truly have to do it all yourself. From motherhood, the great skills of multitasking, completion over time, and flexibility are the key applications I draw on regularly.

TAMMY HARRISON, THE QUEEN OF PIZZAZZ COMPANY

Customer service, marketing, and the ability to sell myself and my expertise—they're my skills, and, frankly, my enthusiasm is catching! When I visit with potential clients, I am able to help them feel the excitement that I feel for my work, and that in turn helps create lasting relationships with them.

LINDA MCWILLAMS, ONCEUPONANAME.COM

My prior profession as a planner and analyst required me to be very organized, a skill that came in handy when I launched Once Upon A Name. You must be organized and a very hard worker to build a successful home-based business. I also had experience working with buyers and suppliers, and that helped when it came time to source inventory. I am a driven person, too much sometimes, but it's a great quality to have when you have your own business.

ROBIN STERNE, WOW! DESIGNS, INC.

It wasn't difficult to choose what kind of business I would launch. I have always loved creating the right image for products, retailers, and events. When you have a passion for your work, it helps you to give 110 percent to your clients. Wow! Designs, Inc. allowed me to utilize my graphic design talents as well as the business skills I learned by working with the team that founded and grew Blockbuster Video into a household name. I am fortunate to run a business that permits me to do something I love and apply lessons learned throughout life.

ALEX POWE ALLRED, AUTHOR AND GOLD MEDALIST

There are two personal skills that I've been able to apply to my home-based business—my love of people and my ability to network. I grew up watching my father, a U.S. diplomat, deal with heads of state, royalty, and other dignitaries. I learned early on the very simple rule to be honest and treat all people with respect. It's amazing how foreign this concept is to people today and how completely powerful it is when you apply it to your customers.

KIT BENNETT, AMAZINGMOMS.COM

Most of my skills are natural God-given gifts. I don't really think I can take credit for the way my mind works. My teaching experience clearly added to my ability to understand playing with children, which is the focus of Amazingmoms.com. The skills I needed to learn to run my new company were computer knowledge and Web design experience. Starting a Web site really meant beginning from square one for me, with a very steep learning curve to overcome.

17

What other businesses did you consider prior to launching your company?

ALEX POWE ALLRED, AUTHOR AND GOLD MEDALIST

For a few years I was a professional animal trainer. I trained Estée Lauder's dog, Doodle the Poodle. Hey, I don't name 'em; I just trained 'em. I did training for Senator Bob Dole, various members on Capitol Hill, and some of the Washington Redskins. It was fun. I thought about doing that forever, because I love animals slightly more than I love people.

SHANNON RUBIO, THESMILEBOX.COM

We researched opening a bookstore for parents doing home-schooling. There is only one in Houston, and the market here is huge. However, the start-up costs were close to $100,000, and we could not invest that much money into a business.

WENDY HARRIS, NATIONAL ASSOCIATION OF MEDICAL BILLERS

I knew that my home-based business would be in the medical billing industry because that's the only industry I've ever worked in. I was confident in my skills, and I knew the business. Initially, I considered opening a medical billing training center. I decided against it because I wanted to reach more people than that. By placing my program on the Internet, I am global. Additionally, I limit my operating expenses by working from home.

VICTORIA USHERENKO, LIAISON IT

I considered several other businesses prior to launching Liaison IT. Among them was developing offshore software for companies in the U.S. or providing real estate services for international buyers. After running into a former business acquaintance who had gone into technology recruiting, I thought it was a good fit for my skills set and personal goals.

ROBIN ZELL, BRAGELETS

Opening a vintage resale shop or antique/craft store mall was my first idea. I am a compulsive person, so there was really no research or anything. Bragelets just kind of "fell" into my lap, and I thought it was too good to pass up. Even though the timing was not the best. But when is it ever?

DIANNE BALLARD, DKB ASSOCIATES

I have always wanted to own and operate a bookstore. I still may do this some day, but right now the consulting field is more lucrative.

Research

Before you invest any money into your idea, it's essential to do research. Solid research will help you identify your competitors, establish your niche, and project the growth potential of your business. The most important thing you can acquire for your new business is knowledge. According to research conducted by Dun and Bradstreet, 90 percent of all small-business failures can be traced to poor management resulting from lack of knowledge. Arm yourself with as much information as possible before launching your company.

Your research needs to begin at the time you are contemplating potential products or services. Start your research with yourself. Is the product you are considering going to satisfy an unfilled need in the marketplace? Will the product or service serve an existing market in which demand exceeds supply? Finally, will the product be competitive? If your business concept allows you to answer yes to any one of these questions, then you are ready to extend your research to other areas.

When conducting market research on your product or service, your goal is to answer these questions:

- Who are my customers?
- What does my customer physically look like?
- What does my customer do each day?
- Where can I find my customer?

You don't have to be a trained research analyst to research your business idea. Analyzing the market is merely a way to gather facts about potential customers to determine the demand of the product or service. The more information you gather about your product, the better you will be able to assess the market and the future demand for it. There are several easy, effective methods to test the validity of your business concept.

You can conduct an unscientific written survey among friends and colleagues, using e-mail, snail mail, or personal delivery of the questionnaire. Utilizing the survey method will allow you to gather demographic information about your respondents and compare it with their behaviors. It's easy to create your own survey by following a standard format.

A good survey begins by gathering data such as age, income, profession, geographical specifics, and family status of the participant. If there are specific details about the person that are important to you, here is where you should ask for them. For example, if you are starting a car washing business, you might ask how many vehicles the respondent owns. The questions may be in the form of multiple-choice or fill-in-the-blank answers. Here is an example of both:

Example one: What is your marital status?

    a. Single

    b. Married

    c. Divorced

    d. Widowed

Example two: My marital status is _____.

The next questions in the survey should focus on customer behaviors. Where do your potential customers shop? How many hours a day are they in their car? Using the car wash example, how often do they clean their car? Whatever it is that would create demand for your product should be identified through your questions in this area.

The final section should inquire about your respondents' present behaviors and their willingness to change. Our car washing business owner might ask, "Would you pay to have someone else wash your car?" "What is the price you would pay to have someone wash your vehicle?" "How often would you pay for this service?" This section will get to the heart of your opportunities and projections.

SAMPLE SURVEY FOR CAR WASHING

Business: _____

Name (optional): _____

Age: _____

Hometown: _____

Income (circle one)

    a. Less than $20,000   c. $41,000 to $60,000

    b. $20,000 to $40,000   d. Over $60,000

Profession: _____

Marital status: _____

Number of children: _____

Ages of children: _____

Number of vehicles in household: _____

Number of drivers in household: _____

Make and model of vehicles: _____

How many hours a day are you in your vehicle? _____

Describe the amount of pride you take in your car:

    a. None

    b. Little

    c. Great deal

Do you utilize your vehicle for business?

    a. Yes (Please describe)

    b. No

(continues)

(continued from page 71)

Who cleans your vehicle?

    a. Drive-thru car wash

    b. Self

    c. Neighborhood teenager

    d. Detail service

Would you pay to have someone come to your home to wash your car?

    a. Yes

    b. No

How much would you pay to have someone wash your vehicle in your driveway? _____

How often would you pay for the service described above?

    a. Once a week   c. Once a year

    b. Once a month   d. Never

Based on your observation of local car wash services, do you see a need for

    a. More

    b. Fewer

    c. No changes

Do you know another car owner who would use the service? _____

Thank you for your input.

You will notice that the sample survey is relatively short and to the point. A trick of the survey trade is to limit the number of questions in order to protect the integrity of the answers. If a survey gets too long, it loses the attention of the respondent and makes it likelier that people are going to give "hurry up and finish" answers rather than valid responses.

Another useful method of research is focus groups. A focus group is a sample of people willing to express their opinions about a product or service. To informally test a new business idea, you can put out the call for volunteers to friends, coworkers, and neighbors. A unique approach to assembling a focus group was made by Amilya Antonetti, owner of SOAPWORKS, who put a classified in the local newspaper, which read "Calling All Moms: Mom looking to start a company. I need your help. If you could create your perfect cleaning solution and body care products, what would they look like? Providing free lunch. Bring your kids!" To her surprise, over 220 women turned out to participate. With your focus group, you can test people's responses to variations of your concept, gather more descriptive oral responses to your questions, and create a network for brainstorming.

Once I had decided to launch BlueSuitMom.com, I prepared a short survey aimed at determining the types of content executive mothers considered useful. I sent the survey via e-mail to every working mother I knew who fit the profile of a BlueSuitMom. I also asked recipients to forward the survey to five of their friends. This gave me the benefit of responses from strangers as well as acquaintances. I received over fifty completed surveys. In addition, I gathered a group of former coworkers who are mothers and gave them pizza in exchange for their opinions. It was a very productive evening. Names, ideas, and suggestions flew all over the room.

A useful trick I use in identifying my market is to visualize individual people. I find it helpful to draw a picture of my potential customers either figuratively or with words. The customer of BlueSuitMom.com is a working mother who makes $50,000 to $75,000 a year and is committed to both her family and her career. When I was preparing to launch our Web site, I found it helpful to write down hour-by-hour what a day in the life of my customer was like, an exercise that allows me to visualize my customers and find places in the day when I can help them. It was a document that I referred to when I was writing my marketing plan as well as when I approached potential investors.

Research will also allow you to understand how your business will stack up against your competitors. Make a list of your competitors and note their strengths as well as their weaknesses. The latter will help you identify opportunities for your business to serve customers in the market. Competitors often later become partners. By making yourself familiar with the services they provide or don't provide, you may find opportunities to create mutually beneficial partnerships.

Since we are all in business to make money, it is important to conduct research that will reveal the revenue potential of your business. This information can be gathered by targeting survey and focus group questions and by researching industry standards if your product or service is already in the marketplace. If you plan to sell homemade doughnuts, for instance, you might want to read the Krispy Kreme annual report to learn about the size of the doughnut industry. The facts included in the reports of public companies can be informative, particularly when you are attempting to build a business in the same industry.

18

What research did you conduct prior to launching your company?

DARCY LYONS, A GARDEN PARTY

By researching the direct-selling organization Web site, we determined there were no other sizable companies doing exactly what we proposed to do. We researched the revenues of companies such as the Pampered Chef. Finally, we researched the sales volume of the gardening retail sales industry and found it was a multibillion-dollar industry.

We felt that the opportunity for creating a profitable niche for ourselves was great.

We did a lot of research on the Web, and all of the information that we came up with confirmed that more and more women wanted to start their own businesses. We also talked to many women already involved with home-based businesses.

LESLEY SPENCER, HBWM.COM

I searched for an association like HBWM.com but did not find anything. I sent a letter to the editor of a local parenting publication about my idea and received some great feedback to reassure me this was a business that was needed.

BECCA WILLIAMS, WALLNUTZ, INC.

I recognized the importance of research from the beginning. I surveyed fifty mothers around the U.S. for their opinions on decorating children's rooms. Some of my questions focused on painting and murals. Their responses provided me with good insights. I also did some informal questioning of mothers that I met about their thoughts on the mural kit concept and design preferences.

ROBIN ZELL, BRAGELETS

I spent a great deal of time researching the Internet sales aspect of my business because I intended to launch a Web site. I believe that research is a very important element to growing your business. I am researching as I go—every day I learn something new, wonderful, and occasionally something scary.

JEANNINE CLONTZ, ACCURATE BUSINESS SERVICES

I did a great deal of research prior to launching Accurate Business Services. I wanted to make sure this was the right business for me. I looked at many different types of industries. Once I decided on the business services industry, I went back to school to sharpen my secretarial skills. I even took a specialized class in legal transcription to broaden the scope of clientele I could approach once I launched my company.

DIANE DESA, A VIRTUAL ASSISTANT

I researched the profession of virtual assistance and knew that it was a relatively new, definitely growing profession. I joined several listservs, the International Virtual Assistants Association, and Staffcentrix prior to starting my business. Membership in these organizations gave me the opportunity to network with experienced virtual assistants.

DEBBIE WILLIAMS, LET'S GET IT TOGETHER

Prior to launching my company, I did quite a bit of research online using search engines, newsgroups, discussion groups on women, and parenting sites, and sending e-mail to others in the industry for advice and feedback. Studying the competition helped me create a niche early on, which is crucial if you are going it alone—there is no use spreading yourself too thin. To set fees, I perused local Yellow Pages for management consultants, trainers, and professionals in related fields. I contacted them to find out a fee range, and then I figured out what the local market would bear. It created a nice network, too, which I highly recommend.

I also read general business books for home businesses, such as those written by Paul and Sarah Edwards—they are a gold mine of information!

DIANE BALLARD, DKB ASSOCIATES

I did quite a bit of research before launching my company. I read numerous books on small-business start-ups as well as on the consulting field. On the Internet, I registered with several organizations such as HBWM.com, Guru.com, and the Management Consultant Network. I also did research on a number of government sites and found lots of demographic information on women's business start-ups. The Small Business Administration site, www.sba.gov/womeninbusiness, has solid information. I found a great accountant who gave me valuable hints regarding the tax and finance issues of the business. My learning continues. I am currently taking an entrepreneurship class at the University of Michigan.

RESEARCH RESOURCES ON THE INTERNET

- finance.yahoo.com: Good site if your research involves large companies. The information includes sector and industry facts in an easy to navigate manner.

- www.bigcharts.com: If you are looking for detailed information on public companies, check this site first.

- www.demographics.com: The site of *American Demographics* magazine. It's filled with lots of search capabilities and basic research information.

- www.census.gov: This is the place to start when looking for specific numbers on just about any niche of the American population.

- www.claritas.com: If you're willing to pay for the most recent numbers for your particular market, this is the place. For a few hundred dollars you can get demographic information segmented down to zip codes in your area.

CHAPTER FOUR

Building Your Business Plan

A detailed business plan is the single most important document in your business. The business plan is a working tool that will change as your company develops and grows. The only components that should not change are your mission statement and goals, because they will keep you focused on your original vision as time goes on. Your target market, exit strategy, and marketing initiatives will be more dynamic, adjusting with events inside and outside your company. You may find after a year or so that the niche market you initially targeted is too small to support your business and must be expanded. You may also pleasantly discover additional revenue streams as your knowledge of the market grows. Opportunities you might not have seen prior to starting your business may become obvious later on. Review your business plan regularly and update it as your company grows or your market changes. I find it useful to always keep a copy of my business plan in my top desk drawer just to look at every once in a while. It is interesting to see how far I've come and how from time to time I've diverted the focus of the company from my original vision. A quick glance at my original plan always puts me back on the right track.

The act of writing a business plan forces you to think about aspects of your company you may not have paid attention to until now. Writing everything down helps you to identify the skills and talents needed to execute your strategy, thus helping you to evaluate your support needs. A well-written business plan describes exactly what is unique about your product or service. A good plan will clearly explain why you believe you have a good idea and the skills to execute it. Even if you desire to set up shop as an independent contractor or freelancer providing a service, I encourage you to go through the exercise of writing a business plan. Besides its practical use, it also serves as a good motivational tool.

Writing a business plan takes thought, but it doesn't have to be difficult. When writing your plan, seek help in the areas of your weaknesses. For many women, these include insurance, accounting, capital requirements, and operational forecasting. Even if you consult with someone only informally in these areas, you will gain a certain level of competency. A little knowledge is better than no knowledge at all.

Prior to the Internet age, it was customary for a business owner to write a five-year business plan. Today, the time has been reduced to three years.

Why Create a Plan?

The process of putting the business plan together, including the thought process before writing it, forces you to take an objective, critical, unemotional look at your entire proposal. Make sure you answer the question "Is this a good idea that's unique and serves a market?"

Your business plan will be a dynamic document. You might choose to have two versions, one public and the other private, as I did in creating the plan for BlueSuitMom.com. The public document can be used to seek financing, while the private version will be for your use in benchmarking your progress. I also use a "deck" along with my executive summary for my public business plan. A deck is a PowerPoint presentation that outlines the major elements of your business plan. I will share a copy of my business plan with you later on in this chapter. Keeping your business plan current will serve you well in many ways. The business plan is the road map for making daily decisions in your business. Should you need emergency funding, an

---

USING A BUSINESS PLAN

A business plan is used to:

- Make crucial start-up decisions

- Gain lenders and financial backers

- Measure progress

- Test planning assumptions

- Anticipate capital requirements

- Correct procedures

---

up-to-date plan allows you to focus on your quest for investors rather than scrambling to revise your old plan. Financial backers and investors use your business plan as the first clue in their decision-making process about you. If you plan to launch a Web-based business, your prospective funders, whether a bank or private investors, will want to see a business plan written to the point of profitability. Personally, I believe that the exercise of evaluating your progress will help you stay on track and focused on your goals.

19

Did you write a business plan and how did you use it?

SHERRY MAYSONAVE, EMPOWERMENT ENTERPRISES

My husband, Stephen, and I wrote a simple business plan that Stephen has used successfully in his venture capital business. He sees a lot of business plans as an investor, and he helps other companies write their plans. Our plan establishes clear PR and marketing priorities such as forming key corporate partnerships. It also includes a mission statement, yearly objective, and biyearly revenue projections, which we update each January 1.

Our plan keeps us on track, and we still operate from it. We use it primarily to check on revenues and for seeing when and where we need to increase specific PR and sales/marketing/partnership efforts. This year, we also used the plan to prioritize the execution of a Communication-Image Certification Program. One objective is to offer one certified communication-image training program a year. It's by invitation only—all applicants must be screened. I did not teach one last year (1999) because I was in the final production phase of *Casual Power*. Once the book was released in October, I went on an intensive book tour for the remainder of the year. Because the book promotions were so successful, I again felt that I was too busy to launch a certification program this fall. Although it is revenue producing, teaching the program is extremely time-consuming for me. But when we went back to the plan and reviewed the corporate partnership and speaking engagement contracts already in place for 2001 and our outlined growth objectives for this year, it became clear that to meet those objectives I had no choice but to begin training some new consultants in the fall of 2000. Our business plan showed me what to do.

Diane Ballard, DKB Associates

Yes. I used three books and followed one of the business plan templates. My business plan follows this outline:

Executive Summary
The Business Venture
The Company
The Product
The Competition
Marketing and Sales Plan
Capital Equipment List

Sales Projections

Pro Forma Income Statement

I wrote that business plan in May 2000 and looked at it again in December. That's when I realized that I needed to look at it more often, because some things had already changed. From now on, I plan to pull it out and review it at the beginning of each month. Also, I discovered that while reading it in December, I felt proud and confident that I was definitely doing the right thing! My current business plan is for two years. If I keep reviewing it monthly, I will have a better handle on where my business is and where it is going. I will have up-to-date and accurate information to use while growing my company.

MOLLY GOLD, GO MOM !NC.

My husband and I built a business plan using BusPro software and then had it reviewed by two venture capitalists and an investment expert who happened to be the best man at our wedding. Like any first draft, it has its fair share of holes and is desperately in need of an overhaul. We refer to it to chart our course and have found that our anticipated main vehicle of sale was in fact completely wrong. Also, we found that the retail process was more strenuous and took longer than we had revenue for! We hoped to get picked up by at least one juvenile products catalog during the first year, but it's taken longer than we expected to even submit our product for consideration. One Step Ahead has finally allowed us to submit, which, after all the delay, seems monumental.

BECCA WILLIAMS, WALLNUTZ, INC.

I did write a business plan for WallNutz, even though I wasn't intending to approach investors for a long time, if ever. I used as a guide an old business plan I'd written during my MBA program, modifying the financial statement and other items to fit the Wall-Nutz concept. I reread and update the plan every couple of months as sort of a "check-in." Did I meet my goals? Has everything gone according to plan or do I need to try Plan B? As long as I keep it up-to-date, it's a living blueprint of the business that guides me, and it grows and changes along with WallNutz.

Dee Ennen, Ennen Computer Services

I wrote a very informal business plan when I launched my company. It was extremely valuable helping me to transfer the swirling ideas in my head to real words on paper. I included the type of clients I wanted to target, the approximate hours I wanted to work, what my fees were going to be, what equipment I needed, what advertising I planned on doing, and my goals. One of my goals was to have several regular clients within three months. Another was to have many of my marketing ideas up and in action by the three-month mark. This meant that I printed my business cards, mailed marketing letters, placed flyers at local college campuses, and placed an ad in the Yellow Pages.

Wendy Harris, National Association of Medical Billers

Yes, I wrote a business plan. I learned how to write it in the entrepreneur class I took. I also received information and guidelines from the Small Business Administration's Web site, www.sba.org. The site is a great resource for small-business owners.

Kit Bennett, Amazingmoms.com

My husband and I created a pretty general business plan. At the time, we were not focused and were not sure which business idea we were going to go with. Amazingmoms is the name that stuck, but I am still officially known by our old name, "Newton Creek Studios." Had we been interested in pursuing investors, we would have been more careful and thorough. My husband used software to write the plan. Now that we are expanding, we have a new partner who has an MBA and, listening to him, I realize we had no idea what we were doing when we started. I really have been doing this by the seat of my pants, so to speak.

Rebecca Hart, Public Relations

I wrote a business plan for my company. I have this advice for women who want to set up their own public relations firms: Your business plan will be the blueprint to your success. It will help you determine if you are ready to go out on your own or not. While formulating your business plan, make sure to ask yourself the following four questions:

1. Do I know what I'm going to do? Defining what business you're in is sometimes easier said than done but is critical to establishing a focus for your business. For example, it took me a long time to come up with my mission statement, which is "My business is helping clients raise awareness and build relationships with key public relations executives. I provide clients with expert public relations counsel, program management, and program implementation services that align with, support, and meet business objectives."
If you don't define what kind of work you do, it will be harder to choose among the myriad of opportunities that will come your way. Also, knowing specifically what you want to do allows you to network with other professionals who provide complementary services.

2. Do I know who I'm going to work with? This is another easy-sounding question that's often hard to answer, but answering it will help you be more effective in your marketing and networking efforts. When you get your first assignments, be sure to set up a good working relationship from the beginning. Make sure budgets are in line with expectations. Ask questions if you're unclear about the project or the client's goals, and be sure you understand how the client determines success. Stay in constant communication, deliver on your promises, and remember to thank clients for their business.

3. Do I know what I'll charge? You don't want to either over or under price your services. The Public Relations Society of America (PRSA) has extensive information—call (212) 460-1459. But here are some basics:

   • Determine a salary level—at what pay would you accept employment with an organization providing the services you are offering, based on previous compensation and industry salary statistics?

- Calculate your cost of doing business—include all the things you take for granted from an employer such as office space, computer, benefits, and administration.

- Add these two figures together to give you a realistic money target. Then adjust for billable time—you won't be able to bill all eight hours in a day. Most independent practitioners find that no more than 65 percent of their work is billable.

4. Do I have a plan to diligently track each of my projects? I track by keeping a record of the type of project, project scope and components, actual time spent on entire project, actual time spent on components, time spent meeting with client, time spent traveling, expenses (phone bills, office supplies, gas/mileage, tolls), fee charged. Later, I evaluate the project to determine where I spent the most time, where I need to improve, did the fee match the level of work I put in. For a similar project in the future, what would I change in the delivery schedule and what should I charge?

Writing the Plan

Writing a business plan is a skill that few of us have learned, and many entrepreneurs and even some seasoned executives find the task intimidating. I've written several business plans for friends and professional colleagues and was apprehensive the first time I did it, but the process comes easy to me now. Like most professional tasks we do, there is a formula and process that once put in place makes this enormous job manageable. Don't think a good business plan requires the writing skills of a Pulitzer Prize–winning writer, because nothing could be further from the truth. The best business plans are written with short, concise, easy-to-understand sentences packaged in a

RESOURCES TO HELP YOU PREPARE
YOUR BUSINESS PLAN

- Business Plan Pro software can be downloaded for free at www.bplans.com and www.ideacafe.com/getmoney/fgr_budget.html. Commercial software may help in writing your business plan.

- Deloitte & Touche's free publication, *Writing an Effective Business Plan* is available online at www.us.deloitte.com/growth/guidebooks/busplan.htm.

- *The Successful Business Plan: Secrets & Strategies* (Oasis Press, 2000) by Rhonda Abrams, available at www.inc.com, offers a downloadable cash flow budget worksheet template, profit-and-loss projection reports, and many other tools for building your business plan.

- *Entrepreneur's Guide to Preparing a Winning Business Plan and Raising Venture Capital* by Keith Schilits (Prentice Hall, 1990).

manner that is easy to understand. Don't avoid writing a business plan because the process intimidates you. Even an imperfectly written plan is an important tool.

As we've already seen from our business-owner respondents, there are many Web sites and software programs that offer business plan templates to make the task easier. One warning about using a template, though, is that if you go to a venture capital firm, they will recognize this cookie-cutter approach and may decline to fund your company because they detect a lack of business experience. Depending on your goals and financial situation, you may want to hire a lawyer who specializes in building business plans. Beware, the cost is expensive: A good plan can cost between $20,000 and $40,000! Entrepreneurs who consider the attorney option are usually those who one day want to take their companies public. If you choose to hire an advisor, the person should remain just that, an advisor. You are going to be the person operating the company, and you should be the author of the plan. You will be the person who must sell the idea, execute it, and build the company, not your advisor. It's your dream. It should be your plan.

Writing a good business plan requires preparation, research, refinement, and discipline, the same elements necessary to execute most business functions. It will take time and patience.

Your business plan should contain the following elements: an executive summary, company description, market information, product or service description, sales and marketing plan, management description, financial information, and an exit strategy. Although there is no required length, most business owners find it takes fifteen to twenty pages to tell their story. If this seems like a lot, keep in mind that your financial spreadsheets may take up to five pages of it. All the pages of your business plan should be typed in 10- or 12-point Arial or Times New Roman fonts.

Now that we know how much you are going to have to write, let's discuss what's going to be included in your business plan.

The executive summary is the first and most utilized part of the business plan. It should concisely describe your product, its uniqueness, the market, your plans for the company, your management team, growth plans, and the amount of money you will need. It can be anywhere from two to seven pages but not much longer—you want to keep the reader's attention. Investors often will ask to see the executive summary before the entire business plan to determine if they are interested in pursuing your idea. The executive summary provides the outline for the rest of your business plan—you may want to think of it as your "Cliff Notes." It touches on the necessary elements of your plan, which you will expand later in the document. Your executive summary foreshadows everything your potential investors will learn later in your plan.

FORMAT AND PRESENTATION
OF YOUR BUSINESS PLAN

- Print on high quality paper on one side only

- Use at least a 10-point font but no larger than 12-point for all text

- Use Arial or Times New Roman fonts

- Include a table of contents that lists each area of your plan

- Number all pages

- Include a cover page with company logo, name, address, and other identifying information

- Maintain reasonable borders

- Eliminate industry-specific words from your document so that a nonprofessional can understand what you are saying

- Include samples of ads or other marketing pieces in an appendix

- Proofread and then have someone else proof it again

- Bind the plan so pages will stay in sequence. Do not staple

- Keep it professional looking. Don't go overboard with flashy binders or inserts

The company description comes next. Here is where you describe in detail the mission or "valuable formula" for your company. What is it you would like to produce or provide to your market? What makes your product or service unique? Is the product currently found in the marketplace? If so, who provides it, and why is your company going to be different? If you are going to produce a tangible product, you need to describe the resources or ingredients necessary to make the item. For instance, Shannon Rubio of TheSmileBox.com would include a description of the gifts she puts into one of her boxes. If she needs 10,000 yellow corrugated boxes with smiley faces on them, she needs to tell the investor where the boxes come from and why she chose yellow rather than blue, if that's important to her product's acceptance. Darcy Lyons's Garden Party business plan includes information about obtaining gardening tools from boutiques and wholesalers. You'll find an example of BlueSuitMom.com's business philosophy and mission statement in the sample business plan I've included at the end of this chapter.

20

Please describe your business philosophy and what makes your business unique

SHERRY MAYSONAVE, EMPOWERMENT ENTERPRISES

I'll give you our philosophy the way it appears in our mission statement:

1. Make every attempt to be responsive to potential customers and clients within twenty-four hours of contact.
2. Form close long-term partnerships with corporations directly linked to our business.
3. Utilize the Internet in these three primary ways:
   a) to create a virtual, instantly accessible brochure about Empowerment Enterprises' services and products;
   b) to facilitate communication and information to

individuals and publications and for writing articles related to our business; c) for e-commerce.

4. Make every effort to retain all rights to my book, *Casual Power*, particularly the illustrations and photography, for flexibility and the ability to maximize its leverage potential.

5. Minimize the number of employees. Offer a Communication-Image Certification Program that produces high-quality communication-image consultants trained in the Empowerment Enterprises' philosophy and the esteemed standard by which Sherry Maysonave works with individuals and corporations. We then work jointly on projects such as corporate workshops and special events. After certification, the trainees will operate their own businesses but will be associated with EE and paid by EE when assisting Sherry. EE refers individual clients to the certified consultants, who pay EE a set referral fee. The program requires an application process and screening. Trainees are essentially handpicked; four were selected out of 600 applicants this past year. They pay a fee to EE to train in the program.

In Empowerment Enterprises' Mission Statement we state that we are devoted to assisting others attain professional and personal success. Our image services and communication programs are custom designed to empower the individual or group, however unique, to easily achieve their goals. It is our belief that success increases your quality of life, your sphere of influence, and your ability to make a positive difference for others. Our philosophy and presentation style is motivating, educational, and inspiring.

MOLLY GOLD, GO MOM INC.

Our goal is to help busy moms organize themselves. We target women with at least one child in preschool and beyond. We find the most appreciative feedback from women with three or more kids. Why target them? Because they are all struggling to strike a balance and have experienced the frustration of multiple calendars completely unsynched. First-time moms don't recognize the value in this, because they don't know the scheduling challenges ahead. For those first-timers who do appreciate planner systems, it's a slam dunk for us, because they want to transfer that skill over to organizing the new tasks associated with motherhood.

MERYL GUERRERO, PARENTING 101

The goal of Parenting 101 is to educate parents and caregivers on the issues they face every day. We strive to bring the best experts and professionals together for a day of parenting education that's not easily available in other places. Parents often don't know where to find the terrific resources in their own communities. Anyone can be a mom or dad but to be a good mom or dad takes patience and some know-how. That's what we provide.

ROBIN ZELL, BRAGELETS

My business philosophy is based purely on personalized customer service. Sometimes a new mother will call me from the hospital after just giving birth to order her Bragelet. A mother's love doesn't get purer than this. I hear the labor stories and share my own experiences. I also take the time to shower her with congratulations. It's very important that we share the excitement of the moment of birth with our moms. It's my goal to maintain this kind of customer service experience as part of my business for as long as possible.

Marketing Information

Next in your business plan will be a description of your potential market. This is a good place to utilize your research and the resources listed in chapter 3. Include demographic statistics, trends in the marketplace, and future opportunities you see that will contribute to your company's success. Describe for your potential investor the size and potential of your market. In BlueSuitMom.com's business plan I mentioned that working executive mothers number over ten million and were the fastest growing segment in the workforce during 1999, according to the Census Bureau. I coupled that to the fact that there were no other Web sites exclusively designed for executive working mothers, to show the tremendous size of the potential market to investors. Make sure you uphold your credibility by citing your sources for your statistics and research.

If there are other businesses that already provide similar products or services, make certain that you describe them in this marketing section. Not only do you not want your potential investors to think you are entering the marketplace with blinders on, but it gives you the chance to explain why your product is different. When my business partner and I launched BlueSuitMom.com, we described why it was important to launch our company on Mother's Day. This timing allowed us to take advantage of the public relations opportunities surrounding the holiday and made BlueSuitMom.com the first site of its kind in the marketplace, an important element to building our brand. We knew from our research that *Working Mother* magazine planned to launch its portal sometime in the summer, and we were determined to beat them to the punch. Potential investors liked our forward thinking and strategic planning.

21

What market are you serving with your product?

JULIE MARCHESE, TWINSADVICE.COM

My market is mothers of twins or multiples. I offer these moms both a book and a Web site with advice and information. My book came first. I started writing it when my twins were four months old, because I could not find what I was looking for in published twin books. I wrote it on Post-it notes that I gathered together once a week, organized them, and wrote. It took ten months. Later, I decided to develop a Web site, because there is not a site exactly like

TwinsAdvice.com. The Internet is also more convenient for a busy mother of twins to go to for support as opposed to having to leave the house for a mother-of-twins club meeting.

JULIE AIGNER-CLARK, BABY EINSTEIN

My market is children from birth to age four and parents who want to expose their children to the arts and humanities in a way that they love. It is our mission to be the leading provider of developmental media products for babies and toddlers.

KAITLAND THORSTENSON, CERTIFIED PUBLIC ACCOUNTANT

My target market is small-business owners who don't need a full-time accounting staff and can't afford a large accounting agency. I strive to provide at less cost the same level of accounting service they would get from a large firm.

SHANNON RUBIO, THESMILEBOX.COM

Our market is mainly professional women in their late twenties to mid-fifties who have Internet access and are used to shopping online. We have very few male clients.

ROBIN STERNE, WOW! DESIGNS, INC.

My clients range from small, home-based businesses to Fortune 500 companies and nonprofit organizations. I've done annual reports, logos, business cards, brochures, billboards, candy bar wrappers, concert badges, and T-shirt art, and I don't mind taking on new projects. If it needs to be created, I'm up to the challenge!

MICHELLE ZEITLIN, MORE ZAP PRODUCTIONS

Our target market is corporate event planners, entertainment production companies, directors, and marketing executives. Many of our clients are Fortune 500 companies seeking high-end, hands-on production and concept development for film, video, and live shows. We customize our presentations for any audience, any venue. We recently produced an industry sales show for thousands at a convention. We supply dancers, singers, acrobats, skaters, musicians, composers, technical directors, and costume designers for our productions.

Sales and Marketing Plan

It takes more than just a good product or service to get people to pay you money! You also need a good sales and marketing strategy, the next section in your business plan. Your marketing strategy should be built on extensive research of your current and potential customers' buying behaviors, perceptions of value, and spending patterns. You'll need to take time to think out your strategy for making people aware of your product and how you will create a desire in them to buy it. Consider traditional means of marketing such as direct mail, sampling, and advertising. Remember also the power of a strong public relations effort. Every marketing professional, whether they represent Proctor and Gamble or McDonald's, will tell you that the most powerful means of marketing is word of mouth. If you can get people talking about you, including the press, you will gain customers. When we launched BlueSuitMom.com, we used the tie-in to Mother's Day and gave the press several angles to talk about us with their readers. Our press releases noted our launch and also talked about the number of executive working women who were celebrating Mother's Day. The end result was thirty news stories in local and national publications and on radio and television about BlueSuitMom.com.

Operational Plan

The next section of your business plan, the operational plan, should include your selling methods, vendor relationships, sourcing information, and a description of your management team. Will your customers purchase your product through mail order, phone sales, or on the Internet? What forms of payment will you receive for your product—cash, check, credit cards? If you plan to have a sales force, whether employees or independent contractors, describe the training they will require and the territories they will cover. Julie Aigner-Clark chose to sell her Baby Einstein videos in upscale toy boutiques. Her plan describes why she chose this approach and why she believes it produced the best results for her company. Today, her updated plan includes the integration of big retailers like Target into her distribution channels.

I'm sure you've heard the saying, "Behind every good man is a woman." Well, behind every successful company is a good management team. In fact, for many potential investors, management experience is the most important predictor of a successful business. Even if you are planning to be a one-woman company, it's important to describe the talents, experiences, and skills you bring to your business. It's okay to toot your own horn here. Remember, what sets apart a successful entrepreneur from the average employee is belief in your dreams and your ability to make it all work.

If you intend to seek investors from strangers, like banks and venture capital firms, make certain they understand how your skills will produce positive results for the company. Potential investors also like to see a management team that is well-rounded. In growing BlueSuitMom.com, you will see that I balanced my creative talents with the technology experience of my partner, Rachael. Your description of your management team should conclude with a list of key advisors, board members, and major shareholders.

Exit Strategy

A business's exit strategy, your plan for getting out of the business, is the section of the business plan most forgotten. But don't let its usual omission diminish its importance. No one begins a business to run it forever. You will need to have an exit strategy in place and will appear to be a seasoned professional by doing so. The exit strategy is particularly important to venture capitalists and investors, because it tells them when they can expect a return on their investment. The greatest upside financially for you as the business owner and for your investors comes with the sale of your company.

Financial Statement

Next to the executive summary in importance is the financial section of your business plan. This section should contain detailed information regarding cash flow projections, anticipated revenue, and expenses. These projections help establish whether and how the business will meet its financial obligations as well as your expectations. It also tells the investor how soon he can anticipate a return on his investment. Unless schooled in finance, few of us have the know-how to prepare detailed financial documents. If you are like me, a creative thinker rather than a numbers person, this area might scare you. My suggestion is to take one step at a time. When you don't know what a term means, keep looking for a definition until you find one you understand. For instance, you don't need a certified public accountant to explain that a "cash flow projection" is a spreadsheet on which you list your expenses and revenue and then match them up to see if you can pay your bills next month.

Even if your expenses exceed your revenue, it's okay, as long as you receive cash in time to pay your expenses. Because your business is new, your early financials will have to be projections. Use accurate and concise cost and income estimates. Don't forget to include unexpected expenses. You will also need to use standardized accounting formats, because this area of your plan will be the most carefully scrutinized by lenders. Don't forget the reason you are going into business is to make money, so this section is just as important to you as it is to investors.

Financial projections that you will need to include are start-up expenses, a profit-and-loss statement, and cash flow chart. In addition, you will need a source fund schedule, a pro forma balance sheet, and historical financial information, if available. You will prepare each of these reports based on assumptions you will establish for your business. Your assumptions should include the size of the market, sales buildup, gross profit margin, payroll, and capital expenditures such as furniture, computers, and equipment.

In an attempt to keep you reading this chapter, I'll give you a layman's explanation of these reports.

- **Start-Up Expense Report:** It's just what it sounds like, a list of expenses associated with starting your company. Many will be one-time costs like office furniture. You should include everything, even if some like phone service are ongoing monthly expenses. Don't forget to include setup fees, temporary help, and renovation costs to create your home office. These expenses will later be worked into your profit-loss statement.

- **Projected Cash Flow:** This is a two-part forecast of when cash will flow into your business and when it will flow out throughout the year. It will help you decide when it's time to make purchases or hire additional help. You won't want to buy your new computer system in a month when cash flow is low. Basically, this report tells you when you can spend.

- **Source Fund Schedule:** If you intend to fund your company through investors, this report identifies the timing for each investment. You might know that Aunt Sue will be investing $5,000 in October and Uncle Henry $2,000 in June. Having this knowledge will help you in managing your company's growth.

- **Pro Forma Balance Sheet:** I call this the "everything" report. It's the mirror into your company's future. If "everything" goes right and all your projections are correct, it will become the statement of your actual finances for this year. It includes all your company's assets, liabilities, and equity. It tells you how much investment money you need to meet your goals and how much of that money will be actual working capital.

- **Historical Information:** If you purchased an already established business, you might be lucky enough to inherit financial information from the previous owner. In this case, your projections will be based on actual numbers.

My advice after preparing your financials, whether you do them on your own or with the help of a software program, is to sit down with an accountant. You want to be sure that your projections, assumptions, and math are correct. A small investment in time and money now eliminates costly surprises down the road.

Another tip is to know the numbers inside and out, especially if you are seeking outside investors. You need to become the expert on your company to sell your concept either to a private investor or a venture capital firm. One of the main reasons cited for venture capital funds not going to women is their lack of financial knowledge about their company. This is not to say that men can explain numbers better than women, but I believe women traditionally put less emphasis on numbers.

Business plans come in all shapes and sizes. Here is a sample of one; all business plans should contain the following information:

Cover Page with name of company, address

Company Mission Statement

Business Description

Strategy

Objectives

Present Market/Market Conditions (include here the size
   of the market in dollars, a description of the market,
   and who the other players in the market are)

Marketing Approach

Operational Issues

Management Team

Financial Projections

Capital Requirements (include how the money will be spent)

Exit Strategy

Conclusion

WEB SITES THAT SUPPLY FINANCIAL PLANNING TEMPLATES

www.toolkit.cch.com

www.inc.com

www.bizmove.com

www.sba.gov

www.entrepreneur.com

As indicated earlier in this chapter, your business plan will change over time. It's not uncommon to see business owners abort one or multiple ideas from their original business plans. It's okay to change direction and try new approaches.

22

What ideas have you changed since your initial business plan?

MOLLY GOLD, GO MOM !NC.

We initially chose trade shows to market our product. It was a bad idea. We based the entire first year of our business plan on the notion that we would sell a few thousand of our product at three different trade shows. We only sold twenty-two. We chose trade shows based on skimpy research I did on the American Baby Group's various consumer exhibits across the country, called Baby Faires. With sponsors like Babies R US and *American Baby* magazine and attendance of 8,000 and more, we thought it was a surefire way to sell 1,000 product per show. Not exactly. Attendees at these shows are mostly first-time, younger parents who are less attached to time management skills learned in the workplace and are generally looking for freebies with absolutely no interest in taking a few minutes to learn about our planner. After two of these fiascos, we realized that the shows were only good to gain company exposure in the market and a place to network—which we did. But, it was an expensive lesson. Next, we went to Book Expo America (BEA) to learn about book stuff. This was enlightening and expensive, with payoffs in the far distance because the cycle for purchasing calendar products for 2001 had already passed. We are just now submitting future calendars for reviews by major booksellers. So we had to change the marketing ideas in our original business plan.

Dee Ennen, Ennen Computer Services

In the category of worst idea, I have a story to share that illustrates a change from our original business plan.

In the beginning when I just had one or two regular clients, everything seemed to work out fine. The clients never needed me at the same time, and I was easily able to handle the work. As I continued to grow and get more clients though, the workload became absolutely impossible to handle. I had two chiropractors, one insurance adjuster, one attorney, and a personnel agency that I worked for on a regular basis. Sometimes they would just have a letter or two to type, but at other times they all brought two or three tapes each to transcribe. Several afternoons at 5:00 I can remember looking at my desk and seeing it completely covered with work to be done by the next day. I used to pile the dictation tapes on my desk by my computer. One day, I had eight tapes that needed to be typed by the following day. Because I was new and didn't want to lose any business, I worked all night and did it. I worked every weekend as well—any work dropped off on Friday I gave back to them by Monday. One of the chiropractors gave me all his work for the week on Friday, and I had to have it done by Monday. I wish I had realized earlier to set limits before I got burned out, but I didn't. What I did discover was that once I set the turnaround times for my clients, they accepted it. One even told me he didn't really need the work back so quickly, but he just assumed it was my policy to complete the job swiftly. I was creating the pressure of deadlines and the stress associated with it, all unnecessarily!

JEANNINE CLONTZ, ACCURATE BUSINESS SERVICES

One idea that didn't work was my first attempt at direct mail. I've learned now through research that I need to put together a better database. What I'm doing now is utilizing my current clients and gearing some postcard mailings to them and a select few potential clients in specific industries (like professional speakers, realtors, and litigation attorneys). The best new clients I've gotten were as a result of word-of-mouth type marketing. That's why I've elected to send my cards to current clients on a regular basis to try and secure referrals. It's important to be consistent in whatever marketing you do. My mailings let my clients know all the different services I can provide for them. The only other advertising I'm doing at this point is the Yellow Pages. I have a one-inch ad that lists some services, and it's worked really well.

ROBIN ZELL, BRAGELETS

One of the worst ideas in our original plan was relying on our Web site to bring in sales. Big mistake! The Internet is truly a World Wide Web with sites being added by the thousands each day. You must reregister your site with search engines about every thirty days because so many are added daily that yours just falls off the planet, so to speak. I really started the Web site to give my customers an alternative means for ordering during late night feedings, naptimes, and quiet moments for new mothers. I felt the site could be changed more rapidly than a brochure, because I knew I was going to introduce new products and a whole new look. I also knew a phone ringing constantly in my home would raise our family stress level—that's why I figured the more Internet orders, the less time I had to spend on the phone.

What finally worked for me was sticking with what had worked for the previous owner, advertising. The only difference was I had to design a new advertising piece that promoted the Web site.

Ready, Set, Go!

Once you complete your business plan, there are two groups who will rely on it: your lenders and yourself. A well-written plan will reassure an investor about the validity of your business and your ability to execute the plan. Almost every lender, whether it's a venture capital firm or government agency, requests a business plan or executive summary or a combination of both. My warning to you is don't wait until someone asks you for a business plan to start writing one. Write it now! Your detailed business plan will help you make critical start-up decisions, anticipate cash requirements, and evaluate your growth opportunities.

For your benefit, I have included the original business plan for my company, BlueSuitMom.com. For proprietary reasons, some names have been changed and confidential information deleted, but it contains enough content to give you a good idea of what a business plan should look like.

BlueSuitMom.com

Executive Summary

BlueSuitMom.com is positioned to be the leading online destination for career-committed mothers. On Mother's Day 2000, we will begin delivering tailored content, community information, time-relevant e-commerce, timesaving interactive tools, and online classes to executive working mothers and the companies they work for. We not only will be the first site to target senior-level working mothers but we also will be the first women's site to offer online virtual classes. We have developed four revenue streams making BlueSuitMom.com both a consumer and business-to-business site:

- Advertising
- E-commerce
- Fee-Based Online Classes
- Corporate Work/Family Balance Seminars

Our Market

The BlueSuitMom.com market is a career-committed mother who on average earns $78,000 a year. According to 1999 Mediamark Research, Inc. (MRI), research conducted by *Working Mother* magazine, the market totals more than ten million women. These women either hold managerial positions within their organizations or own their own businesses. A recent federal population study reported that one out of three women in our market earns more than her spouse. Ninety-nine percent of this group have access to the Internet at the office and are online more than three times a day. Companies have recently recognized the importance of women on the Internet after the 1999 holiday season showed spending by women rose to 66 percent of all e-commerce spending. Since the disposable income of our market is considerably higher than the average female, we recognize the opportunity we have in delivering this niche market to advertisers and retailers. Our market is expected to continue to grow annually due to the management opportunities being offered within the new economy and the higher salaries being offered in the hot job market.

Present Market

Presently, there are no sites that exclusively serve executive mothers. In fact, there are only seven sites that target working mothers in general, and none deliver both e-commerce and content. The closest "competitor" is www.workingmother.com, which merely reprints the content of their print magazine online. As it exists today, an executive mother can visit any one of the women's portals such as iVillage, Women.com, and Oxygen to obtain career and family information, but it is a hit-or-miss situation. The information on the career channels may or may not be written for a woman with children, and the content on the family channels may or may not be written for an executive working mother. In either case, the chances that the information is written for a career-committed mother in senior management are minuscule. The issues facing this market are unique. Executive moms find little use for articles on "flextime," "job sharing," or "saving your Starbuck coffee money in order to take a summer vacation." Whereas articles on "earning more money than your spouse," "separation from your children while traveling for business" and "understanding your stock options" are quite relevant to this group of mothers. Although we have designed BlueSuitMom.com with the specific issues of an executive mother in mind, we feel that due to lack of exclusive working mother sites, we will also attract a large group of aspiring blue-suit mothers.

Products and Services

BlueSuitMom.com provides our market tailored content, interactive tools, community and virtual courses aimed at helping executive mothers balance work and family. Content channels include Career, Food, Family, Health, News, Money, Travel, and Virtual Classes. Within each channel we deliver Q&A with experts, topical feature stories, recent research, chat rooms, message boards, and tips. BlueSuitMom.com also delivers unique features targeted directly to the demographics of our audience such as Ladder of Success (promotion posting for our audience), Female Business Directories, Spotlight on Executive Working Mother of the Month, Exercise of the Week, Job Search Database, Weekly Meal Planning, Small Business Management Advice, Industry Message Boards, and Freebie listings. A relationship with iSyndicate provides real time news headlines. On-site promotions, sweepstakes, and surveys provide additional stickiness to the site and help us rapidly build our database of members. Our biweekly newsletter is used to feature fresh content and drive return visits to our site.

The interactive tools BlueSuitMom.com offers to our audience were designed to meet their specific needs. Interactive tools include fat gram and calorie calculators, stock quotes, illness database, and over 48 financial calculators.

BlueSuitMom.com will be the first women's site to offer virtual classes online. Visitors to BlueSuitMom.com will be able to choose from a variety of course topics, ranging from child development to professional management. Once they have paid a modest fee via our e-commerce store, they will gain access to the class curriculum, assessment tools, homework, and a toll-free conference line. On the scheduled class day/time, the attendee will attend the class via the toll-free line and be able to interact with an instructor and classmates. The class channel not only provides an original revenue stream for our site, it is a "sticky" feature. We believe we will attract mothers and working women outside our market who are directed by search engines to our educational services, thus increasing our page views and e-commerce traffic. We expect substantial media attention for the debut of this original concept in the women's Internet landscape. First-round funding will allow us to enhance the Class Channel with video streaming.

Partnerships

The exceptional management team at BlueSuitMom.com has quickly developed partnerships with key Internet companies. Among our partners are: Meals.com, Headhunter.com, StockPoint.com, WomenFirst.com, *American Baby*, StorkAvenue.com, the *Wall Street Journal*, and Workoutsforwomen.com. It has been our goal to associate ourselves with only the strongest brands and most influential Internet sites in order to build the value of the BlueSuitMom.com brand, establish credibility with our audience, and create a broad base of marketing opportunities. These partnerships represent advertising and e-commerce revenue splits, cobranded pages, and marketing deals that will ultimately increase our visibility and income.

BlueSuitMom.com has built a strong team of content providers as well. Our experts represent published individuals, researchers, instructors, and professional veterans in their areas of expertise. We have also developed relationships with associations such as the National Institute of Distant Relationship Building and Nova Southeastern University Family Center, which can deliver additional value to our audience.

Revenue

Unlike many Web sites, BlueSuitMom.com has created four streams of revenue, which take advantage of both online and offline opportunities. Our multiple cash flow model better positions our company for rapid growth.

The first revenue stream is advertising. We present a unique and exceptional opportunity to advertisers, because BlueSuitMom.com delivers a prequalified, niche market. Advertisers know the value of capturing high-income working mothers who, according to Cyberatlas research, make 85 percent of the household spending decisions. Our demographics are in high demand by retailers, which presents the opportunity for higher CPM's (advertising pricing on the web). Marketers seeking our audience include car manufacturers/retailers, travel organizations, consumer product companies, financial institutions, apparel retailers, and service providers. Due to our very attractive market, we have been able to sign on an ad agency prior to launch.

Our second revenue stream comes from e-commerce. We are testing both inventory and affiliate commerce models. Our e-commerce URL is www.momsstore.com. The name is consumer-friendly and will drive traffic from Web search engines. BlueSuitMom.com currently offers upscale family apparel, gifts, and skin care products. A long list of affiliations with retailers such as Amazon, Omaha Steaks, Petopia, Cooking.com, LLBean, and Priceline.com will offer our audience other areas of shopping.

The third and groundbreaking revenue stream is from our fee-based virtual classes. Visitors pay a reasonable tuition ranging from $25 to $100 for online courses. This is our greatest earning potential since BlueSuitMom.com will be the first women's Web site to offer such a service. Busy mothers struggle to find time to enhance their parenting skills. At BlueSuitMom.com, we not only provide mothers with content but the forum in which to learn, without having to spend the time to find an expert, schedule an appointment, take time off from work, and attend the meeting. We feel that executive mothers who recognize the importance of education and have disposable income will take advantage of our classes. We offer classes in three venues: traditional classroom, lecture hall, and one-on-one. They are priced according to the level of interaction the student is provided with the instructor/expert. The class channel also features personal fitness training and a team of certified coaches facilitating mothers through work and family challenges. Our class channel presents a great tuition revenue stream, as well as a captive audience for advertising income.

Last, BlueSuitMom.com will generate revenue by offering work and family balance seminars and Intranet content to corporations. We will offer half- and full-day training sessions for female management designed to help them manage the demands of work and family. Each session will include assessment tools, role-playing, practical tips, and workshops. The sessions are developed in conjunction with the host company in order to compliment their corporate culture and work/family issues. In the present job market where companies are fighting to retain good talent, we have a substantial opportunity to position BlueSuitMom.com as a human resource tool to America's biggest companies. BlueSuitMom.com will also license content for use on company Intranet sites. Based on content within BlueSuitMom.com, our service will offer companies a tool that can be presented to their corporate mothers as a benefit and position them as an attractive employer for talented working mothers.

Management Team

BlueSuitMom.com is composed of a team of professional veterans from top brands such as Blockbuster, CBS Sportsline.com, Cox Interactive Media, the Miami Herald Publishing Company, and AutoNation USA. The management team has worked together many times within a number of organizations during the past twelve years.

The team is led by Maria Bailey, president and founder. Ms. Bailey has more than twenty years experience in business with a concentration in publishing, marketing, and business development. Most recently, she served as vice president at AutoNation USA, formerly Republic Industries, where she reported directly to the co-CEO during the years when Republic was named as America's number one fastest growing company by *Forbes* magazine. She created and launched the first loyalty marketing program within the automotive industry while at AutoNation. Prior to AutoNation, Ms. Bailey ran Bailey Innovative Marketing, which served clients such as Discovery

Zone, the *Sun-Sentinel* newspaper, and Broward Community College. Her involvement with Broward Community College included serving as executive director of the BCC Foundation, managing assets of over $15 million. In 1990, she created and produced the South Florida Parenting Conference, which today is the largest parenting conference in Florida. She began her career with McDonald's Restaurants and the *Miami Herald*, where she held a variety of management positions. Ms. Bailey is published in *Child* magazine, *South Florida Parenting* magazine, the *Miami Herald*, and *Family Times* magazine. She was an invited speaker at the 1999 International Direct Marketing Conference and will be a featured speaker with AOL, Fisher-Price, and Playtex at this year's International Quality & Productivity Center's (IQPC) conference, "eBaby: Marketing to New and Expectant Parents Online." She is the mother of four children and a marathon runner.

Rachael Bender, vice president of technology, has produced Web sites for some of the Internet's strongest brands. While at a South Florida start-up, she was responsible for all page design, content placement, and server administration, and she developed the e-commerce store. Her contributions at Cox Interactive Media included Web production on GoPBI.com, SoFla.com, Lightening Stalker.com, and Sunfest.org. Ms. Bender not only brings strong technology experience to BlueSuitMom.com but a background in journalism. She spent several years working with and is published in *Florida Today*.

Noreen Conroy, vice president of marketing, most recently managed Sportsline.com's Rewards program, the only in-network online loyalty program. In this capacity she was responsible for increasing page views, repeat site visits, and memberships. Ms. Conroy gained her extensive marketing experience with leaders such as Blockbuster Entertainment, AutoNation USA, Extended Stay America, and Discovery Zone. As Blockbusters' database marketing manager she managed over fifteen customer segmentations, analyzed Return on Investment (ROI), and oversaw a $20-million budget with a sixty-million-customer database. Through her efforts, Blockbuster obtained a 10 percent response rate on direct mail campaigns, increased the length of customer activity, and obtained 1.5 paid rentals for every free one given. Her expertise in database marketing has been utilized to build BlueSuitMom.com's database.

Marketing

We have put a strong marketing strategy in place that will grow as we complete our seed round of financing. Presently, we are leveraging our relationships to execute a grassroots and viral marketing plan. StorkAvenue, the largest retailer of birth announcements in the U.S., will include BlueSuitMom.com's logo on its fifteen million printed catalogs. The catalogs are distributed through Ross Laboratories prenatal hospital network to expectant mothers. Arbonne International Cosmetics is not only providing us with sample facial spas for online promotional use but is also including BlueSuitMom.com inserts in its maternity direct mail campaigns. Because BlueSuitMom.com was a sponsor for Parenting 101, our logo appeared in their ads. In June 2000, our logo will appear in over $40,000 worth of regional advertising for the Parenting 101 conference in South Florida. *American Baby* magazine is highlighting BlueSuitMom.com as a resource for mothers on their Web site as well as featuring our content monthly as part of a promotion. Liz Claiborne is considering cosponsoring our launch sweepstakes giveaway of blue business suits. We have also carefully nurtured a network of professional women's organizations, which we believe will provide strong word-of-mouth marketing. Thus far, we have been able to develop these valuable marketing opportunities without tapping into our marketing budget.

Exit Strategy

Our exit strategy is to position the company to be acquired by a large women's portal such as iVillage, Women.com, or Oxygen. Earlier this year, McDonald publishing, owner of *Working Woman* and *Working Mother* magazines, announced that they would launch a women's portal in fall 2000. By doing so, they will draw attention to the unique market of working mothers. We believe the other women's portals will react by attempting to fill the working mother niche as quickly as possible within their site. It is far more cost effective for them to fill the hole through acquisition as they have done in other areas. Recently, iVillage acquired Parent Soup, Parentsplace, and Familypoint.com in order to fill holes within their content. The latter was acquired for $26 million after being in business for just nine months. It is our intent to establish the BlueSuitMom.com brand and company infrastructure quickly enough to position us for acquisition by one of the big three. Our marketing plan was developed not only to attract visitors but the attention of possible content aggregators as well.

Financing

We are now actively seeking $1 million in seed money to enable us to hire the appropriate talent, expand our marketing efforts, and invest in additional technology. BlueSuitMom.com is presently valued at $5 million based on comparable sites, positioning, and potential growth. Investors will receive equity based on valuation. We will increase our valuation to $10 million by January 2001 when we will seek $4 million in first-round venture capital funding.

Conclusion

BlueSuitMom.com has the elements necessary to be successful: an untapped niche market, an experienced management team, strong strategic partnerships, multiple revenue streams, tactical marketing alliances to support a contagious marketing plan, and the right timing to execute our exit strategy. We will quickly become the leader in reaching executive working mothers. Executive mothers will find the fresh content and interactive tools an important resource in helping them maintain work and family balance. The dependency of our readers will translate into higher page views, advertiser demand, and steady growth of tuition revenues. BlueSuitMom.com is positioned for rapid growth and a high return for investors.

CHAPTER FIVE

Funding

I'm sure you have heard it a thousand times from skeptical friends and family members: One-third of all new businesses fail in the first year. Although there are many reasons for failure, the most frequent cause is trying to start and operate a business without sufficient capital. To avoid this pitfall, you will need to evaluate your capital needs against your formal business plan. Ask yourself these questions: How much money will I need to start the company? How much money of my own do I have to invest in my company? How much money will I need to stay in business for the first year? Some financial experts will advise you to develop a three-to-five-year projection of sales, revenue, and cash flow. I strongly recommend you at least project your profit and losses until you reach profitability. A good idea with not enough funding behind it will probably fail. To begin the process of analyzing the amount of money needed to start your company, consider these start-up costs:

- Incorporations and licenses
- Remodeling needed to create your home office
- Equipment such as fax, computer, printer, copier
- Installation costs for phone lines, additional lighting
- Office supplies: pens, pencils, paper clips, paper

- Legal and professional fees
- Telecommunication and Internet service provider expenses
- Insurance
- Letterhead, stationery, note cards, business cards
- Advertising
- Employee wages and benefits

Also try to anticipate unforeseen expenses. I recommend that you deposit six months of operating expenses in either a savings account or in your business checking account. Should the total amount of expenses exceed $50,000, you might think like a big corporation treasurer and invest a small portion of your operating costs in a short-term certificate of deposit so your money is making money while you wait to spend it. Your monthly expenses will include the following recurring costs:

- Employee wages, including taxes and SSI
- Telecomunication and Internet service provider expenses
- Insurance payments
- Sales taxes
- Maintenance of office equipment
- Advertising and marketing
- Electricity
- Transportation
- Entertaining prospective clients
- Equipment leases

Finding Funding for Your Company

Once you have determined how much money you will need to operate your business, it's time to go looking for it. There are several ways to find funding for your company:

1. Commercial lenders
2. Venture capital firms

3. Angel investors

4. Friends and family

5. Personal savings

6. Credit cards/line of credit

If you decide not to seek outside money to launch your company, you won't be alone. The majority of small-business owners use their own money to finance their start-up costs. Many liquidate life insurance policies, take out a second mortgage on their homes, or use money in savings accounts. Even if you plan to fund your idea yourself, I encourage you to learn about the options I've listed above. You never know when you might need additional money, particularly when you go to expand. It's always good to know your options before it's time to make a decision.

I recently did an interview with *Smart Money* magazine and was asked, "What was the biggest surprise about starting your company?" My answer came quickly. The greatest surprise was I had to devote half of each day to raising money.

23

How do you find funding for your home-based business?

HEIDI PERRY, HOME BUSINESS ONLINE

The best advice I can give on funding your business is "Live within your means!" One of the most common questions I get from hopeful home-based business owners is "Where can I find money to start my business?" My first question to them is "Do you really need it?" Remember, one of the critical things that distinguishes a home-based business from big business is its inherent ability to trim the fat. Before going for a loan, think of creative ways to raise funds. Can you do a joint venture? Is there a low-cost product you can sell immediately and then use the profits to expand? Get creative and see what you can come up with.

I advise never to start a business unless 1) you have sufficient income coming in by keeping your regular job or through a spouse's work, or 2) you have sufficient personal savings to see you through your business's first year. It makes a huge difference in the freedom you feel when you're not bogged down with personal financial matters. However, there may be reasons to seek funding up front, so prepare early for these challenges.

The first thing to do is, establish your credit rating. To get business financing, you need a credit history. If you have always used your spouse's credit card, it's time to get your own. Open a business account in your name. Do some research or talk to a financial advisor to help you get the right kind of credit, a crucial factor when you ask for a loan.

Since bank loans are difficult to get and take a long time for approval, most home-based business owners look for financing through alternative routes such as credit cards, home equity loans, and loans from family members.

If you don't have access to funds from these sources, you will need an airtight, knock-'em-dead business plan to present to potential investors.

Commercial Lenders

Commercial lenders like banks and credit unions can sometimes be a source of funding, although most tend to stay away from start-ups because they have no history behind them. Many larger banks will not even look at your application. But that doesn't mean it's impossible to find loans. Some smaller local institutions tend to be more open to small-business owners. You can also find banks that offer loans through the Small Business Administration. You can either inquire at your bank or visit the SBA Web site (www.sba.gov) for a complete list of participating institutions.

24

Are there ways to gain the favor of commercial lenders for your home business?

PRISCILLA HUFF, AUTHOR

I've taken newspaper articles to my bankers that quote favorable statistics about investing in women's businesses because I want them to know that women business owners are as good risks as men. They have appreciated the information, and it helped make them aware of the women business owners in our area. Here are four tips to help make your bank more "friendly" to you and your business:

- Get to know the bank's personnel and management.
- Rather than make electronic deposits, go into the bank and ask a quick business question. This lets them know you are involved in the business community.
- Treat all personnel and staff with courtesy and respect. If a problem arises with your account, approach it with a problem-solving attitude instead of an accusatory tone.
- Follow the bank's procedures for listing checks, making deposits, and so forth, to lessen mistakes and make your transactions efficient and smooth.
- Take the time to let the president and executives of your bank know why it is beneficial for both of you to work for entrepreneurs in your community.

HEIDI PERRY, HOME BUSINESS ONLINE

Financial institutions are notorious for hesitating to lend money to the self-employed. I know of home-based business owners who are making far more now than they were when they had an employer, yet the bank does not want to lend them the money to expand. The fact is, there is no stability in their income, and they are now a credit risk.

The best idea is to get loans or increase your credit limit while you are still employed and have a steady income. You may also want to consider getting an additional credit card for emergency purposes. Just beware if you are the type who has a hard time resisting credit card purchases! You can get into a real bind . . . real fast.

Venture Capital Firms

According to *Industry Standard* magazine, only 4 percent of the $16 billion in venture capital funding in 1999 went to women-owned businesses. This represents some progress. In 1993, less than 2 percent of $4.9 billion from venture capital firms went to women. From 1998 through the first half of 2000, the percentage of venture-financed start-ups with a woman on the senior management team jumped from 21 percent to 43 percent. The Internet Age has also spawned the growth of several organizations aimed at increasing the number of female-funded companies.

Springboard is a series of nationwide forums that showcase venture-capital-ready companies led by women that are seeking $1 million to $25 million in financing from investors. Springboard sponsors a boot camp, which many women have told me is a must for learning the ropes for launching a company. Women meet venture capitalists, and other female entrepreneurs and coaches help them prepare their presentations to investors. To learn about upcoming Springboard forums in your area, consult their Web site, www.springboard2000.org.

There are several venture capital firms that concentrate on minority- and women-owned companies. Among these companies are the Isabella Fund (www.fundisabella.com), Women's Growth Capital Fund (www.womensgrowthcapital.com), and Viridian Capital (www.viridian.com).

You should go online to review their guidelines for submissions. Do not send anything blindly. Each venture capital firm has its own parameters for proposals. Remember that most venture capital firms

THE LINGO OF VENTURE CAPITALISTS

Bridge funding: cash that carries your company between investment rounds.

Burn rate: the amount of money a business loses monthly that must be funded by capital rather than from profits. This gives investors a feeling for how you manage cash flow.

Due diligence: Process undertaken by venture capitalists, investment bankers, and others to thoroughly investigate a company before financing it; required by law before securities are offered for sale.

Elevator speech: a business plan promo that takes as long as a ride in a VC's elevator.

Pre-money: the valuation placed on your company before raising venture capital.

ROE: return on equity

Runway: the number of months a business can be funded by current assets and operating revenues.

Seed money: equity capital used to prove your concept and develop your product.

Short arms: a VC who enters a first round of funding but is leery about staying in for the second round.

receive 25 to 100 proposals each week. If your proposal arrives and does not follow their guidelines, they will not read it.

Going to a meeting with a venture capitalist can be unnerving, especially when you don't speak the language. Study our lingo guide, and next time a venture capitalist asks you what your runway looks like you'll know not to start talking about an airport! Beyond knowing buzzwords, you must also know what the investor or VC is looking for and tell an interesting story that lets them know you have what they want. Remember that the reason people invest in a business idea is to make money. All too often, inexperienced business owners forget to tell potential investors what rewards they will get from their investment in the new company.

A new source of funding for women-owned businesses launched in 1999 is the Count Me In Foundation. The firm, launched by two corporate veterans, awards start-up money in amounts of $500 to $10,000 to women-owned companies. Consult their Web site for more information (www.count-me-in.org).

At the time I launched BlueSuitMom.com, the Internet gold rush was starting to dry up. In retrospect, I was probably about six months too late to capitalize on the flow of investment money that flooded the market in 1999. Nonetheless, I armed myself with a good, solid business plan complete with a strong management team, good product, and appealing exit strategy and began looking for investors. As you saw in my business plan, I needed to raise $1 million. Fortunately, I had a well-established network of potential funders and proven relationships to help me get started.

A good place to begin is with former employers who might have connections to investors and who already know your work ethic. It doesn't hurt if they are men and can help you penetrate the good-old-boy network that still exists in the world of venture capital. "Networking" and "knowing someone" is still the best way to get your concept funded.

Unlike many small-business owners, I actually had some very qualified potential investors. I had no problem getting in to speak to people, and I also had no lack of advice, but I was not finding money. Fortunately, I finally realized what I was doing wrong. I was not asking for the check! I gave a great presentation and sold my idea, but I never actually asked for the money! I began to ask, and I began to get money.

If you make a cold call on a venture capital firm, it will be difficult to get your business plan noticed in the chaos. Do your home-

---

SEARCHING FOR VENTURE CAPITAL MONEY ON THE WEB

- Capital.com: www.capital.com
- PrimeStreet.com: www.primestreet.com
- Qlender: www.qlender.com
- The Business Finance Mart: www.bizfinance.com
- LiveCapital.com: www.livecapital.com
- Business Funding Directory: www.businessfinance.com
- AngelSociety.com: www.angelsociety.com
- Garage.com: www.garage.com/
- EBZ.com: www.ebz.com.
- Fund Isabella: www.fundisabella.com
- Springboard2000: www.springboard2000.com

---

work. Identify one specific partner at the firm that you want to target and make it your mission to get his or her attention. Send your business plan in the format they require and follow up when necessary. If they request additional information, get it to them quickly.

Remember that investors get their money back only when you go public or sell the company.

Angel Investors

An angel investor is a private investor who puts up the money to get your idea off the ground. Some angel investors stay anonymous, but more often they are individuals who step up to the plate to get your business rolling. When it comes to finding money from investors, it's as important to find smart money as it is to find any money. During the gold rush of the Internet in 1999 when investors seemed to be throwing money at Internet companies, it was the companies with the right names behind them that attracted additional money and interest. You want to find money that delivers not only monetary value to your company but professional experience, insight, and involvement. Investors like to see that you have convinced other business-savvy professionals to take an active role in your company whether financially or intellectually. The old saying, "Birds of a feather flock together," works in the world of investing, too.

25

What are the downsides to funding from an angel investor?

HEIDI PERRY, HOME BUSINESS ONLINE

Angel investors are private entities that are willing to invest in small start-ups. While they are willing to take the risk of investing in your business, they also may want shares and/or to take a position in your company so they can maintain some control. You will have to decide whether the trade-offs are worth it and whether you are willing to relinquish some control.

Loans from Family and Friends

Many entrepreneurs find funding for their company from supportive friends or family. It's fine to be the beneficiary of a generous loan or investment, but you must document it regardless of your relationship. The IRS views a gift from Uncle Lou the same as they do that from a wealthy investor. Be sure to document all monetary transactions to avoid giving the appearance to the IRS that you have received a gift or additional income. You don't need a lawyer to draw up this documentation. Quicken Family Lawyer contains do-it-yourself letters. You should also establish solvency. This proves you anticipate repaying the loan.

26

How did you handle the family loan you received to start your business?

MOLLY GOLD, GO MOM !NC.

We started our company with $35,000, a portion of which was loans and investments from family members. My father is our primary investor, and my in-laws are also investors. For the paperwork on the loans, we executed promissory notes between the company and the lenders with terms of fifteen years and monthly payments. We issued stock certificates from the company to the individuals. It's important to consult an accountant regarding restrictions and rules about awarding equity to individuals. You don't want your investors to have to pay taxes on their stock until it's worth something to them financially.

HEIDI PERRY, HOME BUSINESS ONLINE

If you have a rich, doting uncle, a family loan can be a very good option. Generally, family members are more generous with interest rates and more flexible about repayment schedules. When you hit a slump in your business, family may be willing to accept smaller payments for a period of time until you can get back to the regular payment schedule.

Be sure you put everything in writing and keep to the agreed-on payment schedule. Financial misunderstandings and not paying as agreed can cause bad feelings between family members. Treat family loans as you would any other loans. Be sure to talk through the conditions of the loan and include everything when you write it down. Most of all, stick to your end of the bargain.

Corporate Line of Credit

A line of credit that allows you to write checks against it is one of the most common ways entrepreneurs fund their start-ups. A corporate credit card lets you keep your business charges separate from your personal spending. You will be ahead of the game if you go into your new venture with strong, established credit. This is a smart step many people forget. Depending on the needs of your start-up company, you may be required to sign lease agreements, obtain multiple credit cards, and/or secure a small loan. The less debt you start with, the better, because you are certain to go into additional debt in launching your company.

Think for a minute how many credit card offers you receive a week in the mail. "You have been pre-approved!" shouts at you from the envelope. Although many of the offers have time restrictions on them, I began collecting them in a file during the first month of BlueSuitMom.com. It was a good way to keep emergency spending options close at hand. If you decide to do this, be sure to compare interest rates.

When shopping for a line of credit, consider not only the interest rate and payment schedules but also the benefits. For example, American Express offers a small-business card with a long list of small-business discounts and reward points redeemable for merchandise. The only downside in using an American Express card is that many vendors do not accept it. There are an ample number of Visa and MasterCard cards that also offer low rates and benefits. It is up to you as a business owner to find the line of credit to meet your needs.

27

Why did you obtain a line of credit for your company?

ROBIN ZELL, BRAGELETS

After acquiring my company, it was necessary for me to purchase supplies to produce the Bragelets. Most wholesalers prefer a credit card for ordering over the phone, so I needed a business credit card. I keep my personal and business finances separate. I shopped around for the best rate before I decided on a particular line of credit. You can shop online or off for a line of credit.

There are many institutions that offer multiple rates with various benefits attached. In my case, I chose a credit card with a line of credit attached.

SHANNON RUBIO, THESMILEBOX.COM

It cost my mother and me about $7,000 to start The Smile-Box.com. We relied on credit cards and lines of credit to get us started. My mother, Marivonne, extended herself creditwise to make it happen for us. Fortunately, our sales continue to climb. Our first months of sales were less than $1,000 but now have grown to over $8,000 a month. Our sales each month are at least 50 percent higher than the month before. We feel the personal investment was worthwhile.

HEIDI PERRY, HOME BUSINESS ONLINE

There are several types of credit lines a new business owner may consider. Credit cards and home equity loans are the two most people ask about. Interest on credit cards can kill you if you don't pay it off quickly. Also, credit card rates may jump sharply over time, or the company may impose onerous terms on unpaid monthly balances. Used wisely, credit cards can be a wonderful financing source for purchasing equipment and inventory. However, using credit cards for living expenses is a quick, sure way to experience your business's downfall.

Home equity loans can supply a nice sum of capital if you have good equity in your house. However, use this option only after you have done your market research and devised a good, tight plan for paying off the loan. If you can't make your home equity loan payments, you could lose your house.

Personal Savings

Two-thirds of all small-business owners finance their company from personal savings. You may choose to use part of your vacation fund, retirement fund, or savings account. If you decide to liquidate stocks, mutual funds, or 401K accounts, be certain to consult with your accountant regarding penalties and tax implications. You will want to consider the cost of the money you intend to spend. Selling a depreciated stock may have fewer fees attached to it than a 40 percent tax penalty for selling your 401K.

Remember to document the loan you yourself make to your company. If all goes well for you and your company, the day will come that you can pay yourself back. Your accountant can show you how to carry the loan on your profit-and-loss balance sheet.

28

What about grants and other government loans to women-owned businesses?

HEIDI PERRY, HOME BUSINESS ONLINE

If you are a woman or member of a minority group, government loans are a bit easier to obtain. Sometimes, however, women face gender stereotypes and may find it harder to get loans. Some financial institutions and government offices have departments that cater especially to women-owned businesses. The Small Business Administration's Women's Business Center has a wonderful Web site dedicated to helping women entrepreneurs (www.onlinewbc.org).

Micro loan programs offering $25,000 or less to small, undercapitalized businesses are sometimes available from local economic development departments. Repayment terms usually span from three months to three years. Look in the phone book and call for information.

You may also want to ask your bank about the SBA's 7(a) Loan Guaranty Program. This program is designed for small businesses that lack the collateral to get a conventional bank loan. The SBA guarantees most of the loan, cutting the risk for the bank. In the fiscal year 1999, the SBA guaranteed 43,600 of these loans through conventional lenders.

Very small grants offered by nonprofit organizations such as Trickle Up help low-income entrepreneurs expand their businesses. Preference is given to women, members of minorities, recent immigrants, and those receiving welfare or public assistance. Since this New York–based program began in 1979, it has launched over 67,000 small, typically home-based businesses in 115 countries. U.S. recipients generally receive around $700. While this may not seem like much, a small cash infusion can be just the thing a very small business needs to launch itself. The recipient of a small grant who then establishes a proven track record often finds it easier to obtain a conventional loan later on.

Service-based businesses sometimes use an option called factoring their accounts receivable to smooth out their cash flow. Factors purchase the company's outstanding invoices, usually charging between 4 percent and 9 percent to collect the receivables. For some businesses, factoring is invaluable. However, if your profit margin is slim, this is terribly impractical for you, because the fees will eat up your profits.

Along your journey to find funding you will find advertisements for "free money." I'm here to tell you that "free money" is a myth. There is always a price to pay. When you read the small print and ask questions, you will see that the price is not worth it. Whenever you receive grants or government loans, there is always some program attached, i.e., you may have to take classes or hire employees that match certain criteria. Not that this is all bad—just be aware that there is always a price to pay, no matter how you go about funding your business.

Research and choose your options wisely and always have a solid plan for paying whatever price goes with the deal.

29

Where did you find funding for your company and what were your expenses?

DIANE BALLARD, DKB ASSOCIATES

I raised $4,000 in start-up money for my company through the sale of personal real estate.

One of my greatest expenses was $12,000 for advertising materials like pens, notepads, and fortune cookies with my name on them for giveaways at trade shows. What I didn't use at the trade shows, I give away during appointments. My other big expense was trade show fees of $1800. I also spent $400 on brochures and a banner. Fortunately, I already had a home office with computer and fax so I didn't have to spend money on equipment.

I make ends meet by substitute teaching. I have a substitute's license for Minnesota and Wisconsin. The neat thing about subbing is that I don't have to accept a job if I have appointments or phone calls scheduled that day!

KAREN WILKINSON OLTION, EBUBBLES.COM

We did the rounds with venture capitalists, angel investors, and even banks. Even though I went for funding while the Internet financing frenzy was in full swing, we didn't get in on it. We were considered just a store site with no proprietary technology or dazzling new Internet business model, and investors were simply not interested in us. We did finally get a $1 million funding offer from a venture capital firm that was getting a great deal of high-profile press at the time. The offer included second- and third-round financing as well. The firm had funded another beauty site just months before and would finance them again the next year in excess of $55 million. We were ecstatic! But as quickly as the offer came, it disappeared. Over Fourth of July weekend of 1999, one of the key partners balked at the idea of eBubbles, and the deal fell apart.

Ultimately, we gathered $80,000 in savings, family loans, and bank loans to launch the company. So far, our investment has paid off. Our business has now grown 660 percent over the past eighteen months, and we are looking at almost $250,000 in revenue.

WENDY HARRIS, NATIONAL ASSOCIATION OF MEDICAL BILLERS

I mostly used my savings, but I did get a personal loan from our bank for $5,000. I decided on a personal instead of a business loan because it was an easier and faster way to obtain the money. I would say that the initial setup cost the most. My computer was $600, printer $300, Web site $1,200, training class $1,500, furniture $500, software $600, accountant fees $500, and association fees $1,000. I also spent money on supplies like specialty paper and miscellaneous publications. The bank loan was a three-year loan, and I paid it back in two years.

AMILYA ANTONETTI, SOAPWORKS

I truly believed in our product and that we had a market to serve, so I was determined to find funding to grow our business. In 1995, my husband, Dennis, and I sold our home, secured $120,000 in loans from the Small Business Administration, and set up shop in a warehouse district in northern California. It's been a long haul, but now, five years later, we have our product in 2,500 stores, and our sales are $5 million.

JULIE MARCHESE, TWINSADVICE.COM

My husband and I invested a lot of our own money into my business venture. This was money that we could certainly have used because my husband has not had such a great year. Needless to say, we are living paycheck to paycheck. We gave up the cleaning lady, the baby-sitter, the vacation, and new clothes, all of the extras that would be nice but not absolutely necessary. We have learned to cut a lot of corners just to get by.

NANCY CLEARY, WYATT-MCKENZIE PUBLISHING

When I was looking to fund Wyatt-McKenzie Publishing's Box-is product line, I approached a close girlfriend's millionaire stepfather with a proposal for a $70,000 loan. He did not understand the product at all, but in the process of answering "devil's advocate" questions, I won over my girlfriend's husband. However, this loan was for less money than I was seeking from her stepfather. I made a decision to minimize my start-up expenses as much as possible, to cut out all nonessentials, and find printers willing to barter some of the production costs.

I also decided to lower the quantity on my initial order of boxes. My revised budget was $30,000, which included $10,000 for a PR company contract and $10,000 in "trade" for much of the customizations, inserts, and marketing materials for the Box-is.

I presented my girlfriend and her husband with a proposal for a business loan of $15,000 and 2.5 percent of net profits from the products instead of interest charges and strict payment plans. We have a flexible contract that bases quarterly loan repayments on net profits.

Despite this loan, I still needed another $15,000 to meet my funding goal. As fate would have it, a major computer crash a week later connected me with a local gentleman who had some CD burner software I had lost. He was a retired surgeon who now spent his months traveling the world taking photographs. Immediately, my publisher instincts kicked in. He told me he dreamed of producing a coffee-table book. I knew I could impress him if I helped him create his book with a custom Box-is. In one week, I created a prototype of his two custom Box-is, each containing a calendar of his photos, a journal with a photo on the cover, and stationery with photos in the background. Inside one of the Box-is was a contract for the $15,000 loan—$5,000 of which would be for the production of his custom Box-is to be sent to 50 of his friends for the holidays. I also managed to turn another $3,500 of the loan into a new Web site design for him. By transferring my creative skills to finding funding, I was able to get the money I needed to launch my company.

LINDA MCWILLIAMS, ONCEUPONANAME.COM

I started my company with $5,000 in personal savings. My husband and I didn't like the idea of borrowing the money, so we dipped into our retirement fund. We looked at it as an investment into our future and a way to allow me to stay at home with our children. We have always worked at cutting back, so it wasn't hard to do a bit more. We raise our own chickens, pigs, and turkeys on our small farm. We also keep a freezer full of food and live in an older house that my husband has rebuilt. Every bit helps.

DARCY VOLDEN MILLER, LITTLEDIDIKNOW.COM

I became a rep for several different direct sales companies such as Discovery Toys, 1-800-PARTYShop, and DKFL. I held in-home parties to raise money for my business. My husband gave me the money I needed to get started with these various companies, but I was on my own after that money was invested. Every time I needed more money to put back into the business to purchase business cards, software, and programming. I would go out and sell, sell, sell until I saved enough for the items I was trying to purchase. Plus, due to the nature of network marketing through these companies, I eventually started building teams. This began providing me with a residual income so I didn't have to go out and sell as much to acquire the things I needed.

Once I got the Web site built, I put various affiliate programs into place. This gives me a little extra spending money here and there to put back into the business. The larger my business grew, the more money I began to make through the affiliate programs and direct sales companies.

I also applied for and won several grants. This is a great source of income that is free, and you never have to pay it back. There are some wonderful books out there such as *Free Money and Help for Women Entrepreneurs* by Mathew Lesko. It is packed full of various avenues for grant money. Also, if you do a search on the Web under "Grants," you will be surprised at the amount of links you will find. There really is tons of free money out there, especially for women business own-ers. You just have to put a little work into it!

ROBIN ZELL, BRAGELETS

We borrowed money from my husband's employee stock fund in order to purchase Bragelets. Acquiring a company was a new experi-ence for me. The original owners told me what they wanted for the business, but I offered them less and they took it. Their figure was really based on the supplies they had on hand, plus the trademark. I looked at their balance sheets, but they really didn't tell me anything of value. They were set up as a corporation. I bought the assets of the corpora-tion such as supplies, trademark, toll-free number, and inventory.

30

What financial sacrifices have you made in order to fund your company?

JEANNINE CLONTZ, ACCURATE BUSINESS SERVICES

I started my company with about $2,600 and enough money to pay the bills without my income for eight months, which I managed to stretch out to fourteen months. The one thing we had to give up was our health insurance. That was very stressful. There are not a lot of reasonably priced insurance programs out there for businesses with fewer than five employees. My husband eventually changed jobs just to get health insurance coverage for us. We also had to tighten our belts a bit. We don't go out quite as much, but we share much more quality time together because I work from home. I am not able to go out anymore and charge things on my credit cards, but we still con-sider ourselves financially comfortable.

LESLEY SPENCER, HBWM.COM

When we launched Home-Based Working Moms.com, I quit my full-time job, and we cut back on everything we could. We got rid of cable TV, and my husband took noodles that only cost twenty cents a pack to work for lunch. I clipped and used coupons for groceries, and we set our thermostat to use as little energy as possible. We even got rid of one of our cars, which meant I had to take my husband to the bus every morning and pick him up at night. We've sacrificed, but it has been well worth it.

BECCA WILLIAMS, WALLNUTZ, INC.

We are bootstrapping WallNutz, and this requires us to do without things that friends of our age and educational background are buying. Both my husband and I drive older cars, watch our spending on eating out and entertainment, and limit our clothing purchases. The funding for our company comes out of my husband's paycheck. This is typically several hundred dollars per month. Money for Wall-Nutz is tight although I would like to have more for marketing. We're in a catch-22 situation. I want the product to be more proven before we invest additional money in it, but the better the packaging and marketing, the more likely we are to get connected with a larger distributor.

Growing Your Company Wisely

Once you obtain the financing to launch your company, it's important to use it to get the greatest benefit toward your goals. Watch your expenses carefully but concentrate on the presentation of your deliverables. I always use a gift from Tiffany's as an example of my spending philosophy. You know that the Tiffany's blue box with white silk ribbon holds something special inside. It doesn't matter what went into delivering the box to you; you only care that it's a high-quality, special gift. I applied this philosophy to my business at BlueSuitMom.com. It didn't matter that we were working on leased computers sitting in used cubicles as long as we produced the best information for our market in the most professional manner possible. I remember in our early days when I was trying to convince a large company that we were real players in the Internet world. The company asked that I send them a media kit and formal proposal. I advised them that our public relations department would send it out the next day. Now, let's ignore the fact that we didn't have a public relations department. I just wanted to look as large as the persona I was trying to impress. Within twenty-four hours, we had a full-color media kit assembled thanks to color printers and a Kinko's center. The following week, the company called us to express their interest in BlueSuitMom.com. They never knew that the materials were assembled by yours truly at midnight on the floor of my office. All they knew was they received a professional package that met their needs.

So how do you watch expenses? For starters, treat every dollar like it's your own, whether you have received it from private investors or your liquidated mutual funds. If you wouldn't personally eat lunch at the most expensive restaurant in town, then don't entertain clients there either. Find a cheaper alternative that is appropriate. There are plenty of ways to apply a frugal approach to your business without jeopardizing your professionalism and the quality of your product.

31

How do you manage your young company's finances?

KIMBERLY STANSELL, AUTHOR

Just as becoming physically fit has tremendous benefits, so does making your business financially fit. Whether your business is in a start-up, growth, comfort, or turnaround stage, fiscal soundness is critical to your success path. Here is a set of winning strategies for operating a financially fit firm.

- **Diversify your income stream.** Avoid depending on any one customer or industry, deriving no more than 15 percent of your business from any one client. While it is tempting to

MONEY-SAVING TIPS

- Be careful about putting relatives in key positions.
- If possible, don't quit your day job until your business is making money.
- If you can buy something used, do it.
- Don't try to impress clients with fancy cars and an expensive office.
- Concentrate on the presentation of your deliverables.
- Don't skimp on insurance.
- Look big but spend like a small company.
- Bill your customers as soon as you render the service.
- Don't pay your bills until they are due.
- Buy office supplies in bulk.

grow quickly by becoming a large service provider to a small number of customers, this strategy can make you vulnerable to pressure from those same customers.

- **Keep overhead low and costs in check.** Avoid the good-times syndrome: Don't run up high expenses when times are good, and you won't have to cut back when you hit a lean cycle. Constantly scrutinize margins, cash flow and receivables, and scrutinize every purchase your business makes. Be mindful of unwarranted increases in operating expenses, too.

- **Budget and build up a cash cushion.** Ninety percent of small businesses don't have a twelve-month budget. You'll need one in order to protect the fiscal health of your business. Build up a reserve that's equivalent to several months' overhead expenses; you'll find these numbers in your budget. A stash will enable your business to remain intact during a cash flow drought.

32

How has your financial thinking influenced the growth of your company?

TAMMY HARRISON, THE QUEEN OF PIZZAZZ COMPANY

I didn't start my company with any money because I already had a computer. When the income started coming in, I saved a portion of it and still do, to put back into the company. I now have a complete home office with the latest software to conduct my business.

TERESA KIRBY AND DARCY LYONS, A GARDEN PARTY

We each contributed about $12,000 over the first year of business. Our goal has been to grow slowly and allow the money we make to be returned to the business to purchase product and necessary support items. This plan has worked for the most part so far. Since we have grown at a manageable pace, we have been able to support our consultants and their parties. We have had no problem in making inventory requirements at each of the parties. We have been very disciplined in putting every dime back into the company. We have not yet paid ourselves a salary. I think our biggest sacrifice has been to run a small company for a little over a year now for no pay. We are willing to accept that this may continue for another year or two. It has required a reallocation of cash flow from personal desires to business requirements. Oh well, guess we won't be getting those diamond earrings for Christmas!

KIMBERLY STANSELL, AUTHOR

I think National Small Business Week is a good time to do an annual assessment of your company, including your financial situation. I follow something that Dell Computer Corporation recommends, a five-step plan to help small businesses assess their technology needs. It's the "Five Rs": Rate, Revisit, Research, Realize, and Review. I find it helpful to apply the five Rs to all aspects of my business.

1. **Rate performance.** Look at your company as if you are an outside consultant rating a client's operations. Examine the individual process and steps your company goes through to serve its customers—from the time an order comes in until the final invoice is paid—to uncover opportunities to improve workplace processes. For example, the sales process could be improved by providing notebook computers for the sales team to input orders directly, rather than taking orders on paper to be input later.

2. **Revisit plan.** Using the information gathered during the rate phase, revisit your business plan to determine how the areas identified for improvement align with the company's goals. Then translate the appropriate business goals into a corresponding technology goal. For example, if a company goal is to have faster, more efficient customer service, then you may consider networking computers with a server, enabling employees to share files such as vital customer information.

3. **Research options.** With your technology goals identified, begin initial research for appropriate products and services by benchmarking against similar companies and reading relevant industry publications. Before purchasing, compare vendors not only on price but also on reputation and service after the sale. Remember, when evaluating specific products, it is important to purchase not just what is needed now but what will accommodate anticipated growth.

4. **Realize benefits.** The next step is to realize the benefits the new products and services will provide by installing and incorporating the new technology with your existing systems. To direct the implementation, develop an installation guide and set a target date for the completion of the process. One of the most important parts of the implementation guide should be a training program for everyone in your firm who will use the new system.

5. **Review progress.** Following the implementation, review the process by analyzing again your business and technology plans. Ideally, your company should begin to move closer toward achieving its goals, and operations should steadily become more efficient. Your technology assessment program should be a dynamic process, responding to changing conditions of the business and the marketplace.

CHAPTER SIX

Infrastructure

N ow that you have a business plan that provides a clear and concise road map for reaching your personal and professional goals, it's time to build the infrastructure for your company. By infrastructure I mean your office and administrative issues.

Office Space

The good news is that because you have made the choice to work out of your home, you avoid having a landlord, and your real estate decisions will be minimal. The downside is that when a lightbulb dies, you must play the role of corporate facilities manager and change it. And, if your business plan requires you to hire employees or freelancers who will work in your home, you will need to find space to comfortably accommodate those employees.

Also, if customers will be coming to see you, you might need to locate your office in an area of your home that has a separate entrance. The accessibility of your office will demonstrate the level of professionalism you have decided to exhibit to customers visiting your place of business. Let's face it, it's poor PR to have customers tripping over Legos and homework papers scattered on the floor while walking to your office. However, in this chapter I will assume you are running a business that does not require clients to visit you.

It's very important to find an area of your home away from the traffic flow of the house, that will permit you to work undisturbed. Basements, attics, or guest bedrooms are all good areas for setting up shop. If you can't create a separate space, consider sharing the playroom or den with the family. I have even heard of women transforming the dining room table into the office for a multimillion-dollar business! Whatever arrangements you choose, make your space one that generates feelings of productivity and enjoyment.

33

Where is your office physically located in your home?

JULIE MARCHESE, TWINSADVICE.COM

My work area is mainly my bedroom. The computer is located there, and that's where I keep all my records. I chose this area because I can lock the door to get work done while my husband watches the kids.

I cannot do much when the kids are around, because they want to play on the computer instead of letting Mom check e-mail or fill orders. I do the majority of my work during nap time and after they all go to bed. I get a lot done on the weekends because my husband is around to care for the kids. I try to make my phone calls during nap time, *Blues Clues*, or *Dora the Explorer*.

Sometimes, though, with my kids having temper tantrums in the background, phone calls can be an adventure. That's why I stash Smarties candy in the cupboard. I give them to the kids while I'm on the phone. It works like a charm! I'm sure that parenting experts would be disgusted at such an action, but it certainly helps me, and I don't intend to stop!

My office would make some people laugh. My computer is sitting on a card table with a Dell computer carton under the table for support so it doesn't collapse. It's a pathetic office, but it works out fine under the circumstances that I am in.

VICTORIA USHERENKO, LIAISON IT

I started my home-based business in the baby's bedroom one week after giving birth to my son. For the first six months, I juggled taking care of the baby with conducting research and phone interviews. I tried to make telephone calls and schedule meetings around the baby's nap times. My office consists of a desk, desktop computer, fax machine, and dedicated computer line with a separate voice mail system. My most prized possession is my headset phone combo, which allows me to do several things at once. The best part is that I can hold my baby, feed him, and talk on the phone at the same time. I finally got a nanny after the baby turned six months. I still work out of the baby's room, which allows me to interact with my son throughout the day.

ROBIN ZELL, BRAGELETS

Unfortunately, my office is still my dining room. We are trying to finish our basement so that we can move my operations down there. The dining room looks messy and scary right now. Luckily, it is in the back corner of the house where it gets no traffic. I use the table, of course, and I have a few rolling carts, our home computer, a fax, printer, and a company phone line with voice mail. I used to pride myself on putting the "business" away every day, but I abandoned that idea. It's good that the business is on the main floor of the house, right off the kitchen, because I can work and still keep an eye on my two preschoolers. I can also answer my phone and check orders while making dinner and doing daily chores. I maintain a post office box for company mail.

ALEX POWE ALLRED, AUTHOR AND GOLD MEDALIST

My office. Wow. The office is in the family room so I can get to the kitchen in five steps. I have three baby gates wired together to keep Tommy, who's seventeen months and a maniac, from tearing the books down from my bookshelves and unplugging the computers. Every time the phone rings, I have to leap over the baby gates. There are also two more gates blocking the kitchen because Tommy has been tearing things out of the kitchen and breaking them. Don't tell me to get locks, because he just breaks them. For a while, we used bungee cords, but he used them to step onto and scale the kitchen counters. Argh!

If all the planets are aligned and I am lucky, the girls and Tommy play contentedly in their rooms. Left alone, Tommy can entertain himself nicely. Left alone for too long, he'll burn the house down. There's that fine line....

Basically, I've been very lucky and able to interview most of my people by phone while at the computer. When I interviewed Radu, Marla Maples, and professional basketball players, I've had the kids with me. Once in a while, I'm not so lucky. Last night, I did an interview locked in the bathroom, and last week I interviewed Congresswoman Deborah Pryce in the freezing garage. How many times have I been in the middle of an interview when a fight breaks out, and I leap up from the desk and run for quiet before my interviewee hears the disturbance. This is part of my guilt, because I later think how many times one of the kids went unpunished. My oldest has figured out if a child lets out a yell and I don't come running, I am "working." She knows if I am talking socially she will get into trouble. She's no dummy. I am still working on this situation.

It is so loud where I am that sometimes I just have to turn off the computer and throw in the towel. No way could a man work under these conditions!

KIT BENNETT, AMAZINGMOMS.COM

My business started in the bedroom, and now I am in the utility room with the washer and dryer. Listen, it's a big improvement from the bedroom. We built a "cubbyhole" with two walls to shield the huge piles of laundry from view. I find the melodic rhythm of my dryer soothing. However, each time the timer goes off I jump through the ceiling. I figure this will be a great story to tell some day on Oprah when she is doing a story on Amazingmoms.com.

KAITLAND THORSTENSON, CERTIFIED PUBLIC ACCOUNTANT

Location, location, location. Even though you work from a home office, I believe you also need to be mobile and go out to clients. The number one failure of women in small businesses is thinking that the product is so wonderful people will go out of their way to come to you. This is not the case at all. Even as a home-based accountant, I often take along my portable memory to the client's office and plug into their system. I can sit there, work on the information, and save it. Later at home, I finish up the reports at my convenience.

MICHELLE ZEITLIN, MORE ZAP PRODUCTIONS

I have a phone, computer, and fax in a home office, but my real office is anywhere my clients' events are scheduled. Sometimes it's a theater in New York; other times it's a studio in California. When I was seven months pregnant, my office was at Lincoln Center where we were performing. I toured with my daughter until she was three months old but found that trucking and busing with a baby didn't work well. Most performing mothers either use on-lot day care or have full-time nannies. I spend a few days a week now working in my home office and a few days in my on-site office, wherever that may be.

SANDI EPSTEIN, WORK/LIFE COACH

My office is on the third floor of my home away from the rest of the house. I established the rule that kids are not allowed in Mommy's office when I first started working from home. I didn't want the type of scenario where I sit at my computer and work while my small children play nicely on the floor. My children know that I leave in the morning to go to my office, and I'll see them again at lunchtime. I established that set schedule not only for myself but for my children's benefit. I believe it allows them to know what to expect from me and when.

34

How do you keep your home office organized?

DEBBIE WILLIAMS, LET'S GET IT TOGETHER

Recent statistics reveal that the average executive wastes 150 hours per year searching for lost documents. One in twenty documents is lost and never recovered. When setting up your home office, there are a few basic tricks to keeping yourself organized. Begin by defining your space and then utilize whatever storage solutions are necessary to keep your papers and products together.

Creating a home office is a challenge if you have limited floor space. One way to fashion an office is to use an armoire or unused closet. A card table or banquet table that can be folded and stored when not in use can create additional workspace for special projects. Store files in portable crate systems or in a vertical desktop rack. Hang shoe or jewelry organizers over the doors for office supplies, books, and tapes. Bulletin boards placed around the room at eye level provide easy viewing while you are seated at your desk. Keep your office clutter-free by assigning a dedicated place for everything. Store hanging folders in file cabinets or in portable crates under the desk. Purchase stackable bins for processing paperwork. Purchase a drawer divider for stationery and desk supplies. Inform family members where to deliver incoming correspondence. Utilize a master calendar or wipe-off board for coordinating special projects. Clip or scan articles and file them in a folder for reading at a later date. Maintain a workable follow-up system with an index card file or accordion file. The dividers are numbered 1 to 31, and documents or note cards are filed on the appropriate day of the month for future action.

To create an office on the go, you need a portable system for your car or briefcase. Keep a large sturdy crate or laundry basket in your car for product samples. Small hanging file crates can be used to carry client information or product literature securely to your destination. There are a number of visor and glove compartment organizers to hold small items. Pocket organizers that hang on the back of the car seat are excellent for holding maps, brochures, literature, etc. Use a zippered pouch to contain office supplies in your briefcase.

After you've set up your personal space, take a few minutes a day to preserve it. Write your "to-do" list for tomorrow. Straighten your desk before you quit for the day. Purge your files on a consistent basis. Begin each day with a clear desk and a clear mind and find renewed fervor in the work that brought you here in the first place.

Administrative Issues

Setting up your business's infrastructure will be your first taste of being self-employed and juggling a number of tasks simultaneously. Simple, you say. "I'm a mom. I can do that." You are right. That's why motherhood is such a great breeding ground for entrepreneurs. So let's get started with our long list of details to consider and tackle.

Permits and Licenses

Make one of your first calls a trip to the county clerk's office. Find out about local and county regulations governing permits, tax filing, and registration requirements for your business. You may be required to obtain a county as well as a city business license. One warning: If you don't go to them, they will come to you. If you are required to collect state or local sales taxes on your product or service and you file federal income tax forms, you may trigger a search by your city or state to make sure you have the proper licenses. It's best to start with your city and work your way up through the levels of government bureaucracy.

If by chance you live in one of the few municipalities that do not allow home-based businesses, see if you can file for a variance and special-use permit. Make sure to send a professional proposal to the appropriate official, with complete details of your company, any traffic implications, and letters of support from neighbors.

FEDERAL AND STATE SITES

Several federal and state sites offer great resources for entrepreneurs just starting out.

- U.S. Small Business Administration: www.sba.gov
- Office of Women's Business Ownership: www.onlinewbc.org
- U.S. Department of Agriculture (USDA): www.reeusda.gov
- Federal Business Information Centers (BICs): www.sba.gov
- State Web Sites: www.yahoo.com/Government/U_S_F_L_States
- Consumer Information Catalog: www.pueblo.gsa.gov
- Government Information Locator Service: www.sba.gov/gils
- U.S. Business Advisor: www.business.gov
- U.S. Census Bureau: www.census.gov

Incorporation

Once you have decided on a name for your business, you will want to incorporate. The major reason for incorporating is to give your company a life of its own. In the eyes of the law, this means your company has its own rights and liabilities separate from you or other individuals involved. Several types of incorporation exist. For this reason, I recommend consulting an attorney or accountant to determine what's best in your situation. Incorporation documents must be filed with your state and will require a fee, which varies from $125 to $800. Filing can be done either by an attorney or through an online service. While it is not required that you consult with a lawyer when incorporating, it's a good idea to seek advice on the major points of incorporation to make sure you are covering all your bases. If you elect to use an online service, such as www.corporate.com, you should make sure it is reputable and that you've done your research before filling out any forms.

Once you file for your articles of incorporation, you will receive a corporate kit that includes bylaws, stock certificates, corporate seal, and state rules that govern corporate life.

35

What's the difference between a sole proprietorship and a corporation?

KAITLAND THORSTENSON, CERTIFIED PUBLIC ACCOUNTANT

A sole proprietorship is the simplest way to own a business. Legally, this option views you and your company as one and can be used as long as you remain the only owner of the company. The disadvantage to being a sole proprietor is that you have unlimited personal liability for anything that goes wrong within your business. There is no protection of your personal assets if for some reason your company is sued.

Corporations are different from sole proprietorships. Being incorporated means that the corporation takes on a "life" of its own and, in most states, your personal assets are protected. There are rules, laws, and guidelines that govern the establishment of corporations. In particular, you must get the approval of the Federal Trade Commission. Corporations are accountable to both stockholders and the IRS. Because you are required to make reports on a regular basis, you should hire an accountant, although not necessarily a CPA. There are two types of corporations you may choose: a family-owned "S" Corporation, which is a sheltered corporation in which stocks are not sold, or a regular corporation, in which large amounts of public funds are involved, stocks are sold, and you are accountable to stockholders. You will also need to keep funds in reserve to pay out in the event stocks are returned to you. In trading, another company can "buy" a majority of your stock and literally force you out of business. I would strongly urge that an attorney advise you on forming a corporation, because the laws to protect investors are very complex.

Tax Issues

While you are working with your accountant and attorney on incorporating your business, you should also take the time to establish your future tax practices. My dad always told me there are two certain things in life: death and taxes. As a business owner, you should prepare yourself for the tax man. I recommend opening a tax account along with your business checking account. To avoid tax trauma at the end of the quarter or year, try putting 20 to 40 percent of everything you earn right into a tax account and use the money only to pay taxes. I guarantee this will prevent a panic attack when you get your first tax bill!

Also, ask your accountant to counsel you on taking advantage of self-employment retirement plans.

If the fear of basic accounting and tax law overcomes you, take a class at your local community college. The Small Business Administration also sponsors free and low-cost seminars on every aspect of small-business start-ups. For online tax help for your home-based business, consult the Home Biz Central channel at www.hbwm.com.

36

What accounting issues should someone just starting a home-based business consider?

KAITLAND THORSTENSON, CERTIFIED PUBLIC ACCOUNTANT

The first thing I recommend is to purchase a good basic accounting program like QuickBooks, or even a good carbon-copy check system to write checks *only* for the business. It is very unwise to mix business and personal checking unless you are very careful to identify business entries. Keep a journal of expenses such as mileage, utilities, insurance, or remodeling your office, etc. Setting up an accounting system does not have to be overwhelming, but it is wise, unless you are already familiar with accounting, to seek professional help to set up the initial system. There are also books that give you the basics of an accounting package. Journals and ledger entries are laid out in understandable language, and, if you can add and subtract, that may be all you need.

However, if you plan to invest a large amount of cash and put all your funds into the business, I would strongly advise finding professional help to set up your accounting systems and to guide you. If your business is a partnership with other women, you should draw up a formal contract that spells out what each person's contribution to the business is in cash, in work, and in the knowledge it takes to get the business up and running. Often in a partnership, one partner may contribute a large amount of working capital while the other partner contributes knowledge. A third partner may bring in goodwill that will get the business moving forward rapidly, either because that partner has had a small business before or is part of a large group that will use the business. Those customer contacts are extremely valuable, but are often overlooked as a contribution to the company.

TERESA KIRBY, A GARDEN PARTY

It's important to set up a good accounting system from the very beginning. In our company, I order all of our products and do all of the bookkeeping using the QuickBooks program. I also use this software to file all taxes for all states, whether monthly, quarterly, or annually.

Postal and Delivery Issues

Rain or shine, you can always count on the mail, right? Wrong. Your business mail will not arrive at your office unless you establish a business address for your company. Some home-based entrepreneurs just use their home address because it is the location of their business.

WEB SITES FOR TAXES

- Tax and Accounting Sites Directory: www.taxsites.com. The name says it all. This site is an index of accounting and tax sites. You will find a channel called "Small Business Taxation," which is targeted to small businesses.

- Internal Revenue Service: www.irs.gov. This is the authority on taxes. The site has forms, information, and publications designed to help small-business owners.

- Tax Planet: www.taxplanet.com. Gary Klott, a former tax columnist for the *New York Times*, launched this site. Many of his articles are written with entrepreneurs in mind.

Other business owners rent a post office box as a way to keep personal and business mail separate and maintain the privacy of their home addresses from their clients. Most important, using a post office box makes your business appear larger. I'll talk more about the importance of looking big in chapter 7.

You can rent a post office box at your post office or a commercial mail center like Mail Boxes Etc. The cost varies generally between $7 and $20 per month. Before you rent a box, check out the operating hours of the location to make certain you can access your mail at a time that is convenient for you. Once you've established a mailing address for your business, you don't want to change it, particularly if it's printed on letterhead. Make sure the operation you are renting a post office box from will be around for a while. I remember hearing a story from a home-based meeting planner who went to retrieve seminar registra-

- Small Business Taxes and Management: www.smbiz.com. Good in-depth tax information for small-business owners. The site includes updated tax reforms and has links to other small-business resources.

- Tax Prophet: www.taxprophet.com. This interactive site offers frequently asked questions and tax publications.

- Quicken.com taxes: www.quicken.com. From the great accounting software company comes a site that includes information on payroll and federal and sales taxes. This is the site for the do-it-yourself entrepreneur.

tions from her post office box the day before her event, only to find she could not get her mail because the commercial retailer had gone out of business. Needless to say, she had to deal with angry customers the next day and had to reprint all her company materials with a new address.

If your business requires regular package deliveries, you need to consider some logistics. Delivery services such as UPS and Federal Express are more than happy to discuss delivery and pick-up schedules and procedures with you. A friendly heads-up to your regular postman or -woman may also prove to be helpful. Often, post office personnel are willing to provide postal boxes for outgoing mail. Business owners who live in condos or apartments need to consult building rules and regulations for multiple package deliveries, especially if large boxes will be left in lobbies or there are deliveries using the service elevators.

INTERNET CONNECTION OPTIONS

- **Dial-up account:** uses a modem and telephone line

  Pros: Available anywhere with phone service, most affordable connection type

  Cons: Uses phone line, so you need a separate line. Dial-up service has the slowest connection speeds.

  Cost: $0 to $20 a month

- **Cable:** uses cable television lines

  Pros: Fast speeds, easy installations

  Cons: Not available in some areas. When usage on your cable loop increases, your download speeds decrease

  Cost: $35 to $65 a month plus setup fees

- **Asynchronous Digital Subscriber Line (ADSL):** uses phone line, but you can use the same phone line for voice calls and faxes while online.

  Pros: Connection always on, fast access

  Cons: Unavailable in many areas

  Cost: $40 to $65 a month plus setup fees

- **Wireless:** access through home satellite.

  Pros: Fast download speeds

  Cons: Setup fees as high as $300

  Cost: $20 to $80 a month plus setup

Telephone Service and Internet Access

There was a day when telephone service meant a telephone line that allowed you to receive and make calls. Today, it can mean Internet access and fax capabilities as well as the voice telephone. Since you don't want to miss a call from a customer, make certain it is as easy as possible for your clients to reach you. Most small-business owners will tell you that a separate business line is essential. Ask your phone company about small-business options and special packages that include multiple services like voice mail, call waiting, and toll-free numbers. Since elaborate phone systems can be expensive, I recommend a good answering machine with speakerphone and hold capabilities to get you started.

Internet access has become as important to a business as telecommunication. If you intend to operate a Web site, the speed of your Internet connection is important. Slowest is dial-up service. Most television cable providers offer cable broadband service for a slightly higher cost, or your phone company may offer DSLs.

Insurance

Establishing a home-based business requires additional insurance beyond a traditional home-owner's policy. When you call your insurance agent to inquire about an in-home business policy, you will expedite the process if you have ready a brief description of the details of your business operation. For most small businesses, the best option is a package policy generally known as a Business Owner's Policy (BOP). These policies include property, liability, and crime coverage as well as clauses that cover specialty businesses. A BOP is normally cheaper than separate property and liability policies. Often, business owners consider the value of their assets in determining how much insurance they need. When consulting with an insurance agent make sure you know exactly what the policy covers, what the liability limits are, and how claims are handled.

37

What kind of insurance issues must a home-based business owner address?

HEIDI PERRY, HOME BUSINESS ONLINE

There are many insurance issues you must consider when starting your home-based business. Here are a few descriptions.

Home or Rental Insurance

Check your home or rental insurance policy to see exactly what it does and does not cover. Does it cover your business assets? Be sure to get everything in writing so you have it in black and white later in the event of a crisis. If you are still unclear, get a professional to explain it to you. Purchasing additional business insurance may or may not actually give you extra coverage.

Liability Insurance

Going without liability insurance is something of a gamble. However, at the beginning stages of your home-based business when your budget is tight, I wouldn't worry too much about purchasing liability insurance unless you are providing a critical service to people or companies. For example, if you provide Internet access and your systems crash, you could find yourself in the middle of a lawsuit for the damage it has caused your clients.

I do feel strongly, though, that liability insurance is something you should buy for your business as soon as you are able to. A good rule of thumb for deciding when to add it is to ask yourself, "How collectible am I?" It's fairly safe to assume you will not be sued unless you have significant assets.

You can do online research on liability at dtonline.com/pfa/liability.htm. Another resource is for the State of Wisconsin, but it offers good general information as well: badger.state.wi.us/agencies/oci/pub_list/pi-045.htm

Disability Insurance

This is one of the benefits you give up when you become self-employed. Employers legally must cover their employees for injuries through Worker's Compensation.

While you may not have to do it now, you may want to consider purchasing disability insurance down the road. As your home-based income becomes your livelihood, even a small injury could leave you unable to work regular hours. Since you are your business, your business earnings could seriously suffer. You'll find an interesting article about disability insurance at abcsmallbiz.com/bizbasics/disability_ins.html.

Health Insurance

Paying for health care out of your own pocket is very expensive, and it is one of those things that too many home-based business owners scrimp on. Just remember that one accident or disease could wipe out everything you have. Bad idea. A better idea is to maintain insurance through a spouse or to moonlight with a day or night job until you can afford to buy your own health insurance.

Try to take advantage of employer-supplied benefits before you or your spouse quit your jobs. Get everything fixed—teeth, eyes, glasses, medical check-ups. Use any employer-supplied benefits while you can and do it early enough so you receive reimbursement before you leave the company.

Car Insurance

Working at home makes your commute wonderful—ten seconds flat from your bedroom to your office. Assuming that your business does not require a lot of driving and that you will be using your car a lot less, ask your insurance agency if they will lower your premiums. Of course, if you use your car to visit clients, make deliveries, or for other business travel, you will need to adjust your insurance to cover your driving profile.

Where to Look for Insurance

There are plenty of insurance companies that provide insurance at decent rates for small- and home-based business owners. One way of getting insurance of any kind is to join a home-business association that offers insurance as a membership benefit. Keep in mind that good rates are not the only consideration when selecting a provider. Quality service and quick payment are equally important. There's nothing more frustrating than trying to get service when you're in the middle of a crisis.

You may wish to use an insurance agent to shop around for the best rates on any type of insurance policy. Ultimately, though, you are responsible for your own insurance, and it is an important part of understanding your business.

Patents

A patent is a document issued by the U.S. Patent and Trademark Office (PTO). It grants an inventor the right to use and develop his invention for between fourteen and twenty years, depending on the type of patent protection granted. Patent applications are rigorously examined by the PTO and typically take between twelve and twenty-four months to process. Once the PTO and the inventor agree on what elements of the invention can be protected, they publish a brief description of the patent in a weekly publication called the *Official Gazette*. To apply for a patent, an inventor must file an application and pay the appropriate fees.

Before you file for a patent, make sure you research your idea to verify that no one else is already doing what you want to do. A good place to start is www.corporateintelligence.com. The site offers solutions for researching and licensing trademarks and patents. To get a jump-start on your competition, you can file a priority application which lets others know you have put the ball in motion for a patent on your idea. Many small-business owners elect to file for a patent prior to discussing their product idea with a potential partner or manufacturer.

To begin the filing process, you must first decide whether to hire an attorney or not. The main reason inventors elect not to hire an attorney is the expense. If you are indecisive about the direction to take, you should consult with the U.S. Patent and Trademark Office in order to understand their requirements. Although the process does not require skills exclusive to attorneys, it does demand a great deal of time, knowledge, and diligence. Should you decide to go it alone, there will be many tasks along the way that will necessitate learning new skills and feeling your way through the process. The patent examiners are supposed to support inventors working without lawyers as much as they support inventors represented by attorneys.

38

What are your recommendations for patenting your product?

BETH BESNER, TABLE TOPPER

In the early stages of product research, before you seek investors, I recommend that you contact a reputable patent attorney. Call a local law school and ask to speak to the intellectual property professor to get recommendations.

An attorney will discuss the patentability of your idea and recommend a patent search firm or conduct a search. This may run about $1,500 or more, but I think it is money well spent, especially if you determine that there is an existing patent on the product that you would be infringing on if you develop it. Imagine spending thousands of dollars and then being slapped with a patent infringement suit. I'd also suggest that you consider filing for a trademark for the name of your product. This means doing a trademark search, which you can pay a company to do or do yourself if your library has the CD-ROMS available. Trademarks are discussed in the next section.

You can get Trademark and Patent applications from the Office of Trademarks and Patents in Arlington, Virginia (1-800-PTO-9199, www.uspto.gov).

To patent or not to patent? As to actually filing for a patent, again that is a cost and judgment call. You have more protection if you apply for something, especially if you are going to talk to big companies about licensing your idea. Many companies won't speak with you unless you have a patent or patent pending.

I'd recommend learning more about a provisional patent, which is less expensive and is much less technical than a nonprovisional (regular) patent. However, you must read the instructions and learn about what you can and should claim in the applications—you don't want to be barred from claims that you should have raised in this type of application.

You should know that patents are of two types: utility and design. Utility patents give more protection but are more costly to apply for. Again, we'd suggest you talk to an attorney about the options and learn about the costs involved.

Lawyers' fees for a typical patent application are from $3,000 to $5,000. This does not include the cost of responses to the patent examiner's objections if there are any.

For more information on these topics, check out the newsletter *Dream Merchant*. You can subscribe at www.dreammerchant.net. It's a helpful newsletter for inventors that also lists seminars and programs.

Trademarks

A trademark, mentioned briefly above, is a document also obtained from the PTO. Simply defined, it's a notice to others that a name or mark or logo or business emblem is already in use and owned by someone else. In order to obtain a trademark, you must use the name or mark in commerce that crosses state or international borders. In the case of BlueSuitMom.com, I do business outside of South Florida so our company's name qualifies for a trademark. There are some restrictions to trademarks. You cannot trademark the name of a living person without consent, or living or dead U.S. presidents, insignia of federal or state government agencies, the

U.S. flag, or names that are deceptive or deemed offensive. The filing process is similar to that of a patent. After an application and fee are submitted to the Patent and Trademark Office, they review the name or mark and publish their approval in the *Official Gazette*. If there are no objections filed to the pending trademark, a trademark is granted. The document allows you to use the name or mark for ten years.

Fortunately, applying for a trademark is easier than a patent and does not require an attorney. The application is a short two-sided form that is relatively easy to complete. The PTO offers two electronic registration options on their Web site (www.uspto.gov). The prinTEAS lets you fill in the form online but requires you to print out and mail in a hard copy, and eTEAS lets you both fill in the form online and file it via e-mail.

39

What supplies did you need to start your home-based business?

REBECCA HART, PUBLIC RELATIONS

The first thing I obtained for my company was a separate bank account with a separate business-only credit card. I was advised to keep my business account at a totally separate bank from my personal affairs. It proved to be good advice. I needed a computer with printer since public relations involves a great deal of writing. Next, I had a separate business phone line with voice mail installed along with a dedicated fax line. Even though the fax machine may one day go away, it's still a requirement for my business. Internet access and e-mail were of course a necessity. Since it's important to establish a professional image, I ordered business cards, letterhead with #10 envelopes, and mailing labels. Aside from supplies and equipment, I think the most important support element of a start-up company is a good accountant. I relied heavily on my accountant, particularly to set up my system for paying quarterly taxes. The other thing that it doesn't hurt to start with is some good business leads.

LESLEY SPENCER, HBWM.COM

When starting your home-based business, I recommend keeping your equipment and supplies to a minimum. Take advantage of stores offering no payments or interest for a specified time and get the equipment you need without spending any money up front. Be sure to save enough monthly to pay off what you buy before the time period is up. Otherwise, you have to pay interest fees. The Internet can provide a lot of great ways to save on start-up costs as well. Surf the Web for free services such as fax services and e-mail. I use eFax.com for free fax and Hotmail.com for free e-mail and other business services.

DEBBIE WILLIAMS, LET'S GET IT TOGETHER

Items I bought for my home-based office are letterhead and envelopes, business cards, brochures, postage stamps, calculator, pads of paper, pens, pencils, stapler and staple remover, scissors, tape dispenser, Post-it notes, rubber bands, paper clips, and file folders.

JEANNINE CLONTZ, ACCURATE BUSINESS SERVICES

I have a 266 MHz Gateway 2000 computer with a rewritable CD, a scanner, laser printer, DeskJet printers, and a copier I bought used. I have a business phone and answering machine equipped with caller ID. The faxes come through the computer, and mail goes to a local post office box. This gave me the option of not listing my home address in the phone book.

TAMMY HARRISON, THE QUEEN OF PIZZAZZ COMPANY

To start my businesses I needed a computer, printer, fax machine, telephone, cell phone, and filing cabinet. I also have a Web cam and calculator. Phone calls are difficult because my kids are underfoot constantly, so I have an online answering service. I allow the answering machine to pick up calls, and I return them at my convenience.

All of my customers understand my home-based working life and are more than happy to converse via e-mail.

Technology

Technology has been a contributing factor to the rapid growth of home-based businesses in recent years. The ability to communicate with customers, colleagues, and vendors around the world from a keyboard in your bedroom has literally changed the way we do business. Technology has created the ability for a home-based business owner to work with other home-based businesses to jointly offer more value to their customers. A study published by the National Foundation for Women Business Owners revealed that the use of computers and communications technology has increased the ability of small home-based businesses to work together as "virtual corporations." In this scenario, a home-based public relations firm might partner with a home-based Web designer and a home-based advertising business. Together, the three home-based business owners create a full-service marketing firm and a one-stop shop for their clients. In chapter 7 we will discuss the importance of "looking big," but it's obvious that technology has helped small businesses accomplish the feat of appearing bigger than they truly are. A decade ago, a home-based accountant would probably have only served clients in the local area. Today, the same accountant can serve clients worldwide through e-mail, fax, and instant messaging.

Another important but less recognized development that technology has created for business-owners is anonymity. The anonymity of a virtual relationship may allow you to ask for business that you might be intimidated to ask for in person. I remember sending an e-mail to the editor of *USA Today* when launching BlueSuitMom.com. Would I have picked up the phone to call him? Probably not. I would have figured that someone like that would not take my call. Surprisingly though, he read my e-mail and responded.

Of course, the most important thing technology gives is access to more information than ever, which makes doing business a great deal

---

HOME-BASED BUSINESS SUPPLIES AND EQUIPMENT

Accounting software

Business cards

Business letterhead (8½ by 11 sheets, #10 envelopes)

Business note cards for personal and thank-you notes

Business phone with answering machine

Computer and printer

Copy paper

Fax

File folders

Internet access

Legal paper

Paper clips, Post-it notes

Pens and pencils

Stapler and staples

Tape dispenser and tape

---

easier. Without the Internet, it would have taken several phone calls and an hour of research to determine the appropriate person for me to contact at *USA Today*. Using the Internet, it took five minutes to find the name of the friendly editor and contact information. It's important not only to use technology to your advantage but also to build your home-based business on the right technology.

40

What computer equipment and software do you need for a home-based business?

RACHAEL BENDER, BLUESUITMOM.COM

Choosing a computer for your home office is a confusing and potentially expensive decision. Before buying a computer, you need to accurately assess your future needs. How much you use your computer and for what purposes will affect the type of hardware and software you should buy. If you are running a graphic design business, your computer requirements are much different from those of someone running an accounting business. Unfortunately, with technology, the old saying, "You've got to spend it to make it," holds true.

Here are some questions to ask yourself:

- Will your work primarily be done with the use of a computer?
- How many hours will you be spending at the computer per day?
- What are the primary programs you will be using?

  Word processing

  Accounting software

  Graphic creation software

  Web design software

  Multi-media software

  Spreadsheet or database software

Write down your list of computer requirements and take it with you when you shop at a computer store or do your research online. This will help ensure you aren't buying items you don't need. If you aren't taking pictures of product to upload to your Web site, then you probably don't need to buy a digital camera.

If you will be doing a lot of work with a computer, you should try to buy the best system your budget allows. This way you won't have to upgrade so soon. You'll also want to consider getting at least a seventeen-inch monitor. Consider leasing your computer equipment to save money in your budget for other technology needs.

The technology you buy also depends on your business, but every home office should have these basics:

Hardware

- Computer
- Printer
- Fax machine (or online fax service)
- Copy machine (many fax machines or printers can double as copiers)
- UPS (battery back-up for your computer)

Software

- Word processing program
- Accounting software like QuickBooks Pro
- Web browsing and e-mail

Online services like eFax.com or Onebox.com can replace your fax machine. These services will assign you a fax number and will e-mail you an attachment any time you receive a fax. The service is free to receive faxes. If you'd like to send faxes through one of these online services, it costs about $4.95 per month for an account plus an additional charge per fax.

Onebox.com also gives you access to free voice mail on your assigned fax number.

41

What equipment and software
do you need for starting a Web site?

RACHAEL BENDER, BLUESUITMOM.COM

Starting a Web site for your home-based business is relatively easy when you use outside vendors for your Web hosting and/or Web site design. The first step is to choose your domain name. Domain names are assigned on a first-come, first-served basis, so you may not be able to get your first choice. It costs $70 to register your name for two years. You can sign up for a name at www.networksolutions.com or any domain registrar.

Once you've registered your name, you'll need to decide where to host your site. If you aren't experienced at running a Web site or server, you will probably want to completely outsource the hosting instead of purchasing the server and choosing colocation. For a basic Web site with only a few pages, hosting prices start around $25 a month. Most hosting companies charge a flat fee plus additional fees based on the monthly bandwidth your site uses. There are additional costs for running an e-commerce store with shopping carts, online ordering, and credit card processing. To process credit cards on your site you will need to open a merchant account. Many hosting companies have online forms to walk you through this process.

To build or update your Web site you will need a Web editing program such as Homesite, Frontpage, or DreamWeaver. You will also need a file transfer protocol (FTP) program and image editing software.

Payroll

If you choose to hire employees, you will need to manage your company's payroll and file the appropriate taxes involved in paying wages.

WEB SITE TERMS

Bandwidth: Amount of data transferred for a given amount of time. This term also means the amount of data you can transfer through a connection.

Colocation: When you own a server but have it located at a Web hosting facility, they provide an Internet connection for your machine.

Domain name: The unique name that identifies your Web site. In the example www.example.com, the domain name is example.com

FTP: File transfer protocol. Used for transferring files from one computer to another.

Merchant account: An account with a third party company that provides credit card processing. They handle receiving payment from the credit card companies and depositing it in your account.

The small-business accounting software you choose for your company most likely has payroll functionalities that allow you to manage your payroll and provide tax information. Another option is to hire a payroll management service. These companies will do everything from issuing your payroll checks to filing your employee taxes. Unless you intend to hire at least a half dozen employees or multiple hourly paid workers, you probably won't need this service right away. Onvia.com (www.Onvia.com) allows small-business members to describe the service they are seeking and obtain bids from their network of providers.

As an employer, you are responsible for withholding Medicare, social security, and income taxes on each employee. Most small businesses elect to file these taxes quarterly to reduce the tax shock that can occur when the tax man knocks. This is another time when consulting an accountant can serve you and your business well.

Hiring Help

There will come a day in the life of your home-based business when you will need or want to hire others to help you fulfill your customers' needs. Hopefully, you will be so successful in attracting clients and selling your product that you will eventually be faced with the happy dilemma of maintaining the status quo or growing your company. It won't be an easy decision, particularly if you've built a business on your personal talents or relationships.

I remember going through this dilemma when I owned Bailey Innovative Marketing in 1996. The name says it all. The company grew rapidly because I leveraged personal relationships with people who wanted me to apply my talents to their projects. The problem was that everyone wanted me personally and not a younger associate or employee. The other problem was that I didn't fully trust an employee to make the impression or decisions I would make when meeting with clients. My options were to remain a single-employee company and simply maintain the client base I already had or acquire help to grow the business to include clients I was currently turning away. Ultimately, I created a pool of resources that included several different types of employees and grew my business.

Among the different types of employees you can add to your business are full- and part-time employees, family members (sometimes known as volunteers), and independent contractors, also called freelancers.

Regardless of the type of help you decide to get for your business, acquiring employees will mean additional work for you. Not only will you be filing tax forms or doing the paperwork to pay their salaries, commissions, or fees, you now must become a full-time cheerleader and manager.

In trusting others to represent you and your business, it is imperative for them to fully understand your product or service and possess some of your commitment to the business.

Full-Time and Part-Time Employees

Your employees will bring their own thoughts, life experiences, and personal challenges to your company, and some of these may not mesh with your ambitions and goals. No one will have the same passion and dedication you have to your ideas and dreams. It will be up to you to manage these relationships, and at times it may be a challenge. If you accept that going into the relationship, you will save yourself a great deal of disappointment later. That's not to say that you should not expect an employee to adhere to the standards you set. It is important to clearly describe your expectations to your employees and to set well-defined goals and daily tasks. Since most people work to be paid, make sure to put all commission requirements or your compensation program in writing so that both of you understand how wages will be earned. Be specific in outlining how and when they will get paid, how you will calculate their wages, and how working for a start-up company may have effects on their pay.

Don't assume that the relationship will work. Clearly list how employment can be terminated. If you set up a probationary period, make sure you both understand the dates and duties involved. Lastly, it is a good practice to have all employees and vendors sign a non-compete or nondisclosure agreement. This is a document that says your employee will not disclose any of your unique ideas or concepts to a competitor or apply them to a business he or she starts in the near future. You can download a NDA, as it is called for short, at Onvia.com (www.news.onvia.com/x18278.xml).

Family and Friends as Employees

Family and friends may be the first to volunteer for a position within your newly formed company. This is a good sign because it means either that your passion is so great it's contagious or that they are watching you work so hard they want to lend a helping hand—both reassuring gestures that you are building your company on the right foundation. However, be warned of the challenges that come with hiring a family member or a friend.

If the working relationship goes sour, you can't exactly fire a family member and walk away from the situation. (Terminating your aunt's employment may make for some very uncomfortable holiday dinners.) I once, while managing a McDonald's, had to fire my own sister. Her revenge was to gain employment at Burger King and give me the silent treatment at home for a week. Think long and hard about your present family relationships and how the daily challenges of running a new business may modify them. Many people do hire family members to help, and sometimes gain successful results, but it takes open communication and predetermined guidelines for conflict resolution, among other things.

Employing friends can be equally challenging. We're familiar with friends' behavior, often in certain environments other than the workplace. The ability to maintain a close friendship with an individual doesn't necessarily mean you can work side-by-side with him or her every day. Unless you have successfully worked with a friend in the past, I would use the same caution when hiring a friend that applies to hiring a family member. You don't often see a person's work ethic while lounging around the pool or watching old movies on the couch. My best friend of twenty years, Audrey, and I had the opportunity to work together for AutoNation. Although we held different responsibilities, we worked close enough to learn that we didn't work well together. Her dedication to the organization and my desire to fight for my ideas could have damaged our friendship had we not recognized it and made a pact to keep work and friendship separate. When deciding if hiring your friend is the best choice for you and your business, the best test is to weigh the value of your friendship against the value your friend will bring to the company. You can find a good employee on Monster.com but it's more difficult to find a new friend.

42

Do you have family members working for your home-based business? What challenges arise from family employees?

SHERRY MAYSONAVE, EMPOWERMENT ENTERPRISES

My husband, Stephen, is the vice president of marketing for Empowerment Enterprises. He joined the company two years ago. He first became involved when I was reviewing the publishing contract for *Casual Power*. He negotiated terms with the publisher that gave us the primary rights to the book. After that, he became involved in many decisions for marketing the book. What really drew him in beyond the advisory stage was when I began to be approached to be a spokesperson for clothing manufacturers and other image products. Everyone wanted exclusivity but because of Stephen's business experience, expertise, and vision, I have remained an independent expert. I am not paid to say particular things about any products, which we felt would diminish my credibility. However, there were numerous companies still willing to work with us under this set of rules. Stephen has driven those partnerships far beyond what anyone ever conceived their potential to be, making them truly win-win for both sides. Needless to say, I am extremely grateful to have him on my team, especially acting as managing partner.

When we first began working together, I think there was a time when Stephen had to learn that I am the creative force behind the company. There are times when I must recharge my creative battery even though he can operate his marketing machine at high speed with few breaks. Once we recognized the talents we both brought to the table, the better the working relationship got. We also make it a point to have time together when we don't discuss business. I think the fact that Stephen has other professional interests allows us to manage a good working relationship with each other.

KAITLAND THORSTENSON, CERTIFIED PUBLIC ACCOUNTANT

The only employee I have is my daughter, Dawn, who works under my guidance. I don't feel like I face any challenges working with her. I am truly a blessed mom and find that my daughter, who has a good head on her shoulders, is doing just fine with the customers I left in her care. She worked for me and with me from the time she was fifteen years old and now is happy being a student and working to finish her degree in pre-law. I am very proud of her. She has three children and is making her own life.

MERYL GUERRERO, PARENTING 101

I work with many family members to put on our annual Parenting 101 conference. I no longer look for outside volunteers to help me because so many of my family members are willing to work. I only count on those who are committed to the goals of this conference and passionate about the mission behind teaching parenting. They include my husband, mother, aunt, father, and brother-in-law. One year, my aunt flew down from New York to help me. When I asked nonfamily people who weren't as committed to do it, they really didn't get the job done. I once had thousands of brochures to distribute to local retailers and schools prior to a conference. I gave boxes of them to volunteer helpers to distribute. When I followed up, I found the boxes left behind tables or under desks. Now, my family members help me do that job.

I've only been put in an uncomfortable position once, when I used poor communication in setting expectations. I would rather have someone tell me they can't do something so I can find someone who can, than to have them not do what they agree to do. I treat family members the same as other employees except for my mother. She knows I might lose it once in a while with her, and she's agreed to let me abuse her with extra work or by expressing my frustrations to her. With all my family members, I make sure I put everything in writing, just as I would for an employee.

BECCA WILLIAMS, WALLNUTZ, INC.

I rely heavily on volunteers to help me get things done. My husband advises me and packs murals, and my parents, in-laws, and friends have helped staff WallNutz booths. I repay my friends in different ways. Tomorrow, I'm going over to one friend's house to finish a mural in her daughter's room. We swap our talents to help each other. My husband gives advice or helps pack boxes whenever I ask. He's still waiting for the money to come rolling in, but he's really pleased that I'm pursuing my career and enjoying staying home with our daughter.

When I begin hiring employees, I'll be looking for people who are willing and able to dig in and help with anything that needs to be done, from dealing with important vendors to packing murals. The only way we're going to grow is if all the people involved are committed to WallNutz's success. To encourage this commitment, which may not be glamorous at times, I'll offer them equity in the company so that they are personally invested in WallNutz.

Independent Contractors and Freelancers

Independent contractors and freelancers offer good solutions to growing your company, without assuming the financial responsibilities of full-time employees. Although they hold different titles, the only real difference between an independent contractor and a freelancer is the amount of work they will accept and the time they spend on it. Independent contractors usually contract for longer periods of time with a certain company, or for an entire project, while a freelancer is often willing to accept short, one-time projects. Many writers or designers are freelancers, and often maintain a full-time day job in addition to their freelance work.

Both independent contractors and freelancers allow you to increase your resources without adding the burden of quarterly employment taxes and the expenses of employee benefits such as health insurance. However, this does not mean you are off the hook with the Internal Revenue Service. At the end of the year you must provide to both contractors and freelancers a 1099 of fees paid to each. Consult your accountant for detailed tax requirements before you hire any employee. Most often, independent contractors and freelancers are experienced professionals who, like you, have made the decision to be self-employed. Many are eager to obtain new work and anxious to provide their skills to you, and the Internet has made it easy to find them. One such site is www.netmommies.com. The founder, Corliss Hale, has gathered formerly employed women who are now staying home with their children but are willing to do freelance work. Both HBWM.com and BlueSuitMom.com also offer directories of women who offer services such as typesetting, Web design, accounting, marketing, and public relations.

Like most decisions you will make, this choice of employment has its pros and cons. Although it gives you the flexibility to manage your overhead costs, it also forces you to relinquish a certain amount of control, particularly related to the amount of time you dedicate to your business. You can generally rest assured that a full-time employee is working for you during the time you're paying them, but if you retain an independent contractor for the month, you risk being one of four clients paying them to get a job done. Where you fall on the contractor's priority list will depend on your relationship with him or her and the enthusiasm he or she has about the job. Also, when dealing with freelancers or contractors, you must rely on an independent person to represent your company the way you would. Some business owners believe only a full-time employee will hold the commitment necessary to do the job right.

There are plenty of good and bad employees in any employment status. My personal experience with working mothers has allowed me to interact with hundreds of very qualified professionals seeking a way to balance work and family by accepting freelance work. I think the right chemistry between my employee and myself far outweighs the employee's title. As the old saying goes, "Want something done? Give it to a busy person!" As far as I'm concerned, no one fits that description better than a mother working from home.

My advice when hiring any employee is to obtain a sample of the person's work, clearly describe your expectations to the potential employee, and each discuss your professional goals. If the chemistry is there, you should be able to work out the rest of the details.

43

What are the issues involved in hiring independent contractors and freelancers for your home-based business?

REBECCA HART, PUBLIC RELATIONS

I employ a few independent contractors who do work with my home-based public relations company. The independent contractors I work with come highly recommended from professional colleagues. For the most part, they are members in good standing of the Public Relations Society of America (PRSA) and are accredited. Our arrangements are very simple, but probably not the most fiscally responsible. We bill with no hourly mark-up and refer each other on projects with no referral fees, figuring that what goes around comes around.

DEE ENNEN, ENNEN COMPUTER SERVICES

I use independent contractors to do excess work that my clients need me to complete. I was very fortunate in finding back-up help in some of the businesses that I did typing for. Often the secretaries there were looking to make extra money, so I hired them to work for me. One of the best advantages is that they are familiar with the work already. I've also found back-up help through the Internet and people I have met by e-mail or through my chats. I send e-mails or fax the work to them and they send it back by e-mail when complete. I often use my independent contractors to proof my work, and that is extremely instrumental to the success of my business.

Dependability is a must when selecting independent contractors. They also need to be very dedicated to their work and strive for perfection. I always proof their work. I pay my contractors a set fee and mark up the product to my clients.

DEBBIE GIOQUINDO, PERSONAL TOUCH TRAVEL

I have two independent contractors who work for me. They came from another travel agency in our area. I had worked with them in the past and, when they heard I had gone off on my own, they approached me about working for my company. They have their own set of clients, and they work as they feel fit. Some weeks it's full time, some weeks it's part time.

I felt like I was taking a risk initially hiring independent contractors. You have to feel confident that they will represent your company and uphold the same business standards that you set for yourself. The kind of independent contractor I look for is someone who acts like a professional and is caring. I need individuals who are serious about the travel industry and who give personal service to their clientele. I prefer an agent who researches itineraries and doesn't just book the client in the least expensive trip because of price. Price isn't always everything. They have to know if a hotel is in a bad neighborhood or five miles from the beach. They have to be trustworthy and sincere. My independent contractors work from their homes. When their documents come in, they either come to my home to pick them up or we meet somewhere.

JEANNINE CLONTZ, ACCURATE BUSINESS SERVICES

I have two part-time independent contractors who work when I'm on a deadline or have a lot of projects in the works. I also network with other business support service owners to handle overflow work. Employing independent contractors removes me from the tax and insurance liabilities of hiring a full-time employee. I find people through friendships and networking. I look for ambitious people who are willing to put forth the time and effort necessary to make the business prosper.

Outside Vendors

Outside vendors offer the same flexibility as independent contractors and freelancers, but on a larger scale. Outside vendors run businesses that serve other, sometimes smaller businesses. The relationship tends to be long term although the frequency depends on your need for the service. Outside vendors are normally paid on a per project basis and may have a special pricing arrangement with you. For example, a public relations firm may use ABC printing as an outside vendor for all printing. ABC printing may charge the public relations firm $500 to print a press kit that the PR firm will mark up to $800 for the client. By using the same vendor on a regular basis, you can obtain better pricing and establish an understanding of your quality standards.

Examine the vendor's work quality, references, and capabilities carefully, as you would with anyone you choose to represent your company.

Outside vendors pose the same challenge that independent contractors and freelancers do as far as getting your work prioritized. If your top client needs printed brochures by tomorrow, it's difficult to convey the importance to another business owner who has other urgent jobs ahead of yours. Long-term relationships with your outside vendors will help you gain their loyalty for your work.

Another way to uphold relationships with your outside vendors is to pay on time for services rendered. Most vendors will bill on a monthly basis with discounts applied if paid early. Take advantage of these savings and cultivate your relationship at the same time.

Check with your local Chamber of Commerce, Small Business Bureau, Yellow Pages, or online to find outside vendors.

44

How do you deal with outside vendors for your home-based business?

BECCA WILLIAMS, WALLNUTZ, INC.

I have an outside organization in place that can handle large volume packing and shipping should our company take off. It took some time to iron out the logistics of our needs. It was the combination of understanding my vendors' capabilities, building in some "oops" time, and making sure that I underpromise delivery times to customers. Both my printer and transfer paper supplier have short lead times once an order is placed. They were the easy pieces of the puzzle; my fulfillment piece was more difficult. It took some searching, but I eventually found an organization that employs disabled adults to package and drop ship the murals. They took one of my mural kits and did a time study to estimate a per piece price. Since then, they've changed to a per hour charge, but now they offer drop shipping. This allows me to offer the kits through a number of different Internet retailers that require drop shipping that I couldn't have handled alone. I simply fax over the orders to the fulfillment center, and they do it. The system hasn't exactly been tested yet, so I'm sure there will be some kinks. Which is why I promise vendors to ship the product within four days of the order, when I actually believe we can get them out the door the same day.

REBECCA HART, PUBLIC RELATIONS

I use some outside vendors to do various tasks within my company. I hired a Web designer, bookkeeper, and freelance photographer. I pay each of these professionals on a per project basis. I made the mistake once of doing a trade with a computer consultant. I later decided that I'd rather be a paying customer so that I can get full attention. When looking for good, reliable, and qualified service providers, I rely heavily on personal and professional referrals. I found my Web designer through another professional organization, the National Speakers Association (NSA). I found my bookkeeper through my accountant, and I worked with my photographer at my former place of employment.

MOLLY GOLD, GO MOM !NC.

I've hired several outside vendors. First, I hired the lawyer who handled the incorporation. He got us the official papers, the Go Mom seal, and the stock certificates, and he filed all the necessary state and local papers. He was my husband's personal lawyer so it was easy to find him. We now use a law firm with specialists in intellectual property, trademark, etc. They are a big firm and can meet all our legal needs. My bookkeeper I found through my sister, who owns a medical billing company called Psychbiller. Using these outside vendors has been a good experience, but some vendor relationships present challenges. Our current printer is an example. The account rep lied to us all week about the status of our calendars. She assured me that our job was on the press, and delivery was just fine for this past Friday. The truth emerged Saturday morning that not only did our calendars not go to press, but the blue line was never shot. The result was we won't get the first 25 percent of product for two weeks. We lost two whole weeks of production because of their irresponsibility. In retrospect, I should have kept tabs on the status of our job.

WENDY HARRIS, NATIONAL ASSOCIATION OF MEDICAL BILLERS

I hired an outside vendor to design my Web site. It didn't take a lot of effort to find my designer. I employed one of the instructors I met while taking entrepreneur classes at the local community college. His name is Dave Borland from Utrax. He gave a very good class so I looked at some of the sites he designed. After viewing his work, I felt confident in my decision to hire him. The best part was that he gave me a good price because I had been in his class.

DEBBIE WILLIAMS, LET'S GET IT TOGETHER

I use a virtual assistant for occasional work such as distributing press releases, a legal advisor for reviewing contracts, and a Webmaster for special projects such as creating forms, programming, and advising. Whenever possible, I exchange services or barter, and this has worked quite well for me.

CHAPTER SEVEN

First Obstacles

Y ou have your home office set up, your business plan is complete, and now you find yourself sitting in your office looking into an empty computer screen. Now what, you ask? Chances are, it's time to take on your first challenge if you haven't already experienced it. Depending on the type of business you have selected to launch, your first hurdles will vary in complexity. If your new company provides a service like public relations, graphic design, bookkeeping, or even dog-sitting, your first challenge is to find customers. On the other hand, if you have chosen to design, produce, and sell the next great widget, it's time to figure out how to take your idea from concept to consumer product. Either road will present you with the necessity to learn, problem solve, and cope. These experiences in conjunction with working long hours on low wages create high hurdles to jump.

Nevertheless, you need to convince yourself that no task is too big to overcome. It's time to draw on the passion and determination that led you into your own business in the first place. I recently heard a successful businessman describe entrepreneurship as a long race that requires persistence rather than speed and ultimately delivers a feeling of fulfillment. It's ironic that I built the business plan for BlueSuitMom.com while training for the New York marathon. I may not be fast, but my strong steady pace allowed me to cross the finish line in Central Park, and it has enabled me to survive the Internet fallout of 2000. Tenacity will go a long way in helping build your company!

Approach your initial challenges with excitement and perseverance. Apply problem-solving skills you've learned in other areas of your life. Can you recall a day when a pipe broke and flooded your house? Cleaning up and repairing the damage seemed like a huge undertaking at the time, but I'm sure you broke down the problem into smaller tasks and eventually restored order to your home. It's no different when challenges arise in your company. Do you need packaging for your product? Begin by finding a box maker, then a graphic designer, then a fulfillment house to package the product. Take one step at a time until you accomplish the goal. Remember, there is no better way to find an answer to a problem than to ask those who have already done it. Most people take pride in helping others and enjoy providing the answer to somebody's question.

45

What was your first major obstacle?

DARCY VOLDEN MILLER, LITTLEDIDIKNOW.COM

Looking back, I created my first challenge myself by creating self-doubt. My mind seemed to constantly be filled with questions: Could I really do this? Could I make enough of an income to provide a living for myself? Will people believe in me? Will I be able to make all those dreams in my head come true? What if I fail? Do I have what it takes to run a real business? Those fears were almost paralyzing. But I knew that, no matter what, I didn't want ever to look back on my life and say, "What if . . . ?" So, I just jumped in and kept the faith. I knew I could always say, "I tried and gave it my best shot."

I also faced a huge learning curve. I had discovered the Internet only two months before I came up with the idea for my business. I knew that the best venue for my business would be this "Internet thing." Needless to say, I had a lot of learning to do. Especially when I decided to build my Web site myself. The best books I read to help me build my business on the Internet were *Start Your Own Business for $1,000 or Less* by Will Davis and *Making Money in Cyberspace* by Paul and Sarah Edwards. Both of these books were monumental for me. The Edwardses's book was an excellent resource for me, because it taught me everything I needed to know about the Internet in "idiot" form, such as what a banner is and what HTML is. It's funny to look back now and think that I didn't even know what a banner was! We all had to learn this at one time . . . even Jeff Bezos! I also took courses over the Internet on learning Web design and HTML. It was very much a learn-and-build, build-and-learn process.

PRISCILLA HUFF, AUTHOR

I believe that lack of self-confidence is often the first obstacle entrepreneurs face. Most people have self-doubts when starting a new venture, including many women. "What if my business fails?" "How will I balance a business, family concerns, and my regular job?" are some of the considerations that erode a woman's confidence. A good way to grow your confidence is to find other women in business or find a mentor and discuss any fears and concerns. Most women entrepreneurs are willing to share some tips and help one another succeed through encouragement and assistance in finding the right resources to get the new business up and running.

ROBIN ZELL, BRAGELETS

The first obstacle I faced was lack of knowledge for making my product. I had to learn how to make bracelets. Who in their right mind buys a bracelet company without ever having made a bracelet? One of the first bracelets I made was for a returning customer who was very particular. She wanted it a certain way, a certain pattern, etc. She called me when she got the bracelet and told me she just "cried when she saw it." I thought this was going a little overboard. She told me I put the clasp on upside down, and it didn't lay flat. I asked her to send it back, and I would fix it. I hadn't put the clasp upside down. It turns out that the previous owner of Bragelets was left-handed and strung beads in the opposite direction I did, so she naturally put the clasp on the other side of the bracelet. That customer has ordered from me since, but I make sure I put the clasp on the other side the way she likes it. Silly little stuff, but what is no big deal to me is a big deal to someone else.

JEANNINE CLONTZ, ACCURATE BUSINESS SERVICES

The greatest obstacle I faced was getting focused and motivated to cold call on potential clients. It was easier to sleep in and do the bonbon and soap opera thing than to cold call potential clients. My cold-calling strategy was to take my brochure, a cover letter explaining my business, and some business cards and visit area businesses. I hated it. It was hard to find out exactly who I should be talking to, and prospects did everything they could to dodge me. My task was made more difficult because the secretaries or receptionists I had to go through at first thought I was trying to take their jobs away. Cold calling is a continuing educational process!

BECCA WILLIAMS, WALLNUTZ, INC.

My greatest obstacle was created by my health. I quit my full-time job several months before my daughter was due, with the intention of launching the business before she arrived. Unfortunately, I became ill with pre-clampsia and couldn't work as much as I wanted, and ultimately Capra came into the world five weeks early. A couple of months after she was born, I actually got to work on the business full time. The absence of childcare assistance made the process of building my company much slower than I expected. Because Capra was premature, the first months of her life were dedicated to getting her to eat, eat, and eat some more. The rest of the time I spent pacing the floor comforting a colicky baby. Once that was all over, I spent her six hours of nap time every day feverishly working on WallNutz. I think I was partially motivated by the delay in starting the business. I was ready to go into production on the product and anxious to show the kits to retailers. The other source of motivation was the need for outside contact. Before starting back to work, I felt like a walking, talking milk cow whose only purpose in life was to nurse my child. Having business meetings let me break out of being only a mommy.

LINDA MCWILLIAMS, ONCEUPONANAME.COM

The biggest obstacle I faced when starting my business was gaining support from my friends and family. I found my friends were better about it. My family sort of thought it was a passing interest because "everyone was trying to work on the Internet." It got to the point that I didn't discuss it with anyone. My husband was supportive provided it didn't cost us anything and it made money. The reality is you don't just publish a Web site and become an overnight success. It requires a lot of work and determination and sometimes a lot of "let that comment slide off" attitude. I am determined to make this business profitable, and I will! Let them all eat their words! Determination is a necessary attitude for survival.

MOLLY GOLD, GO MOM !NC.

My first obstacle was going from concept to tangible product. It was a long journey. Long, not laborious, is the best word, because it was so exciting and so complicated and emotional. Like having a baby, there was so much uncertainty magnified by anxiety. I first researched my idea at the patent office. It was daunting, but luckily I had a friend's husband at the patent office who guided me through it. This was before I was even remotely interested in the Internet, and I had no idea if the trademark and patent library was live yet. Ultimately, www.pto.com became our final resource as we protected ourselves with every copyright and trademark that applied. We relied on Internet resources and filed directly without an attorney. Shame on us, because an attorney should have been our first step. After I played around with the idea, I let it sit. Always bouncing it off others, always receiving "that's awesome" reviews. I finally decided to proceed and happened to meet a designer who was enthralled with the project. Together we met with focus groups, and I redrew my concept over and over until I was happy with the final product. We made the mistake of not securing a final prototype on our first design. The results were quality problems on the first shipment. My advice is to touch, smell, and see every ingredient, part, and component of the product you produce.

DARCY LYONS, A GARDEN PARTY

I think setting up the partnership with a friend and then having differences was our greatest obstacle. The great thing about Terry and me is that we have known each other for fourteen years. We were roommates at one time and shared a bathroom—you get to know a lot about a person when you have to share a bathroom! We have a pretty good understanding that we each have different strengths and weaknesses. The tricky part—as in a marriage—is learning to respect those differences and realize that when the strengths are combined, the sum is much greater than the parts alone.

From the very beginning, we told ourselves we would not allow this company to put our friendship in jeopardy. If that were to occur, we would dissolve the business and remain friends. I think this says a lot for women—because I don't know many men who would be able to do this. Luckily, our disagreements are relatively minor, and we are able to step back, listen to each other, give each other the time needed, and then move on.

Our greatest disagreement came when we were selecting an accountant. My husband and I have a relationship with an accountant here in San Diego who we are very comfortable with. We wanted to use his services, but Terry wanted to find an accountant who was not our personal accountant. I just couldn't understand why she would not want to use someone with whom at least one of us had some prior experience. It took me a while to understand her point of view, but in the long run we agreed on a different accounting firm.

We have also found that we both must agree on the products that we sell. Terry has one product that she is "in love with" and I have one product that I am "in love with." We each hate the other's "love child." We have yet to sell either one of those products!

LARA PULLEN, ENVIRONMENTAL HEALTH CONSULTING, INC.

The greatest obstacle I experienced when starting my company was handling the rejection I received from queries I submitted to publications. I was unaware of how difficult it is to break into magazines. I spent a lot of time studying how to write a query and how to pitch a story, and yet rarely would I ever get a response from an editor. I would even send the required self-addressed stamped envelope! This was frustrating, and it seemed like I was wasting my time. Finally, one editor did respond, with a note encouraging me to pitch a slightly different story. I jumped at the opportunity and spent time researching this new story. I never heard back from him. I was frustrated because it seemed to me that he had made me waste my time.

Months later, he did contact me. He had moved to a new job on a health Web site and had brought my file with him. Evidently, one of the reasons he left his job with the magazine was because he did not have the freedom to encourage new writers or use different stories. He wanted me to write for him at the new place. I have written many stories for him since.

TAMMY HARRISON, THE QUEEN OF PIZZAZZ COMPANY

The first challenge I encountered was helping men to understand working with a home-based company. Women had no trouble understanding that I was a home-based working mother, but men needed some education. Not all men need help understanding what women do at home. The trouble I had was with men in certain professions. The types who think they need to be in control of everything around them are the ones I have had the most difficulty with. The attorney I worked for was a man, and I think part of the trouble we had was because I worked under his nose for two years before leaving to have my first child. He was so used to being in control that he had his wife work there so he knew what she was doing all the time! He knew I was a productive person when I worked from home, but he could not control what I was doing or watch me do it. I believe that was the problem, but I did continue to work for him for two years from home until the big case we were working on was ready to go to trial. He never did get comfy with my not being in front of him. Ultimately, we went our separate ways. I do receive notes from males thanking me for being so open with what I do and wondering how they can help their wives get into the same type of situation. Support is all that is necessary, and the willingness for change.

I have found so many people who are fearful to become home-based because of the changes they will have to make. I have to earn a person's respect, whether I work in the corporate world or from home. Trust is a vital issue with all aspects of life, so it is a major factor in being home-based as well. The best way to ease the transition of being respected in an office and being respected at home is to work at it.

46

How did you figure out how to make your product?

BECCA WILLIAMS, WALLNUTZ, INC.

I developed my product by trial and error. I first started with the thought of a sticker-like stencil where you stuck the whole thing on the wall, then peeled away pieces to expose the wall for painting. The concept worked, but research showed that the cost of production was too high. Several times, I went through brainstorming, creating a prototype, testing, and investigating volume production costs. When I finally devised a method where cost was okay, I made the decision to stop investigating other methods of transferring the design to the wall. I'm sure there are better methods out there, and I'll figure them out eventually, but at this point in the business, my time is better spent marketing the product.

JULIE AIGNER-CLARK, BABY EINSTEIN

I could picture in my mind the educational videos I wanted to create. My husband and I produced the first video with our home video recorder. We did all the production in the garage of our home. Once we had the product we were seeking to deliver to our customers, I went to the phone book and began calling videotape reproduction companies. This certainly was not the best or cheapest way to get copies of our video produced, but it was an easy answer at the time. Eventually, we found a duplicator who was willing to produce a large quantity of our tapes for the right price.

AMILYA ANTONETTI, SOAPWORKS

In order to discover the most natural cleaning alternatives, I literally hung out with the old people in a retirement community near my home. I asked them how they got food coloring out of their carpets or stains off the walls when they were younger. I knew that a food stain on a carpet fifty or seventy-five years ago was a much harder stain to remove than the same food stain on treated carpets today. The older women told me about concoctions of borax and vinegar or baking soda and water. I then spent hours experimenting with different mixtures in my kitchen. Once I found a solution that was safe for my child and worked around my house, I gave it to neighbors to try out. Some agreed that it worked well while others told me it worked for this but not that. I just kept mixing until I found the right recipes.

By asking business owners who produced their own products, I learned that I needed what's called a formulator. A formulator is a professional who mixes stuff. There are wet, dry, and solid formulators. I soon discovered formulators were all over the place. Most are inventors who just enjoy inventing.

While the formulator did his mixing, I created an advisory board to advise me on the must-have ingredients and the ones to avoid. It seemed funny to go back to the formulator and say, "I need you to make this but it can't have this, this, and that in it." Once the mixtures were finalized, we sent samples to friends and just kept streamlining the process until we were happy with the product.

NANCY CLEARY, WYATT-MCKENZIE PUBLISHING

When I conceived my Box-is idea—which, in essence, is really an oversized cigar box—I looked for specialty manufacturers that produced a variety of notable children's products. One source in Singapore I found through my publishing organizations. As an entrepreneur, I think it's important to immerse yourself in your market through magazines, professional organizations, and clubs. This way, you have a wide selection of manufacturers at your fingertips. The other source I found in China through a chance meeting with a woman who introduced herself as a book printer.

The decision to print overseas was based on the price difference—but really it came down to the customer service I received from the Singapore sales rep, who is located in Berkeley. They Federal Expressed a prototype to the specifications of my quote. I received it in two days—from Singapore!—and the power I felt as I held my idea in my hands sealed the deal. It looked great, and they had proved they could deliver.

If you want to manufacture a product for your business, the first step is to find a graphic designer with packaging experience who understands your vision. Mock-ups are the key to success. I can't tell you how many "fake" products I have produced for clients to hold up in infomercials, print in pre-production sales brochures, or post on Web sites. The clients use the prototype to gauge consumers' responses before going to the expense of mass-producing the product.

47

What was the biggest surprise you experienced when you started your business?

DARCY MILLER, LITTLEDIDIKNOW.COM

The biggest surprise for me after starting my business was that it was the best thing I ever did for myself in my life! It is truly the most rewarding, challenging, satisfying, gratifying, wonderful, intense, and passionate thing I've ever done. It is also the most scary, stressful, and worrisome thing I've ever done. It's a good kind of scary and a good kind of stressful. Really, the biggest surprise is that I found myself. I realized that owning my home-based business is just where I belong. There's nothing that makes me happier, nothing that makes me more satisfied, and nothing that returns to me more than what I put into it. There is also nothing that makes me feel more whole except being a mother. I can truly say that I love what I do. I can't wait to get up in the morning to "go to work," and I don't want to go to bed at night. I am truly amazed at how much fun it continues to be after more than a year of hard work and low pay. I am sure it is directly related to working with a friend.

TAMMY HARRISON, THE QUEEN OF PIZZAZZ COMPANY

The biggest surprise was, I am sought after! Someone hears about me and others follow, which is so exciting. To be deemed an expert in my home-based field and then to have people find me for work is unbelievable. The Internet is *huge*, and I am a part of it. My husband had been bugging me for years to learn Web design, and I resisted because I thought there were so many other more talented people out there doing it that I could not be successful at it. Once I got into it and realized how many people were looking for my type of talents, I was amazed!

Another thing that has surprised me is, though I've been working on the Web for less than two years, most people have great trust in my abilities! I am self-taught in everything I know, and that doesn't scare people away! I believe that is a valuable lesson to anyone wanting to start an e-business—it is the motivation behind you that makes you trustworthy and successful, not necessarily years of experience.

Since HBWM.com was my first client, I was excited that I was being paid for my learning curve as an advertising representative. I remember the first real request for proposal (RFP) that I toiled over for a big advertiser. Most advertisers give you about forty-eight hours to respond to an ad campaign proposal, so I spent the entire forty-eight hours working through it. I had never done this before! Lesley at HBWM.com had never filled one out, either, so she was not much help! Finally, I asked my husband, who has a Ph.D. and has filled out numerous RFPs, and he laid the groundwork for what we should do.

Then, just after Christmas in 1999, I had a house full of holiday guests from Texas when the phone rang. It was the advertiser calling to tell me they accepted our proposal and had over $10,000 to spend at HBWM.com! I tell you, there is so much truth to living on adrenalin from one big sale! The month that their money came through, I made more on just that one sale than my husband brought home!

KAREN WILKINSON OLTION, EBUBBLES.COM

Honestly, we were very pleasantly surprised at the enthusiastic response of shoppers (particularly women) to our concept and product mix. It was an almost immediate confirmation of our perception that there was a definite void in the bath and body retail world that ebubbles.com was conceived to fill.

As we saw it, female consumers were presented with basically three "same-old" forms of body care product mixes: 1) the mall-based chains of manufacturer/retailers like Bath & Body Works, who offer what we consider to be a very teen-oriented range; 2) the drugstore variety of lower quality, mass-produced brands like Calgon and Suave; and 3) high-priced ancillary body care products of the mega-cosmetics companies like Esteé Lauder, Clinique, etc.

The chances of finding something new and different—a luxurious milled soap that was really made in Provence, France, or a pure aroma-therapeutic treatment bath oil from a famous German spa—were slim-to-none without a lot of digging around. We were thrilled to receive such positive feedback right off the bat from women all over the U.S.!

RACHAEL BENDER, BLUESUITMOM.COM

My biggest surprise was the emotional tie I developed for our company. When you start a business, it really does become your baby, and sometimes it is hard to separate the decisions you need to make for the company from what you had hoped would happen.

I also don't think I had an accurate grasp of how difficult it can sometimes be not to bring home a steady paycheck. Luckily, my husband's income covered our needs, but I think, psychologically, women need to validate our importance in our families and to ourselves by earning a good living. I wasn't prepared for the fact that sometimes I felt like I was not contributing anything to my household, even though I knew that if I put my full effort into the business, in the end good things would happen.

DEE ENNEN, ENNEN COMPUTER SERVICES

My greatest surprise also created my greatest obstacle. I was surprised at how much work I had from the very start of my company.

My first mailing of letters was to chiropractors, and I got two chiropractors who wanted to have their work done on a daily basis. This work required transcribing tapes of daily notes and narratives. Then my marketing efforts at the printers started producing lots of work. I received two additional business clients through this means as well as numerous individual clients. And as if that wasn't enough, the flyers that I placed at schools started producing papers. At that particular time I was offering twenty-four-hour service. My clients would drop off their job on Monday, and I promised to have it done by Tuesday. That worked out well when I had just a couple of clients, but, as new clients came on board, I could hardly keep up with all the work. I did two things. First, I tried to do it all and worked incredible hours. Then I realized I just couldn't keep that up, so I changed my policy and offered forty-eight-hour service. I also got a back-up secretary to help. I still made money on the work she did for me, and it took enormous pressure off me.

Managing Disappointments

The road to success doesn't come without its moments of disappointments. Remember, you must go through fire to get steel. The irony to experiencing times when people may let you down or major clients change their minds on hiring you is that these events often seem to result in something positive. Each of us can remember when we felt disappointment about something that didn't happen and later felt thankful that it didn't. Maybe it was a high school boyfriend who dumped you, and you later realized he would have made a terrible husband. Or a promotion you missed, only to find out the position was later eliminated during downsizing. Garth Brooks wrote a song that says, "Some of God's greatest gifts are unanswered prayers." You don't have to be religious to relate to the reality of this line.

Each day that I look at our two daughters, whom we adopted after years of infertility, I feel thankful that I didn't get pregnant when I wanted to. If my attempts had been successful, I might never have experienced the positive outcome of adoption.

I can still remember the euphoria I felt when I received a verbal commitment for almost a million dollars in funding for BlueSuit-Mom.com. The money allowed us to come out of the gates with money to spend on advertising and a full-time staff. My entire body was shaking for days, and my heart pounded so hard that I could barely sleep at night. However, the day that the check was to be delivered came and passed. Calls to our investors were not returned. I could see the writing on the wall, and the disappointment was intense. I had promised friends jobs, placed orders for equipment, and gained a significant amount of confidence knowing that respected businessmen were willing to invest in my idea and skills. Probably the greatest part of my disappointment though was the fact that they didn't just come back to me and say their financial situation had changed. Quickly, we revised our business strategy and limited our spending to the most necessary items. Then came April 2000 when Internet funding came to a halt. and well-known Web brands began closing their doors. We held to our bootstrapping approach to building our company even when other investors stepped up to the plate with money. Today, a year and more than 200 defunct Internet companies later, BlueSuitMom.com is still growing and surviving the New Economy fallout. There have been many times in the past twelve months that we actually have been thankful that we did not receive the million dollars of funding. We would have gone the way of fast-spending companies and might not be around today.

48

What was your greatest disappointment?

DARCY LYONS, A GARDEN PARTY
The greatest disappointment I experienced was that I couldn't perfectly balance everything in my life: running a business, running

a home, running a family, running my personal life. I thought I could do it all. I couldn't. Something had to be sacrificed. And, because I had to sacrifice some things, it threw off the equal balance of "the wheel." I realized that because running my home lost its place on the priority list my husband and son suffered. I found that my husband, my biggest supporter, was becoming my biggest saboteur, because I couldn't care for the home and family as I once did. I know that eventually I will find that perfect harmony, but right now I'm still looking.

MOLLY GOLD, GO MOM INC.

My greatest disappointments always come when we are rejected by publications that we feel we share a connection with their audience, like *Parents* magazine, which refused to review our product last month. The frustrating part is, I feel the editor bases the rejection more on a personal application than on consideration for the magazine's audience. I take it personally, foolish as that may be. I suppose that's a direct result of my creating the product in the first place. My husband says it's all about sales. You've got to sell yourself to people and make their job easier. The twenty-five nos you receive won't matter when you finally get that one yes. You have to not take it personally and realize that the only person who will look out for you is you. So if you make your approach so very simple, eventually you'll fill one need and then another.

That is what you focus on, the next great success. Frankly, I think both the press and retail are the two rudest segments to work with. They'll tell you no along with how you're just one in a number—they only care about what meets their needs. You have to outsmart them by meeting their need in their way, like a timely press release that is good enough to reprint verbatim.

DEE ENNEN, ENNEN COMPUTER SERVICES

My greatest disappointment came when my publisher backed out of representing my book only days before it was supposed to go press. I was completely devastated. Here I had worked so hard and long on my book. At first, I just couldn't believe that it had really happened. This publisher had pushed me so much to make this book the best it could be, and now it seemed that it all was a waste of time. I'll be honest—it took a while to get over it. Then I decided that instead of just giving up, I'd self-publish my book, and that's what I did. Today, I make so much more off the self-published version than I would have from regular publishing. I believe because I had this happen, I was more determined than ever to make it work.

KAREN WILKINSON OLTION, EBUBBLES.COM

It's very interesting that what was my greatest disappointment at the time has really turned out to be a blessing in disguise. As I mentioned earlier, we worked with some venture capitalists in the spring of 1999. We were extremely disappointed when the deal fell through, especially as the holiday season was fast approaching, and we were still in the very rudimentary stages of building the site itself—a monumental task. We danced around a bit with private investors in the next few weeks, then my husband and I decided, okay, it's now or never if we are going to "go live" by Christmas. We bootstrap-financed it ourselves and got to work, applying the same principles to our company as any other small corner retailer just starting out. We have continued to grow slowly.

As it turns out, the other beauty site the venture capitalists funded with over $60 million went bankrupt, while we've continued slowly but surely to build a small and loyal customer base. We speculate that if we had received the funding, we too would be shut down today.

LESLEY SPENCER, HBWM.COM

I was disappointed when I realized I couldn't please everyone. No matter how hard we try, we cannot. It was hard at first and still is on occasion, because we as humans want to be liked, and we want to please. There are millions of people with unique personalities and differing needs. As one person, I cannot possibly be everything to everyone. I have to focus on who I can help and do my best to help them as much as possible. If I cannot help them, I try to refer them to another person or organization that may be able to.

Self-Motivation

Most entrepreneurs can be characterized as self-starters and self-motivated individuals. But even the most energetic entrepreneur can run out of steam at some point while starting a business. The trick to managing your drive is to identify your motivations from the beginning and focus on them in times of fatigue, frustration, and boredom. This is where having a strong set of goals established for yourself and your company is beneficial. Whip out your business plan on a regular basis in order to reflect on the motivations that brought you to where you are today.

Even the most motivated individual will experience moments of procrastination. Procrastination normally surfaces when we are facing a task that we either are not committed to doing or are afraid of doing. Although you are committed to your business, you might be less committed to paying your sales taxes on time or cold calling on customers. Certain tasks just naturally fall to the bottom of your priority list. Owning a small business forces you to do things you might be unfamiliar with or just plain dislike. I remember the first time I had to file quarterly employment taxes. The Internal Revenue envelope sat on my desk for weeks. I couldn't even bring myself to open it. I knew there would be things I didn't understand and small print I'd have to ponder. Unfortunately, as the boss, there was no one to whom I could pass the envelope. There's no time like the present, and eventually I realized I was spending more time fretting over filling out the form than I would doing it. The funny thing is, the anticipation is always worse than actually completing the task.

To jumpstart your motivation, set a goal, pick a day, and assign a task to that time. Commit to yourself that no matter how you feel, that is the time you are going to accomplish your goal. Focus on what you can get out of completing the task. In the case of my tax envelope, I could look forward to a clean desk, even if only temporarily.

49

What is your advice for staying motivated?

PRISCILLA HUFF, AUTHOR

I recommend setting some realistic goals and focusing on the steps to achieving them. Make sure you write those goals down, because business experts say a person is more likely to reach her goals if she has them written down. I have a weekly work chart I fill out and each morning I make a to-do list from that chart. At the end of the week, I analyze what I have been able to accomplish.

It is also very important to keep a positive attitude. It will help you go forward, even when it seems you are just spinning your wheels, or making mistake after mistake. I find, too, that networking with other entrepreneurs—helping them with a lead or information or referral—seems, somehow, to stimulate more opportunities coming back my way.

NANCY CLEARY, WYATT-MCKENZIE PUBLISHING

I love what I do—even more now that I am designing for my own benefit. Now, someone comes to me with their idea, their dreams, and the adrenaline rush of creating something beautiful in a matter of hours is just awesome! The change in my role from "paid designer" to "publishing partner" allows me to pour my heart and soul into a project because I know I will make a percentage of the sale, and every one of those products that sells just gets the Box-is brand out there further.

JORJ MORGAN, COOKBOOK AUTHOR

To stay motivated while I'm working on a deadline, I break down the tasks into doable segments. Then I plan out my week, setting goals of how many segments of writing or recipe testing I need to complete each day. I always leave extra room in the schedule for unexpected interruptions like a child home with the flu or a car that has to go into the shop. I easily reach my goal by finishing small segments of work. I reward myself by getting up from the desk and doing something fun like peeking at my favorite daytime soap or reading a new magazine or even baking a batch of double chocolate chip cookies. Then it's on to the next task.

DARCY VOLDEN MILLER, LITTLEDIDIKNOW.COM

I surround myself with like-minded women who share a common mission and vision. Fortunately, with my business, these women are built right in. I knew that keeping each other motivated and encouraged would be the key to our success. We're founded on the idea, "There is strength in numbers." We turn to each other for encouragement, motivation, and support on our ventures. Any time one of us needs a little dose of encouragement we go to our group and are assured that a number of women will be there to give us just the boost we need. Building a business is hard. If you can find support in your times of weakness and need, then you've got it made.

ALEX POWE ALLRED, AUTHOR AND GOLD MEDALIST

There is a section in my new book, *Passion Rules,* that talks about the reasons to go into business or not to go into business for yourself. One thing sticks out in my mind. Yes, you must find your passion, believe in yourself, take charge, and be willing to take risks. But one reason not to go into business is a lack of self-motivation. This is the time to be really serious with yourself. Everyone likes the idea of working from home, but there are some people who should not. Whether you are going for the gold or making a go of the business world, you have to be able to cheer yourself on always. Bottom line: If you need someone else to motivate you, self-employment is not for you.

Motivation is an important part of my life. As a former athlete, and even today when I'm at the gym, I play little games with myself. The object of the game is to see how much I can do in a certain time frame. I lifted this much last time, how much can I do now? During my work time, I make myself lists, and I see to it that by the end of the day or week, I have completed the list. I take those lists very seriously, maybe too seriously. I have another friend who uses the list method. She's got lists all over the place, and she's always making new ones. I keep telling her, "Make one list and only one list. Treat it as though it were the mission statement to your business. Each week is a new mission."

Another biggie I talk about is putting things off. Statistically, women procrastinate more than men. Interesting and true. As an athlete, I knew a lot of competitors who dreaded training. They dragged themselves to workouts and put off their trainers and coaches. They made up excuses and whatnot. But training is part of the bargain, right? I always charged through the workouts and somewhere along the line convinced myself the workouts and training were better than the actual competition. If you want to be a success, I mean, really want success, you've got to enjoy getting your hands dirty. CEO Lynette Reed of Illume Candles, who I interviewed in *Passion Rules*, says she really didn't *love* what she was doing until she actually began making candles herself, getting her hands into the wax. That was when her company took off, more than tripling its sales.

GWEN MORAN, MARKETING EXPERT AND WRITER

One of my biggest regrets is that I didn't learn to ask what I didn't know early on. I was twenty-six when I started my business and faced challenges because of my age. For me to admit that there was something I didn't know was tremendously difficult, because I often had to convince prospects I had the skills despite my young age. When I did start opening up to other agency owners, sharing challenges and questions, I was shocked to find out that most of them were facing exactly the same issues I was facing! Once I learned to ask what I didn't know, my stress level was relieved, and I felt a great sense of comfort and motivation.

It's critical for entrepreneurs to find an outlet that relieves the stress of owning a business. Spouses, boyfriends, girlfriends, and close friends can quickly tire of your obsession with your enterprise. More than one business owner has found herself faced with marital difficulties and a diminishing circle of friends. While burnout can be a challenge to avoid; it's even more of a challenge to overcome once it's set in. It's helpful to organize lunches or dinners with other groups of entrepreneurs or find a mentor who will be willing to discuss your challenges. You also need to take time away from your business—at least one day off per week and a vacation or two each year at the minimum. If you play golf, get out on the links to blow off some steam or find a hobby to tear you away from your business.

Stress

Most entrepreneurs will tell you that stress is synonymous with owning your own business. Just as heat rises, so does every challenge, hiccup, or problem that your company will encounter. Whether you are the sole proprietor or employ a team of a hundred, every problem will eventually reach your desk. How you react to each episode of trepidation will determine the level of stress you encounter. Stress is caused by a rush of adrenalin in our body as part of a fight-or-flight reaction. Although the surge in adrenalin can create a positive boost of energy, too much can result in loss of self-confidence, lack of productivity, and anxiety. Long-term adrenaline exposure will divert your body resources to your muscles rather than areas that control body maintenance. This is why people who experience long-term stress tend to be sick more often. Ask my husband, Tim, and he will tell you that every January 2, I come down with a terrible cold or flu. It's as if my body finally gives out from the hectic pace of all the holiday activities.

Operating a home-based business presents two channels for developing stress. There is the stress of running your company and the stresses that arise from working from your home. Picture this: You are on the phone with your largest client. After weeks of convincing him you can handle it, he's about to offer you a project that could help you double your profits this year. Suddenly, your two toddlers decide to test their vocal cords arguing over the last Oreo cookie. Or, that same client needs his project completed by 5:00 P.M., and your computer decides to crash. Working from home forces you

---

WARNING SIGNS OF STRESS

- Negative thoughts
- Short-term physical symptoms such as cool skin, fast heartbeat, rapid breathing, and tense muscles
- Trouble making good decisions
- Difficult situations seem a threat rather than a challenge
- Feelings of anxiety, frustration, and short temper
- Long-term physical symptoms such as frequent colds, back pain, digestive problems, and sexual disorders
- Feelings of being out of control or overwhelmed
- Changes in eating habits
- Irritability
- Reduction in personal effectiveness
- Change in work habits
- Neglect of personal appearance

---

to deal with the number one contributor to stress: loss of control. Often, you have no control over whether your children are going to be hungry at the moment your customer calls or when you can work and when you can't.

Being in control is largely a matter of attitude. Often the difference between being in control and not being in control comes down to investing in yourself. Whether it's breaking away for a hot bath or running a few miles on a treadmill, it's important to find time for you. Someone once asked me why I run twenty-six-mile marathons. Part of the reason is because it gives me time to be alone and think while I maintain my weight. But the main reason I do it is for the unknown. After each marathon I've run, something good has happened in my life. Once it was the birth and adoption of my youngest daughter; another time it was the launch of BlueSuitMom.com. I'm not sure why it is, but achieving one goal in my life seems to create momentum or karma in some other area. That's why I run, to keep goals in my life and to know that I control whether or not I reach them.

Just as your business plan is important to the growth of your company, an action plan to manage personal stress will help you keep control in your business and grow as an individual. A good idea is to set goals for self-improvement and to control the factors associated with your stress. You might decide to start each day with meditation or end your day with some type of exercise. At BlueSuitMom.com, we have a policy that everyone must take Friday nights off regardless of what's on our plate. Even if you must force yourself to sit down on the couch and do nothing, taking control of your time will go a long way toward managing stress.

50

How do you deal with the stress of being a business owner?

SHANNON RUBIO, THESMILEBOX.COM

I feel like I am still learning how to deal with the stress of running my own business. What I have learned is the importance of taking time for me. I have a lot of things I love to do that I didn't allow myself time for like reading, playing my guitar, and working out. Now, I make an effort every day to do something. Even though I may fall asleep reading, it makes me feel better knowing that even a small part of the day was for me. I also think exercise is a great stress reliever.

My advice for women starting out in their own businesses is to try and build as much support as you can from family and friends. A strong support system gives you a sounding board. My other piece of advice is to pick a business that you love because you end up living and breathing it! And always be aware of *why* you are at home, whether it's for your kids or to have a flexible schedule. Keep that goal in your head for when things get stressful.

ROBIN ZELL, BRAGELETS

When things get stressful, I take a few days off. Sometimes I just don't answer the phone. I call a friend or my mom and vent and swear I am going to close down this darn business! The problem is that I regret later taking a break from work. I ultimately spend a few hours, even weeks, chasing my tail and paying for it. The most frustrating part of the day is 5:00 P.M., when I have spent a couple of hours working because the little ones were playing so well. I then head upstairs to find out I have a five-hour mess to clean up. The whole house looks like a bomb hit it because I did some work. One step forward, three steps back. That's when I question if it is worth it.

DARCY VOLDEN MILLER, LITTLEDIDIKNOW.COM

Luckily, I am a pretty low-key person and don't get stressed out too easily. I'm probably a bit whacked, but I love talk radio. I am able to lose myself in other people's dilemmas. It makes me realize that my life is pretty darn good! Other stress relievers for me are to go outside with my kids and, of course, catalog shopping!

I probably feel the most stress when I am on the phone with a customer, and one child is trying to see how far he can spit Fruit Loops off the balcony in my office, and another is doing his loudest Hyena-Gorillasaurus imitation. I am sure the person that I am speaking with will hang up on me and immediately phone Child Protective Services because they are certain there is some sort of toddler torture going on at our office. At that point, it's time to go outside for a few laps around the swing set for the kids, and the new Dean and Deluca catalogue for me!

ALEX POWE ALLRED, AUTHOR AND GOLD MEDALIST

When I am stressed, exercise is the key for me. It is the way that I am able to reduce tension and shrug off things—like losing documents or interviews or having little people drive me insane! I think when we are stressed out we tend to lose our perspective on things. Finding out at the last minute about a school project or assignment from a client can seem much bigger than it really is if you are already on edge. I'm a jock at heart, so I will always choose sports to let off steam. Someone else might try something different. I have a friend who is into crafts and craft meetings. Because she is isolated during the workday, she uses her hobbies to meet with other people and relax.

KAITLAND THORSTENSON, CERTIFIED PUBLIC ACCOUNTANT

My way of dealing with stress is to make sure I always set aside private time for myself. Even in the years when my children were young, there was a big old floppy chair in my bedroom, and when I was there with the do-not-disturb sign in place, they knew that it was Mom's downtime. Long hot soaks in the hot tub also seem to relieve my stress a great deal. I do go on a treadmill at least three times a week for a minimum of thirty minutes and have worked up to a five-mile-an-hour rate that also helps to work out the stress. My advice to young entrepreneurs is never, ever let the business run you. It's important to remember that you are the person in charge. When it becomes such an obsession that all you are doing is work and more work, then it's time to look at what it is you are truly trying to achieve and if you are using work and business to block out some problem in your life. For me it was a bad marriage and issues from childhood. Now, when I sit down to work, it is for my pleasure, not just for money. If I didn't enjoy the work, I wouldn't do it. If the ownership of the business is driving you into stress, then it is time to look at what is going on.

SANDI EPSTEIN, WORK/LIFE COACH

Stress management is essential for your own health and the health of those around you. Too often, entrepreneurs immerse themselves in their work, which over time can detract from being a whole person. These basics are important for me: exercise, a social life, a support system of family and friends, and set hours when work is out of the picture. These preventive measures sound simple, but it is surprising how frequently we ignore them!

KIT BENNETT, AMAZINGMOMS.COM

I actually find it less stressful working at home. For me personally, office politics caused more stress than my work now. When I feel overwhelmed, I work on my art. Pottery, painting, and gardening are all very important to me. I also try to meditate or pray daily to feel inner strength and calm. I also make sure my husband and I get time alone on Friday or Saturday evenings. It may be a date night or a video after the kids are in bed. Mindless entertainment at least once a week helps to settle my brain.

Starting your own business is an exciting and rewarding adventure. You must be determined, strong-willed, and very patient. As we all know, hindsight is 20/20. I went into Amazingmoms.com pretty blind, and my vision is not yet perfect. However, here are the issues I keep in mind. Maybe they'll also help you:

1. To avoid conflicts, get full support from your children and partner.

2. Make a schedule and stick to it. Otherwise, when your children see you being pulled in another direction, they may vie for your time and attention, making your life more difficult.

3. Create a separate office space.

4. Keep personal and business finances separate.

5. Make a business plan and have it reviewed by experienced business people before you take any other steps.

6. Plan how you will get help when you need it. A friend or family member may be willing to help you out part time.

7. Keep checking in with yourself. Are your priorities in line? Are you still on the right path?

8. Be flexible and creative with your time when necessary.

9. Get a separate phone line for business.

10. Don't make promises to your children that you may not be able to keep.

11. Do *not* quit. Owning a home business is hard, but it is worth it.

51

Can you describe your toughest times and how you handle them?

BECCA WILLIAMS, WALLNUTZ, INC.

I try to have a priority list and cross off tasks as they are completed. I do get discouraged from time to time and think, "Maybe the kits aren't a great product and that's why retailers aren't carrying them. Maybe parents don't really want to buy something that requires effort." This usually happens after I've been negotiating with a buyer who finally says she's interested. When the deal falls through for one reason or another, it is a serious disappointment, especially since it is a rigorous process to tailor the pitch to that specific retailer.

Miraculously, right around those times, a customer will send an e-mail that says how impressed she is with the site and that she's so happy to have found the kits. Or, I'll use one of the kits to help friends paint their child's room, and I realize that this is really an easy and fantastic product. What motivates me is knowing that this product is going to be gangbusters when enough of the kits get into the hands of end customers.

KAREN WILKINSON OLTION, EBUBBLES.COM

When I get into fear and anxiety, it's usually over financial issues at times when I'm just not taking time enough to get some exercise or quiet time to myself. I have a trick to "get grounded" that my friend Mary taught me. It *really* works! I stop and actually lay on the ground (sometimes in my house, but most times outside on the grass or the patio), put my legs out together in front of me, and stretch my arms all the way from my sides. I hold my hands palms down onto the warm brick or cool grass and breathe, breathe, breathe. I concentrate on feeling the ground or earth through the palms of my hands first, then try to pick up the feeling through the rest of my body while letting frantic thoughts melt away. Nothing like using the ground to get grounded! It's a great form of meditation that really works for me!

A long, very hot bubble bath also works for me. I actually light candles and close the door for absolute silence if I feel stressed and overwhelmed and need a good therapeutic soak. I'm absolutely convinced of the efficacy of aromatherapy, too, and I think the breathing in of steam in a hot shower or bubble bath enhances it. If I need to de-stress, and immediately get peppy again, I choose eucalyptus and/or a peppermint blend. But, for relaxation, nothing really beats good old lavender.

Lastly, I keep a file of compliments and unsolicited feedback from women and men who took the time to tell us how much they appreciate eBubbles, our customer service, and our products. If I ever have any doubt about why I'm doing this whole thing, this file reminds me.

LINDA MCWILLAMS, ONCEUPONANAME.COM

There are times when things get tough. I think that's to be expected when running your own company and managing a family. When those days happen, honestly, I cry in the shower. Nothing grand about that but it does help sometimes. At other times, I just try to take stock of everything I feel I've accomplished. I try to remind myself that I am doing this for my family and me. I want to be home but also need and desire to be creative and supportive of my family financially. I have always worked. I like to work. I need to work and feel productive. I am not only nurturing my family, I am nurturing myself. This has been hard to convey to my husband, and that's when it's stressful. I won't stop trying to get it through his head!

JULIE MARCHESE, TWINSADVICE.COM

One of my personal weaknesses is taking on too much and then becoming cranky and overwhelmed staying up late night after night to complete tasks. Ninety percent of these tasks are work related, and getting them under control helps me to feel more in control the following day. I will continue to pull late nights until I am back in control of my schedule.

DEE ENNEN, ENNEN COMPUTER SERVICES

I used to thrive on stress. I loved the challenges and the sense of achievement. I used to do ten things at once and do them accurately. It all caught up with me, and I started having medical problems. Obviously, it's not a good thing to have medical problems when you are self-employed. When you can't work, you have no money coming in.

Today, I take breaks and go out for lunch instead of just grabbing something out of the refrigerator. I only do one or two things at a time. I reorganized so that I don't waste time looking for things. I learned to say no. That was hard, because when I say no, I'm turning down money, and it's hard to do that sometimes, especially with three kids. I learned that even "good stress," i.e., a new client, media attention, etc., can be harmful.

I relax more today. I try hard not to constantly be in a hurry. There was a day when every second counted. Now I try to not plan as much, and so I keep a looser schedule.

RACHAEL BENDER, BLUESUITMOM.COM

I'm afraid I don't deal with stress very well. Basically, when I feel too stressed, I take a step back and do something else. I take a nap, go to the beach, or even veg out on the couch. If I'm really, really stressed, I impose a no-work-for-twenty-four-hours rule and focus on something else to clear my head. This is hard to do, but afterward I always feel ready to jump right back in.

I felt the most stress when my business partner and I were looking for venture capital funds to keep the business going until we could generate enough revenue. All the times we were turned down were nerve wrenching, because I realized we could be one of those businesses with potential that might fail because we didn't have money to pay the bills. I've always been far more stressed by things that were out of my control than by the mounds of work I want to do. At least I know that if I set the right priorities and work fourteen-hour days, I can get it all done. I can't always control the actions of others.

CHAPTER EIGHT

Networking

How well you network plays an important role in getting your business started. Networking is how you will acquire your first customers, and it is your access to resources. I like to think of networking as my way of gathering information. Imagine yourself at a cocktail party hosted by your local Chamber of Commerce. If you were a fly on the wall, you would hear the members asking each other questions: Where is your office located? What kind of telecommunication system do you have? How many employees work for you? Where do you get your bottled water? Do you have a copier? These fact-finding business owners are busy looking for new opportunities for their companies. The practice of questioning each other allows them to determine the needs of prospective customers and formalize plans to meet those needs.

In the same way, you can establish channels of information for yourself where others give you the lowdown about finding vendors, executing your sales plan, and learning from their mistakes. If your new business requires you to package your product in a box but you are lost as to how to do this, you'll want to call on someone who already puts a product in a box. Where does he get his boxes? If that's the wrong type of box for you, where else might you look? Chances are, another business owner can help you find the right packaging for your product. My point is, don't ignore networking by thinking it is only attending meetings, shaking hands, and exchanging business cards. Networking can happen on a school playground, on the phone, through e-mail, and at the supermarket. Networking savvy is about developing contacts, getting the word out about your business, and acquiring useful information.

Networking is a skill that does not come naturally to many people. More often than not, a person who is a poor networker is noticed more than someone who does it well. I'm sure you know a few of these folks. They are commonly referred to as brownnosers or fakes. They shake your hand and give you a business card as their eyes survey the room for their next victim. They show little interest in you or your needs. It is important to remember that the most beneficial contacts are those based on mutual respect, trust, and sincerity.

There are different viewpoints on networking and utilizing contacts. Many see networking as a means to reach their goals by leveraging the contacts, skills, and knowledge of others. I've always believed that it's more productive to give more than you expect to receive from a new contact. As I built my network of the home-based business owners you see in this book, I thought about what I would give back to them in return for the many e-mails I sent filled with questions that I needed answered in a short time. Whether it was giving away space on BlueSuitMom.com that I could otherwise sell or passing along a product to a potential distributor, I felt it was important to establish the bond required for a long, mutually beneficial relationship. I've always believed that what you give will come back tenfold when you least expect it. Besides, who can't use a new friend or two? By creating a strong network, I now have forty new resources for information, forty new believers in my product, and forty new friends I can call on in the future. Multiply that 40 by the 3 friends they can refer me to if they can't help me, and suddenly I have 120 places to go for answers. Chances are, if I ever made purple widgets for dogs, someone in this group would know someone who knows something about marketing and selling widgets to dog owners!

I've had more than my share of opportunities to learn networking skills and, unfortunately, more than enough times to embarrass myself by doing it wrong. Can you imagine how terrible I felt the night I told a group of people at dinner how the business model of a newly launched million-dollar company was flawed and destined to fail? No sooner did I express my opinion than I learned that the business owner and author of the business plan was seated right next to me. Mortified is a good word to describe how I felt. My number one rule: Always know to whom you're speaking before you express an opinion.

Another time, I was on a plane seated next to a young stockbroker. I'm always amazed at what perfect strangers will say to each other on a plane, and today was one of those days. As we sat on this five-hour flight, the young man began trying to impress me with his knowledge of a businessman who lives in my area. He proceeded to tell me why this nationally known individual's companies had lost the favor of Wall Street and what a terrible person this man was. He apparently did not read my body language, which would have told him that I was uncomfortable with this conversation or that he should allow me the opportunity to respond. Unfortunately, after an hour of "impressing me" with his "firsthand knowledge," acquired from a friend of a friend, I informed him that not only was he wrong, but the man he so terribly described was my boss and a family friend. In fact, he had attended my wedding. Needless to say, the remainder of the flight was very awkward for the young man. Remember, you never know who the stranger you're speaking to is, or who they might know, so make sure you find out before you dig yourself a hole.

Prior to attending a networking event, read the invitation or meeting notice carefully. Often, an invitation lists special hosts or board members who will attend. If you see a name on the list that might be a potentially good contact, find information about that person before attending the event. You can often look in the archives of your local newspaper online or in the prospectus of a company to find biographical information. I always go to networking meetings with an informal strategy of who I'd like to meet and what I might speak about to strike a chord with that person. I then follow up the next day with a handwritten note. You don't always have to go for the jugular the first time you meet a new contact. Remember the best relationships are built over a period of time.

52

What is your secret for
effective networking?

GWEN MORAN, MARKETING EXPERT AND WRITER

The word "networking" has almost become a cliché, but it's truly one of the most important skills a business owner can learn. With today's technology, the potential for networking is tremendous. The title of Harvey Mackay's book, *Dig Your Well Before You're Thirsty,* is tremendous advice for building an effective network. If your relationships with people are based on genuine interest in others and a spirit of reciprocal assistance, life and business are infinitely easier. While who you know isn't everything, it sure counts for a lot!

I frequent a public relations and marketing forum on the Internet that has great information that I use for my clients. I met a gentleman there who owns a public relations firm in Arizona. We became e-mail buddies. He has given me invaluable advice that really helped me to grow my business. It was three years until I actually met him face-to-face at a national conference!

SHERRY MAYSONAVE, EMPOWERMENT ENTERPRISES

Networking can be a very valuable tool to building your business. Here are some techniques I use that may be helpful to others.

1. Start with a strong belief in your product or service. Be confident that you are adding value. Expect opportunity to knock, that new business is simply waiting for you! Write down monthly or even weekly goals of exactly how many new contacts you need or want to make. Read the goal aloud daily and take two minutes to visualize meeting these new people. Feel grateful, even before anything happens. Keep your eyes open. Seize any unexpected or expected opportunity. Actively seek out new groups. This works. Watch your network miracles abound!

2. It's not so much who you know as who knows what you do well. Find out the names of the powers that be in your community, group, company, or industry. Seek a way to make a positive, memorable impression on them, making certain that they understand what your products, services, or expertise is about.

3. Never discount anyone. You never know who will turn into a gigantic lead.

4. Defining moments often come at the most unexpected times: Always look the part.

5. I try to make others feel important when I am speaking with them. I strive to make a genuine connection. I make and maintain eye contact and do not look around the room for my next contact while they are speaking.

6. Use a positive handshake. I always slide my palm all the way along the palm of the other person, even with the end of their palm, including when shaking hands with wimpy men who just grasp my fingers!

SANDI EPSTEIN, WORK/LIFE COACH

Simply stated, networking is putting yourself and your ideas out into the community. I network to learn more about what I do, to broaden my client base, and to see what other areas of work or personal development are interesting to me. Conscientious networking is essential to business and personal growth. You should feel relatively natural and unforced. Meet and connect with people because you are interested to meet and learn from them and to share yourself with them. Try to make it a comfortable experience. Otherwise, others will feel your discomfort, and you won't get a positive return.

JORJ MORGAN, COOKBOOK AUTHOR

I find it very easy to find something in common with almost everyone. When I meet someone, I start talking about children or their occupation and then move on to food. Everyone has a connection to food—whether they like to cook or not, everyone loves to eat! I always keep business cards with me that give my Web address, and I pass them out to everyone from the saleswoman in a gift store to the young man at the next table in a restaurant. I offer them the opportunity to learn about preparing food at home and encourage them to pursue the information on my Web site. If they are not interested, that's fine, too. I also believe that I can learn something from everyone I meet and try to listen carefully to what they are saying.

53

How did you gain new business contacts when you started your company?

DIANE DESA, A VIRTUAL ASSISTANT

I looked to my family and friends when I started my company and sent them all a brochure I had produced about my new business. I spent about $500 to have a brochure professionally prepared and printed, and to do an initial mailing. I am selective who I send it to because of the high cost of production. I send one to individuals I meet at networking meetings who want to know more about what I do. When I mail a brochure, I also include an "It was nice to meet you" note. This system has been quite effective so far.

SHERRY MAYSONAVE, EMPOWERMENT ENTERPRISES

I get my business contacts everywhere! I joined every organization and association I could: Chamber of Commerce, Women Business Owners, Toastmasters, Leads, Rotary. I've particularly enjoyed being a Rotarian, because the membership is primarily professionals and serious business types. I found the Rotary lunch meetings to be a friendly networking oasis, and when I travel, I can attend meetings in other cities. I also enrolled in seminars and workshops, both business related and personal growth varieties. I found the people there open to learning and change and extremely helpful in growing my image business. In the beginning, I often reduced my fees in exchange for referrals, on a sliding scale basis. The trick is not to approach this loosely. I discussed my system thoroughly with my client (corporate or individual) prior to rendering my services. The referrals had to be for viable contacts who agreed to book a certain number of hours or a workshop with me in the next two months. If the appointments did not pan out, the client agreed to pay my full fee. This avoids people playing the system by getting their friends to agree and then canceling out. After I learned how to work it, this approach brought me a lot of new contacts. Clients had a monetary investment in their referrals following through, and they made all the phone calls to prod slow referrals to schedule their appointments with me. If you don't set it up this way from the beginning, the people who don't send you referrals have a tendency not to call you back with repeat business, even if they want to, because they feel guilty.

DEE ENNEN, ENNEN COMPUTER SERVICES

I established contacts through direct mail, advertising in local papers, press releases, Internet message boards, and online chats. My best networking came from sending professional letters to targeted groups. I went though the phone book and selected all the businesses that I felt could use my word processing services and sent letters and business cards to them all. Since I wanted to specialize in legal and medical transcription, I targeted those areas first. This approach was very inexpensive and was well worth the minimal cost and time it took. I would definitely do it again. In my letter, I outlined my services and stated my specialties and said how I could benefit their company. I used phrases such as "Your work can be done on an as-needed basis" and "We supply fast, accurate services."

For marketing my book, I networked on message boards and in chat rooms. I helped other people start their own businesses and at the same time promoted my book.

ROBIN ZELL, BRAGELETS

To establish new contacts for my business, I did a mail announcement to a network of people. I also sent e-mails to every person in my address book. Other helpful relationships developed with the women in my moms' group when I put on a display at our meeting. I also get a lot of business from people who see someone wearing a Bragelet. They call and say, "My neighbor just got a bracelet from you, and I want one just like it!" Word of mouth is the best advertising for my business. It's like the old shampoo commercial: "I told two friends, and they told two friends, and so on and so on." Word of mouth is definitely my best friend. Especially when money gets tight, and I cut back on paid advertising. Word of mouth keeps me afloat.

TAMMY HARRISON, THE QUEEN OF PIZZAZZ COMPANY

I build new business relationships through e-mail. E-mail is my link to the world. I use it daily and have difficulty going a whole day without it! Not only do I receive great responses from the articles I write, I also get e-mails from people who have heard of me and who want advice on working from home who have a ton of kids like I do! When visiting via e-mail, I try to be professional as well as personable. One warning: Do not send e-mail that you would not want your mother to read!

Here are some dos and don'ts for using e-mail:

Tip 1: Personalize your e-mails. This is a real biggie in all communications between you and other people. Go to the person's Web site if they have one so you know what it's about and then say something nice about the site so they know you have looked at it. Then, put yourself in the other person's shoes and try to determine what type of response is appropriate. As long as it's true, I don't mind writing what people want to hear. Make sure to put names into your address book. Next, always use a personal salutation. It's not difficult to get that person-to-person, eye-to-eye feeling with e-mail if you hone your skills. Never let your e-mail look like spam: "Dear sir or madam" looks bad if there is a name available somewhere on the site. If, when looking at a site, the only name I can find is the owner, I write directly to them. People love getting compliments and will see that the e-mail is properly forwarded. Last, include info about yourself when appropriate. It is very important in building relationships. I usually mention that I'm the mother of three children and how much I enjoy their site. Appear to be a real person and not some marketer just generating e-mails.

Tip 2: Keep your e-mail short and provide suspense so that readers must respond in order to get their questions answered.

Tip 3: *Never* use "I will" or "We can." Always write in generalities, as this could save you from making legally binding promises that you may not be able to keep.

Tip 4: Send individual e-mails to avoid spamming. Never send a dozen of the same message. The name that you write in the "To" window should be their name and not their e-mail name. If you do not know a name, put the Web site or business name in there. Work an e-mail correspondent the same as you would someone on the telephone! I am long-winded (can you tell?), so my e-mails tend to be wordy and detailed. After you communicate a time or two with someone, you will adapt yourself to their writing style and can communicate effectively.

JULIE MARCHESE, TWINSADVICE.COM

I obtain new contacts by surfing the Internet and finding leads that may fit with my niche. I contact people either by e-mail, letter, or phone. I also look "outside the box" by contacting organizations that are somewhat related to the twins/parent/medical market like health insurance organizations, formula companies, diaper companies, publishers, and other parenting Web sites.

I will contact anyone I believe can strengthen the success of my business.

Associations and Organizations

Membership in local and national associations and organizations is a great way to network. The benefits of such groups are that they often present a learning experience as well as an opportunity to meet people and spread the word about your business. The Toastmasters

WHEN LOOKING FOR GROUPS TO JOIN, CONSIDER THE FOLLOWING FACTORS

- Frequency of meetings

- Size of membership

- Accessibility of members to each other through a membership directory or e-group

- Purpose of the group: Is it social or philanthropic?

- Cost of membership and what you receive for your dues

- Involvement opportunities

- Location of meetings: Particularly for national organizations, are there local chapters where you can meet other members?

organization, for instance, focuses on teaching public speaking, while Women in Technology International (WITI) spotlights the latest trends in technology for its members. Most local newspapers run a weekly or monthly listing of meeting times for professional organizations in the business section. You might look at the newspaper's online edition if you don't find it in the hard copy.

The level of involvement you decide to pursue with your membership is a totally personal decision. Most groups eagerly welcome new members who are willing to work on committees or special projects. Since first impressions are important, make sure you clearly understand the group's expectations should you decide to take an active role.

54

What associations or groups have been helpful in establishing new business contacts and resources?

JEANNINE CLONTZ, ACCURATE BUSINESS SERVICES

I belong to several philanthropic as well as professional associations. What I found was that getting involved with networking groups and charitable organizations got me out in front of those target business owners, giving them an opportunity to get to know me. I have the opportunity to peddle my wares in a more relaxed atmosphere.

DIANE DESA, A VIRTUAL ASSISTANT

I joined two local networking groups, Business Networking International (BNI) and American Business Women's Association (ABWA). Joining helped me to educate people about who I am and what I do. People are very interested in my profession because it's new. As a new member, I was required to give a short presentation about my profession, and I used the opportunity to explain what a virtual assistant is, what she does, and how it all works. Networking in local groups really helps to get the word out. One of my best clients was a referral from someone in my BNI group. This particular client is a professional fund-raiser who works on his own and has specific goals about the outcomes he wants from his business. I take care of the details of his business, which gives him the time to do more networking within his area of interest. There are only two other virtual assistants in the San Antonio area who belong to AssistU, a national trade organization, so getting "out there" and educating people really helps. The AssistU registry is very helpful in securing clients. People who go to the registry already understand the concept of a virtual assistant, know they need one, are ready to let go of certain aspects of their business, and want the collaborative relationship having a virtual assistant brings.

PROFESSIONAL ORGANIZATIONS FOR WOMEN

- American Association of Home-Based Businesses (AAHBB) is a non-profit organization for those who run businesses from their homes. www.aahbb.org. No fee for membership.

- American Business Women's Association (ABWA) offers entrepreneurial opportunities to women business owners by connecting members to business. www.abwahq.org. Dues vary.

- American Small Business Association (ASBA) is a partnership of small-business owners with the shared goal of running a profitable business. The ASBA seeks to leverage the collective buying power of many small businesses. www.asbaonline.org. Yearly dues: $60.

- Association of North American Businesses (ANAB) offers services and resources to small businesses. www.anab.com. Yearly dues: $14–$100.

- Formerly Employed Mothers at the Leading Edge (FEMALE) is a network helping home-based mothers keep in touch with other professional women. They publish a newsletter and have local support. www.communityresources.net/female.html. Yearly dues: $24.

My clients who come through the registry have various needs, and I only respond to the ones who I think are a fit for me. Since I don't like to do bookkeeping, when someone comes through the registry seeking a bookkeeping virtual assistant, I immediately delete those. The registry is helpful in making sure of a beneficial and productive match between virtual assistant and client.

- Home-Based Working Moms (HBWM) offers home-based mothers the opportunity to network and share resources. Membership includes newsletters and support system. www.hbwm.com. Yearly dues: $44.

- National Association for Female Executives (NAFE), an organization of the Working Woman's Network, provides resources and services through education, networking, and public advocacy. www.nafe.com. Yearly dues: $29

- National Association of the Self-Employed (NASE) was formed by a group of small-business owners seeking group buying power for goods and services. www.nase.org. Yearly dues: $79.

- National Association of Women Business Owners (NAWBO) provides education, resources, and networking for women business owners in 70 local chapters. www.nawbo.org. Yearly dues: $50–$100.

- Women in Technology International (WITI) is dedicated to the advancement of women through technology. Local chapters offer informational meetings and networking opportunities. www.witi.com. Yearly dues: $150.

LARA PULLEN, ENVIRONMENTAL HEALTH CONSULTING, INC.

To put me and my company in front of more people, I became more active in my community. When I was just starting out, I tried everything that I could think of. I spent time at the "dog park" meeting other dog owners and talking about what I did and what they did. As it turned out, the owner of a Labrador proved to be a very good contact. Talking to him resulted in a good job for me with Chicago's Museum of Science and Industry.

I joined the local Chamber of Commerce, but this did not work for me, perhaps because the members were not my market.

I attended public meetings on an environmental issue in my village. When questions arose that I could answer with my expertise, I spoke up. After one public meeting, I introduced myself to the head of the public health department and told her that she should hire me as a consultant on the issue because I knew the subject, was local and therefore easily trusted by the community, and was a mother with a small child (also increased credibility). She hired me the next day.

I also volunteered to organize our village block party and got to know the people on my block very well. I had a couple of leads from this that I probably could have pursued harder, but didn't because by then I had plenty of work.

I am also active in the National Association of Science Writers listserv.

55

How do you continue to establish new contacts for your business?

KAITLAND THORSTENSON, CERTIFIED PUBLIC ACCOUNTANT

Most of my business contacts are by way of word of mouth, although I receive some referrals from local computer stores and use their bulletin boards to post notices. I've even developed a network of clients in California through word of mouth. There is nothing like a friend who knows a friend who needs your services. Once a year, I fly to California from the Midwest and do my sister and her neighbor's taxes for them. It is a great way to take a small vacation that is usually paid in full by the business I generate there.

Kit Bennett, Amazingmoms.com

I establish new contacts by searching the Web and sending e-mails. Finding the appropriate contacts is imperative. I begin by searching for like-minded sites, using similar keywords as the ones on Amazingmoms.com. I also go to similar sites and look at their links pages. I continually ask myself, "Who is my audience, what do they look for, and what is it they want?"

I don't approach huge corporate sites directly. They won't give you the time of day. Smaller sites are okay. Hundreds of successful links from smaller sites may prove valuable in the long run. The fact that I am small does not lessen the impact I may some day have on the Internet. Don't be intimidated by competitive sites: There is room for everyone. The advice I give to a newbie is to take the risk and make the contact. The benefit of being on the Web is that rejection is not so hard. One of my tricks is to contact a site's advertising department. Sales people will return e-mails or phone calls. A good sales person knows that a lead made today may not pay off until next year. One time, I contacted the ad sales department at NBCi.com to ask about pricing. The sales person and I spoke for quite some time. She sent my information to a colleague, and the next thing I knew, Amazingmoms.com was a featured site for the SNAP network. Lesson learned? Sales people are well-connected and may very well spread the word about your business.

When I write an e-mail to a stranger, I first give a compliment. I say, "I was visiting your site today, and I'm very impressed with the quality of your content" and "Thank you for providing such a valuable resource to families."

Then I introduce Amazingmoms.com and myself. I ask if there is any way we can work together through reciprocal linking or shared content. When it's appropriate, I send an article, recipe, or family game idea for them to use on their Web site. They love free content.

Debbie Williams, Let's Get It Together

I put my networking efforts into building my Web site and then visiting related sites to network with others. I needed to learn all the aspects of Web design and went to find others like myself who were self-taught. I call it networking, but it is really marketing. One thing I learned is that business evolves rapidly when you share ideas.

Online networking, or "Internet-working" as I fondly refer to it, is the best way I know to expand your professional network. Not only can you meet people from all parts of the world with diverse talents, but by using e-mail, you bypass the gatekeepers and get to reach an important contact directly. The rules of business have changed so much in the past few years, and nowadays it's easy to take advantage of the opportunities this technology provides.

Shannon Rubio, TheSmileBox.com

My mother and business partner, MariVonne, is the networking arm of our business. She belongs to American Business Women's Association (ABWA), Business Professional Women (BPW), and several small Chamber of Commerce and networking groups. This is her arena. She goes to many events and hands out cards to everyone. She says, though it's hard at first to gain the confidence to go network on your own, in the end it is worth it. She says that after a while you get used to it and begin to enjoy it. I believe that if you have any level of self-confidence at all, you can network, because it is so important to building your business. One thing that I do when I have to go to these things is bring a friend. It gives me the moral support I need to enter a room full of strangers.

Maintaining Relationships

Once you've made the contact, it's up to you to build the relationship. Many business owners underestimate the value of good relationships and the time it takes to cultivate them. A networking strategy is an integral part of growing your business. After twenty years of being in business, I do networking every day. I do it without even thinking about it. Each day, I read several newspapers to keep abreast of industry trends, of people who were promoted to new positions, and of newcomers to our business community. Should I see someone I know in the Promotions column, I send a handwritten congratulatory note merely to maintain the relationship with the person. Sometimes, I see an interesting article in an out-of-town paper and send it to an acquaintance who might find it interesting. These small efforts put my name and my company in front of the people I need to know and who need to know me.

Another part of my networking strategy is to keep an up-to-date and accurate Rolodex. I organize it in three ways: by name, industry, and company name. This way, if I forget a name, I can still find it in a particular business. Each time I meet someone new and acquire a business card, I follow up with a handwritten note, mentioning the meeting. This reinforces the introduction regardless of how short it was initially.

Don't forget to include customers in your networking strategy. It's always less expensive to keep an existing customer than it is it find a new one. Besides, people like to know their business is appreciated. Take the time to maintain your relationships with your best customers, particularly if they send you new customers. It's always a nice gesture to acknowledge customer referrals with a thank-you note, accompanied by discounted merchandise or additional product.

56

How do you maintain relationships with business contacts?

ROBIN ZELL, BRAGELETS

Although I maintain relationships by giving discounted merchandise to loyal customers, I think the most effective way to maintain relationships is through customer service.

I try my best to make sure everyone is happy, because word of mouth is my best advertising. I am selling bracelets to moms who deserve something nice, and delivering the best possible product is a personal issue for me. It makes me feel bad sometimes when a customer checks on her order by sending me an e-mail with her order number. I don't know order numbers, just people's names and their children's names. I really hate it if I spell a child's name wrong. I know how that irritates people. It bothers me, too. I don't want people to look at their Bragelets and have bad feelings. I moved into a house like that once. The sellers were so obnoxious during the sale of the home that by the time we closed on it, I hated that house! The feeling just never faded.

DEBBIE WILLIAMS, LET'S GET IT TOGETHER

I maintain most of my business relationships via e-mail, either individually or by participating in discussion lists. I use my e-mail program as a contact management file or fancy Rolodex. I make notes about birthdays, spouses, kids' names, where they live, and what their interests are, both business and personal. I then categorize or sort my contacts by topic such as colleagues, journalists, leads, clients, and so forth. Then, when someone asks me if I know a good business coach or online marketing expert, I refer to my virtual file and find someone to refer them to. Although I haven't met many of these colleagues, we have a strong network online and are able to find what we need or help each other find someone who knows where to find it.

Beyond networking, I use e-mail to notify colleagues of industry news, similiar to writing FYI on a sticky note and passing an article around the office. It's a great way to share newsletters, news stories, and contact information.

For local colleagues, we've found that it really helps to make routine appointments with each other or, even better, to have a standing appointment for coffee or lunch. Getting together once a month in a central location gives us the chance to share industry news, client leads, and to brainstorm.

TERESA KIRBY, A GARDEN PARTY

We do not have an advertising budget per se, but we keep product on hand so it is easier for us to send free merchandise to a company or individual to promote A Garden Party. Everyone likes to get something for free, and Darcy and I really believe in our product and know that it is an appropriate gift. Word of mouth is an important advertising vehicle for us.

JEANNINE CLONTZ, ACCURATE BUSINESS SERVICES

I maintain good relationships with people through personal contacts, whether it's a handwritten thank-you or dropping by their office with some of my homemade salsa. There's no group of people that deserves more of my attention than those that send me business through word-of-mouth marketing. For this reason, I need to keep my name at the forefront of my clients' minds. Not only for their next project, but also in case they know someone to refer me to. My business boasts "as needed," so I have many clients who only use me every once in a while. I've had clients tell me that my reminders and promo items (letter openers, pens, magnetic calendars) keep my name fresh in their minds.

I had a situation about six months ago when a client—I'll call her Marge—asked me to do things I wasn't interested in doing, but I did them anyway to accommodate her. Afterward, since she was on retainer, I gave her the "five-day" notice as outlined by the contract, completed all current tasks, and refunded her the unused portion of her retainer. I suggested other people who might do the tasks she was looking for. I figured I'd never hear anything from her again. About a month ago, I got a call from a new prospect who said she'd gotten my business card from Marge—too cool! The new prospect is now one of my best clients. You just never know. I always say, "Never burn a bridge," because you never know where it might lead you!

Overcoming Intimidation

Introducing yourself to a perfect stranger can be intimidating, especially if you are a small-business owner. Everyone tends to look larger and more experienced than you at first. Keep in mind the unique qualities you bring to your company and the needs your business can fill for others. Whether you are walking into a room or calling a larger company to purchase your product, draw on the self-confidence that allowed you to launch your own business. Often, your passion for your company will carry you through uncomfortable moments when you need inner strength.

I recently learned an important lesson about my approach to entering a room full of strangers. I was describing to a good friend, Paige, a problem I was having with my son Owen. I complained to Paige how each time I took Owen to a birthday party, he clung to my hip until he surveyed the room and found a child he was comfortable playing with. I couldn't understand why he didn't just enter the room and immediately begin speaking to the other children. Paige, who is very outgoing, quickly pointed out to me that I did the same thing at parties. She said she'd noticed for years how, when I entered a room, I surveyed the crowd carefully before approaching anyone. Seems that the same behavior I criticized Owen for exhibiting was one he'd learned from me. Today, I prepare myself mentally as I reach the door to a party or meeting and immediately walk to the center of the crowd to begin introducing myself.

Intimidation can also set in when you are calling on executives at large corporations. Belief in your product will carry you through these moments. When we were launching BlueSuitMom.com, I was calling on major brands such as the *Wall Street Journal, American Baby,* and Liz Claiborne. Although I sometimes felt like I was looking up at a 500-pound gorilla, I focused on our unique product and the benefits a relationship with us could deliver to these biggies.

57

Do you ever feel intimated by big retailers or strangers?

BECCA WILLIAMS, WALLNUTZ, INC.

My heart beats a little faster while I'm dialing the phone to introduce myself to a new buyer, but I'm not intimidated approaching large retailers. Sure, I'm impressed that getting a contract with Michaels means being distributed in more than 600 stores, and I would love to have that contract. But Michaels isn't the only craft store in the world, and the craft industry isn't the only place to market my kits.

There are literally thousands of stores where my target customers shop, so just because one large retailer says no doesn't mean the next will, too. In fact, a buyer at Michaels told me no, and I just thought, "Fine. One of these days, another retailer will help me prove that you should've said yes, and then you'll be convinced to carry the kits."

MOLLY GOLD, GO MOM !NC.

I have moments when I feel intimidated, but mostly I jump right in and ask directly for what I need, and that helps me get through it. I lose my fear when I am seeking information or showing how I can be a part of what others are doing. I think people appreciate clear communication about intentions. At least, I know I appreciate it. If you don't ask, you'll never know. I always try to make some connection with strangers. If it's a member of the press, I might look for a commonality in our work styles. I never try to fake the areas that I'm not astute in like venture capital and accounting issues. When I encounter those topics, I simply state my ignorance and defer all those issues to my dad. I can honestly say that the financial and business issues of our business intimidate me. I am an idea, marketing, and image person. If it's financial stuff, I tend to squirm and avoid it.

There are times when I'm intimidated by other women who seem to know the right people and have got their act together. As we struggle to gain our legs, I think, Oh my, I'm so not that woman! I don't work full time at this. I don't research to validate my Go Mom! attitude. I run on my instincts. But therein lies the answer to your question. Instinct leads me when I feel intimidated. I also remember what my husband always tells me, "You are the only mom who can teach other moms about how to be a Go Mom." Somehow, in teaching these other moms, my product will provide its financial worth. I'm intimidated by the thought that if I choose Go Mom !nc. all the time, my family will continue to suffer, my parents will be financially strapped, and my marriage may be damaged emotionally. I have such high expectations for myself as a stay-at-home mom, but I recently realized that my mothering has suffered because of my business. So will my priorities of marriage, family, Go Mom !nc., in that order, sustain a slow-moving, costly launch for the company? That question is far more intimidating than anything else.

ALEX POWE ALLRED, AUTHOR AND GOLD MEDALIST

There was only one time that I was intimidated, and that was because I was very young and unprepared. I spoke to Queen Noor of Jordan and pretty much made a fool of myself. Older and wiser now, I make sure I've always done my homework before I talk to someone. I've talked to celebrities, star athletes, Olympians, politicians, and, most recently, a Pulitzer Prize winner. I don't get nervous or intimidated because I look at it like this: They have some valuable information, whatever the topic that I want. I'm asking them to talk about themselves. Right there, that takes the pressure off me.

This is where believing in yourself comes in handy. There's a woman named Cris Dolan. Featured in *Glamour* and *Working Woman*, she is a real hotshot. (She's also a former athlete I bunked with.) She is one of the most sought-after troubleshooters in the nation. She is incredibly confident, because she knows she knows her stuff. Recently, she went to be interviewed for a job, "Just to see what they had to say." Her interviewers quickly found out that Cris was there to interview them. She went in with the attitude, Why should I come to work for you? Not everyone can have that kind of confidence. She tells me she wasn't always that way, but she learned the art of selling herself and believing in what she stood for.

When you are thinking about becoming self-employed, you become your brand name. You have to market, package, and sell yourself. My advice is to get started right away and sell, sell, sell!

SHANNON RUBIO, THESMILEBOX.COM

I have never felt intimidated, although recently I experienced a situation that came close. I was at the Dallas Gift Market, which is a very large gift show with hundreds of large vendors and distributors. Walking the aisles of the show, I soon learned that many vendors lack respect for Internet-based companies. The behavior they demonstrated to companies with a dot-com after their names was so bad that I could easily have felt intimidated. Instead, I left the show only feeling annoyed by their behavior.

SANDI EPSTEIN, WORK/LIFE COACH

I don't think I feel intimidation in asking for someone's business because of the approach I take, which includes the following: 1) I seek out clients I can best help. In the case of my consulting, I target companies, under $100 million in revenues, that are too small to hire the big consulting firms; 2) I develop a network of colleagues that specialize in other areas of the business; 3) Most important is attitude, attitude, attitude! I approach my potential clients with the desire to help. If I can't help them or sell them the product they need, they will tell me so. My job is to help clarify for them what they need and show them what I can provide to fulfill that need. If it isn't a fit, I feel it wasn't meant to be. Getting clients in consulting and coaching seems to have a lot to do with personal chemistry. That means I usually get the business if I walk out of a "sales" meeting feeling connected to the potential client and their problem and knowing that somehow I added value to their understanding of their needs.

JORJ MORGAN, COOKBOOK AUTHOR

I feel that you really have to believe that what you are offering has tremendous value. My first attempt at writing a cookbook yielded some pretty stinging criticism. Publishers and agents commented on everything from the title—which was, shall we say, not terrific—to the way in which the recipes were grouped. I chose to learn from every criticism and made e-mail responses. After that, I researched my target market and tested and retested each recipe. I assembled a group of thirty e-mail buddies to test each recipe. I only knew a handful of these testers personally. Most of them signed on to test because they enjoyed the recipes I posted on my Web site. Each Monday, I sent an e-mail with the titles of twenty or so recipes. The testers sent me return e-mails, choosing the recipes they wanted to test that week. In one ten-week period, we tested 250 recipes! You do the math. I kept every comment and worksheet that the testers sent back. Not only did this feedback provide the basis for editing the book, but it also provided the direction of the Web site. I was able to determine what a recipe reader wanted to know that was not included in the text of the book. This is the information that is posted on the Web site. I then edited and retested and edited some more. When the testing was over, I knew that I had produced a good book. I had the confidence given to me by all of my testers and Web site readers. Armed with confidence and a belief in the value of your project, intimidation is easy to overcome.

Dressing for Success

SHERRY MAYSONAVE, EMPOWERMENT ENTERPRISES

A professional image is a huge component of successful networking. If you are inappropriately dressed or poorly groomed when attending a Chamber of Commerce meeting, you risk damaging your business and your professional reputation. You will certainly not be remembered in a positive light by the people you hoped to network with. Dressing to look like a professional, being impeccably groomed, and maintaining excellent posture are all essential to commanding respect and creating interest in you and your business.

My Top Ten Dress-for-Successful-Networking Tips for Women

1. **Attract, don't distract.** Look businesslike but not boring like a corporate filing cabinet. Wear a stylish suit or pantsuit. A well-coordinated outfit of dressy tailored separates is also an option. A tailored jacket, one that fits you well, is essential when wearing separates. Dress with simple, elegant flair.

2. **Power up, don't clown around.** Choose colors like black, navy, rich shades of red, dark green, and dark brown and solid-color fabrics for your basic pieces. Contrasting or coordinating colors can be added in blouses, tops, or scarves. Avoid large loud prints or sweet floral prints.

3. **Wear "armor."** Bare arms make us look like socialites, not businesswomen. Long sleeves are essential to a take-me-serious look. Yes, this is true even in warm climates.

4. **Get a leg up.** Hosiery is non-negotiable. Naked feet and bare legs that are okay on some social occasions do not command respect in the business environment. Avoid wearing white hosiery with dark shoes and a dark skirt or pants. Blend your hosiery to your shoe color and hem color for a put-together look.

5. **Put your best foot forward.** Shoes tell your secrets. For business wear, shoes must have closed toes and heels — no scandals, please. Classic and stylish two- to three-inch pumps walk you toward success faster. Your shoes must look new — nicked heels or scuffed toes scream loser. Ideally, your shoes should be as dark in color tone or darker than your hem. Unless it's a networking picnic, do not wear flat shoes, even if you are six feet tall.

6. **Look important and successful.** A successful image attracts people. The quality of your accessories is the key. At the minimum, accessorize your outfit with important-looking metal earrings that flatter your face shape and coordinate well with your outfit. Add other jewelry if appropriate. Your jewelry must look expensive, even if it isn't. Avoid noisy bangle or charm bracelets. Cutesy or whimsical jewelry or accessories convey little-girlish, overly playful, even rebellious attitudes.

7. **Have perfect timing.** A businesslike metal watch adds enduring strength and power to any business image.

8. **Exude confidence.** Standing tall and wearing tastefully applied makeup conveys high self-esteem, confidence, and that you pay attention to details. Women who consistently wear simple makeup earn 20 to 30 percent higher incomes. It's worth the effort. Be sure to finish your face with a smile.

9. **Get "a head."** A stylish haircut that suits your face shape and hair type is a must! If your hair is longer than shoulder

length, do not wear it down. Wear it up or tied back. Avoid wearing cutesy hair accessories and absolutely *no* banana clips—they do not win in the game of business networking.

10. **Forgo the "bag lady" look.** Don't carry so many items that you look like you're shopping or have the baby with you. Tote only one organizer (the zipper type that looks tidy when closed) or a soft-style briefcase, polished and in mint condition. Do not carry a purse in addition to one of the above. If you need money for the event, carry it in your organizer or briefcase. Carry your business cards in your pocket.

Asking for Help

Asking for help is difficult for many people. I remember my early professional years when I was in a management development program. Every six months, I had one evaluation in which I had to describe my greatest weakness as it related to managing people. Every six months, I answered, "Delegating work." It wasn't that I was afraid no one could do the job as well as I could; I was afraid to ask for help. I'm not sure why I developed this trait: Perhaps it had something to do with being the oldest of nine children. The fact of the matter is, I never learned how to ask for help. Ironically, none of my so-called mentors during this particular program ever addressed my weakness with me. I just kept on working long hours and taking on more projects. It wasn't until I was president of a large volunteer nonprofit group that I realized it was impossible not to ask for help and also that people actually like to help. Another important lesson was that I certainly was not helping myself by not asking. As you start your home-based business, there will be many times you may need help, whether it's answering an accounting question or finding a manufacturer for your product. Regardless of how big or small your need is, don't be afraid to ask, especially if you are asking another entrepreneur. Take advantage of the experiences of veteran business owners. Most are glad to help.

58

How do you ask for help?

BECCA WILLIAMS, WALLNUTZ, INC.

There are so many sources that I use to get help, it's hard to list all of them. Little Did I Know.com, a group of mom business owners, has been a great source for Internet marketing ideas, input on the product, and emotional support. My father-in-law has a lot of business contacts in the area, and he's introduced me to people who advise me on marketing the product to retailers. The Senior Corps of Retired Executives (SCORE) has also been helpful in providing advisors. When I need help with staffing a trade-show booth or packing the product, I ask my husband or friends to donate their time. My vendors and potential vendors are all helpful. They have a vested interest in seeing WallNutz succeed and often research ways to improve their part of the kits or refer me to their contacts.

BETH BESNER, TABLE TOPPER

When I began designing our Table Toppers, I had to start from scratch in finding a manufacturer. I started by picking up the phone, describing my product, and asking people if they were capable of producing it. Of course, it wasn't just one call. It was a process of elimination. Asking for help is like a game of telephone where you call one person who might tell you to call another who might have a friend who knows someone, and so on. Operating your business will always require you to ask others for information or know-how. I'm fortunate that I tend to be aggressive, and I'm not afraid of asking for what I need.

KIMBERLY STANSELL, AUTHOR

The help many small-business owners need is only one request away. Think about it. You're just shy of reaching a goal. The missing link may be a piece of information or a professional courtesy. You're surrounded by untapped sources of support from your clients, suppliers, colleagues, and friends. They've probably already said, "If there's anything I can do to help you, let me know." Don't let the opportunity slip by. Here are a few ways others can help you along the way:

Make an introduction or arrange a meeting. You can build new relationships faster when an associate introduces you to others. Your contact can share with you key information about a prospect. They can also tell the prospect a few things about you, your business, and the value of your products or services.

Serve as a sponsor. Some of your sources may be willing to fund or sponsor a program or event you are hosting. Ask them to lend you a meeting room or equipment, use their company name, or donate money or other resources.

Distribute information. Ask your contacts to distribute your marketing materials. For example, a dry cleaner could attach a coupon from the hair salon next door to each customer's plastic cleaning bag. Or, your flyer could be inserted inside an associate's newsletter.

Publish information for you. Ask your sources who may have the influence to get information about you and your business printed in various publications. If you know someone who has media contacts, ask them to recommend you as a quotable source or for a feature story.

Make the connection between what you need and the people who can supply it.

Make and use a wish list. You'll begin to see how simple requests that others fill for you can make a real difference in your business.

CHAPTER NINE

Time Management

Smart business people recognize how equally important both time and money are to the success of their businesses. Ironi cally, the same people who give so much consideration to how they spend money give little consideration to how they spend their time. For entrepreneurs, time and money are both available in limited quantities. No matter how great your business plan, if you don't have the funds or the time to execute it, it's unlikely your concept will succeed. Bearing this in mind as a business owner, you should make the same effort you put into developing your budget to creating a strategy for using your time wisely.

I remember as a young child my father giving us the same speech every September as we were about to start the new school year. He always sat at the head of the dinner table and said, "This year we are going to set priorities." Even though the priorities only lasted for the first few weeks of the school year, my siblings and I understood that to be successful, you must set priorities. As adults, we may think we know what our priorities are, but do our actions carry out our thoughts? Look at your day, today, right now. Can you account for your time? Will you feel productive at the end of the day? If you answered no to either question, it's time to stop and change your time management plan.

The first step in creating a time management plan is to write down a short list of business and personal priorities. Items might include generating new sales, finding funding, exercising, and spending more time with your family. Literally write them down so you can see them. Then say them out loud so you can hear them. This little exercise forces you to use more than one of your five senses, which means the chance of you retaining the information is greater.

Next, look at how you presently spend your time. Are there things you are doing that you don't need to do? Sometimes, we get into such a rut that we don't even think about how we spend our time. Look especially at the small things. Let's say you can eliminate ten two-minute chores. That means you've gained twenty minutes in your day. That's enough time to read the newspaper or walk one mile. I evaluate my time at least once a month. Last month, I realized that every night I pick up my children's crayon bucket before going to bed. It wasn't that my three older children, Madison, Owen, and Keenan, neglected to put them away after using them; it was Morgan, their two-year-old sister, who would sneak the crayons out of the cabinet later. Every night, I was performing the same ritual of picking up multiple Indian red and sunburnt orange crayons. After evaluating my daily chores, I realized that putting the crayons into a plastic-lock container would save the five minutes it took me each day to collect all the crayons into the bucket. Once I asked myself if picking up crayons was what I wanted to do with my time at the end of the day, I immediately found a way not to.

How much of your time is directed to one of the priorities you've listed? Since you have limited time, anything that doesn't contribute directly to helping you meet your goals is disposable. I'm not being unrealistic. If you are a mother, I know firsthand there are going to be chores you must do during the day that have nothing to do with finding customers or spending quality time with your family. You must make doctor appointments, pay bills, and pack lunches. You can put these tasks in your discretionary time account.

Next, it's time to turn to a calendar. If you don't already have some kind of schedule keeper, it's time to invest in one. It doesn't have to be a fancy daytimer or Palm Pilot. Your mission is to have one place where all your appointments, priorities, and schedule are consolidated. As a working mother, I elect to keep all my business appointments on the same calendar as my family schedule, since most of my business and home activities are interconnected. I would be remiss if I didn't mention that Molly Gold, a contributor to this book, created an excellent time management system for moms. You can find it on her Web site, www.gomominc.com.

The final step in creating your time management strategy is to fill in the time slots of your daily calendar. Look again at your list of priorities. Block off a time when you go calling on new clients and put your hour of exercise down as well. If you allocate a specific time to each task, you are more likely to complete all of them. Start your day with the most important tasks—the beginning of the day is the most productive time to jump into the things that mean the most to your business. The later into the day you push them, the less likely you will be to complete them.

Schedule some free time into your day as well. It seems that every phone call and e-mail contains a new task you must complete. Rarely does someone contact you and not want something, even if it's just a yes or no answer. The only way to stay caught up with your unscheduled tasks is to have unallocated time in your calendar. Stick to your schedule and reward yourself for doing so.

The second most important element to budgeting your time is focus. Finding focus is often more challenging to home-based business owners because of all the distractions that exist in your house. Maybe the laundry is calling or the soft couch is reaching out to you while you walk to the kitchen for your fifth snack of the morning. I've heard that the *Oprah* show calls out to many entrepreneurs even when the television is off. Recognizing the hurdles you have to overcome is the first step to focusing on priorities. Determine what time of day is your best time to focus and schedule your priorities for that part of the day. The more focused you are, the more productive you will be. I know that I cannot focus when my two-year-old is pulling out drawers or coloring the walls in the next room, so I don't attempt to do things that require concentration. I save those tasks for after the children's bedtime. This approach saves me from feeling discouraged

---

TIPS FOR EFFECTIVE TIME MANAGEMENT

- Realize that the traditional rules of time management don't work for everyone. Find a system that works for you and your family.

- Technology has increased our sense of urgency. Apply human judgment to determine what's really important.

- If you don't want to do it or don't need to be doing it, then stop doing it. Filling time with useless and unproductive tasks is taking the path of least resistance.

- Use a to-do list. To get a jump start, prepare your list the night before.

---

or frustrated when I can't accomplish my goals, yet permits me to cross a few items off my to-do list. There's no sense setting yourself up for failure, so always find a task that fits the situation at hand.

I once read an essay on time management that I thought was extremely insightful. It started out by saying there is no such thing as "I can't find the time," because we can't lose time. The writer explained that because time is something we live, it can't possibly be lost. According to his thought pattern, time management is merely the choice we make on how to use time. He spoke to the point that there is no way we could ever have enough time to do everything we want or should do with our time. That's part of being human. Recognizing this, it's up to us to choose those things that are important to us and then assign time to them. It's up to us to take time from one activity to give it to another. Once we realize that there just simply is not enough time to do everything, it's time for us to delegate the tasks we decide not to devote our time to doing. Delegation is a part of

- Link more than one task together, such as stopping for stamps on the way to the grocery store.

- Never touch a piece of paper more than once. If it requires an action, do it while it's in your hand.

- Find ways to speed up time-wasting tasks, even if you need to rearrange your home or office.

- Realize that there are only two solutions to completing a task. You must either hire someone else to do it or roll up your sleeves and do it yourself.

- Focus only on tasks that increase your profits.

- Schedule unallocated time once a week to catch up.

time management. A good business manager will create a network of freelancers or contractors who can support their business goals by performing particular tasks.

59

How many hours a week do you work at your home-based business?

DARCY VOLDEN MILLER, LITTLEDIDIKNOW.COM

I work somewhere between forty and sixty hours a week. Sleep is the governing factor for the amount of time that I can put into my business. For the time being, I have to work when my son goes to bed or is napping. His bedtime is around 9:00, and I go to work immediately. I usually end up working until 2:00 or 3:00, or even sometimes

4:00, in the morning. I go briefly to bed and get up when he awakes around 7:00. I can keep these crazy hours for only so long before it all catches up with me. Then I end up having to take a night or two off to catch up on my rest. Then, it's back to the same cycle again, except now I have to play catch-up for the nights I've taken off. I know that it won't always be like this. If I could, I would work 24/7 on my business. I think that when you know you've truly found what it is you love to do, the hours you work don't seem like hours at all. I look at forty to sixty hours a week and think, "Is that all?"

GWEN MORAN, MARKETING EXPERT AND WRITER

I always laugh when people tell me that they're going to start their own businesses so that they can work their chosen hours or reduce their work schedule. I've met hundreds of entrepreneurs, and I've never met one who has told me that he or she works fewer hours than when they worked for someone else. You must be prepared to work many hours when you're starting a business. Someone once told me that a business goes through the same phases that a baby does—and when it's an infant, it needs constant care.

However, once your business becomes more self-perpetuating, you have to learn to pull back and take advantage of the increased self-sufficiency of the business. I almost fell into the trap of staying in the office for hours poring over new projects, growth plans, and reviewing employees' work for clients. My "Aha!" moment came when an old college friend came to town. I met him and his wife for breakfast, and he asked me, "But what do you do for fun?" I realized that I had been going on and on about my business. He remembered me as an outgoing, fun-loving individual—not the single-minded person that I had become. That helped me realize that I needed to "get a life."

Now, I make it a point to take at least one day off per week—usually Sunday. I plot my time carefully. My husband and I schedule time together, and I try not to schedule meetings on Mondays. That's my office day when I get paperwork done. It also takes the pressure off me so I don't have to work on the weekends. I know I'll have a day to review projects, return phone calls, and generally organize my week.

I recently interviewed the author Gil Gordon, whose book is called *Turn It Off.* His time management model is to look at the week as a pool of 168 hours. You decide which hours you want to be on 100 percent, which you want to be on 60 percent, and which you want to be on zero percent. His Web site, www.gilgordon.com, contains great information about time management.

KAREN WILKINSON OLTION, EBUBBLES.COM

I work on the average about eighty-five to ninety-five hours a week on eBubbles. Because we have yet to accept a large investment of any type, I wear a lot of hats and am involved in just about every aspect of the company at this point. On a daily basis I do customer service calls, personal shopping with customers, order packing, product photography, copywriting, database management, and of course, the dreaded bookkeeping.

JORJ MORGAN, COOKBOOK AUTHOR

I work until a task is complete. I prioritize everything and work way in advance of deadlines. I always have a "Things-to-do" folder, and I plunge into that pile when I have extra time.

LINDA MCWILLIAMS, ONCEUPONANAME.COM

I work at least forty hours over a seven-day period. My day starts at about 5:30 A.M. With everyone else still sleeping, it is one of the most productive times of my day. My days end sometime between midnight and 2:00 A.M. Again, everyone else is asleep, and I get a lot done. My children and husband govern this big time! If I could send everyone away for four hours a day, I would be able to do everything I need to in a few days! Of course, that would defeat the entire purpose of staying home with the kids and working at home. It has been hard balancing work and family. There are many days I hear them saying, "Are you at the computer again?" It can get very discouraging when you know the family is not always behind you 100 percent, even though they know the alternative is I leave the house for work like before. Sometimes I have to remind them of this, and sometimes I have to tell myself to walk away from the work until the late evening so I can give my family my time.

JEANNINE CLONTZ, ACCURATE BUSINESS SERVICES

I choose to work a lot because I love what I'm doing. I may work fifty-five to sixty hours most weeks, but it's at my pace, and when I want to work. If I want to spend a day shopping or going to a movie or visiting a friend, I can. To make up the time, I work on Saturday and Sunday, or in the evenings. Working from my home gives me incredible flexibility. The other side of the fifty-five- to sixty-hour coin is attendance at meetings. That is an integral part of my business. It is where I do my cold calling, and I think it's important to be visible at meetings and get involved. That's how prospective clients get to know my commitment and me. It works wonders for me. I also enjoy it immensely. Most of the charitable groups I'm associated with do fund-raisers to help kids in our community. That's important to me. And I like being associated with other business people who share my goal for a better place for all of us to live. It all makes for a good client base, too.

KIT BENNETT, AMAZINGMOMS.COM

My schedule is governed by my to-do list and the needs of my children and is very strange. Some weeks I work sixty hours and am up until dawn sitting at my computer. I take time off from work to go on class field trips, school breaks, and after-school activities. In a perfect world, I would work from 7:00 A.M. until 3:00 P.M. However, life would be boring if it were perfect—that's why I'm self-employed! I don't fit into a nine-to-five lifestyle.

I anticipated long hard hours when I started my business. I hoped that my Web site would become more automated so eventually I could work fewer hours. That is not how it has worked out. Amazingmoms.com is like a child. Right now, it's a toddler and still needs hand-holding through every step. I'm very surprised that I have become such a workaholic. Never in my wildest dreams did I think I had that in me.

When I lived in San Francisco, I used to cross the Golden Gate bridge daily and watch the painters working on the bridge at death-defying heights. Each day, I watched them making progress, painting up and down the towers. I realized that it would be months before they completed their task. So long in fact, that by the time they finished, they'd have to start painting at the other end again and never get the satisfaction of completion. I swore I would never be a bridge painter! Well, here I am ten years later, a bridge painter. My job never ends. I have to set limits or I will lose sight of my family.

KAITLAND THORSTENSON, CERTIFIED PUBLIC ACCOUNTANT

I love the tax season, because it means more work for me. The rest of the year, my accounting tasks amount to twenty hours or less per week. I have clients scheduled so I only deal with them one at a time. But the arrival of the tax season means long hours, less sleep, and other less than healthy behaviors. I try to work only from 6:00 to 9:00 at night during the week and from 8:00 A.M. to 8:00 P.M. on Saturday. Sunday is always my day of rest. That means the phone goes on hold, and the message on the answering machine is "This is God's Day. I am taking the time to thank him for my blessings and honor him by devoting this day to him." I try to accompany my tax season hours with good music while I work in seclusion. I drink lots of water and try to stay as organized as possible. When I get stressed out, I lean on my friends and family.

60

Has owning a home-based business freed up time for other things in your life?

LESLEY SPENCER, HBWM.COM

Working at home has allowed me to make better use of my time. The time I used to spend commuting, I now work. I also start dinner, wash clothes, and take care of other household duties between working. I also save time by doing my shopping during the week while the stores are not so busy, and if needed I can make up work time in the evenings or weekends. With my office in my home, I can work anytime I have extra time or need to send a quick fax or e-mail.

JORJ MORGAN, COOKBOOK AUTHOR

My home-based business allows me to be accessible to my family—my hubby, three boys, father and mother and brother, sister, nieces, and nephews. From packing lunches to the dreaded science projects, I'm able to lend support and make sure things go as planned.More important, I'm there when we need to talk, which always seems to occur on their schedule, not mine! There is one important parenting fact I have learned: When your kids are ready to talk, you'd better be ready to listen. Working on my own schedule also allows me the freedom to pursue projects like chairing a community fund-raising drive or cooking festival food for 40,000 attendees. I actually enjoy those extra undertakings.

61

What are your secrets for setting priorities and managing a business?

RACHAEL BENDER, BLUESUITMOM.COM

When we first started building BlueSuitMom.com, the tasks that needed to be done by date of launch seemed overwhelming. So, I wrote down all the projects and the major steps we needed to take to accomplish each task. I then divided the tasks into three categories: "Must be done by launch," "Would like to be done by launch," and "Do after launch." After prioritizing the projects this way, I set deadlines for each step. This also allowed me to focus only on this week's goals. During any downtime or when one section got completed ahead of schedule, I focused my attention on the "would like" list. I also grew to realize that, although perfection is the goal, sometimes I had to compromise and do something less well than I would have liked. To this day, I organize our projects into "must" and "want" categories.

NANCY CLEARY, WYATT-MCKENZIE PUBLISHING

My secret to prioritizing is journaling, journaling, and more journaling. My journals of the past two years are the blueprints for my product design and marketing this year. If I hadn't finally paid attention to my journal entries for the past ten years, I never would have conceived my "Box-is" product line. I would still be fixated on my white legal pad with its endless list of client jobs. Nowhere in my client notes of my design company were there any hints of my true dreams and goals. The priorities and goals that mattered were written in my personal journals.

WENDY HARRIS, NATIONAL ASSOCIATION OF MEDICAL BILLERS

My secret to setting priorities is to take a deep breath and say to myself that I was really born an octopus. I tackle my most urgent task first and then the minor ones. When I feel overwhelmed and frustrated by my workload, I take my dog for a fifteen-minute walk. I also find it useful to refer to my original business plan to make sure I am on track with my goals.

DEE ENNEN, ENNEN COMPUTER SERVICES

I set small, realistic goals in order to accomplish my larger goals. I need to feel that sense of accomplishment you get when you complete a task. Each day I set mini-goals, and I write them down in my Daytimer so they become part of my day. I also have learned to prioritize myself throughout my day and stay focused on the task at hand. It's important to use that focus both in your role as a business owner and also as a family member. If I'm working, I concentrate on my work. When I am with my children, I am with them all the way.

JORJ MORGAN, COOKBOOK AUTHOR

I write everything down and then rewrite the list until my jobs are done. I learned a lot from Stephen Covey's book, *The Seven Habits of Highly Effective People*. I also learned a lot while studying special education in college and later when managing schoolwork with my child who has dealt with certain learning disabilities. I've learned to break every task down into smaller parts. If I have a 1,000-word article due, I start with an outline and write one or two paragraphs at a time. When my publisher required a hundred more recipes in order to complete the book, I divided the recipes into sections and completed one section at a time. My best secret for setting priorities and achieving goals is to realize there is a positive solution to every problem, as long as you allow enough time to find it!

Lesley Spencer, HBWM.com

My secret for setting priorities and achieving goals is my belief that God and family come before business. If my priorities are in line, setting and achieving my goals is much easier, because I am focused on what is important.

I feel it is important to set personal goals and priorities when starting a home business and to continually review those goals on a regular basis. You need to know what's important to you such as your faith and religion, your husband, your kids, your business, your fitness and health, recreation, etc. Without setting all your priorities, your business can easily become your priority, and you may risk neglecting your marriage, your children, your faith, or your health. There are so many duties and tasks in running your own home business that it's important to find balance. You don't want your business to affect other areas of your life negatively.

Rebecca Hart, Public Relations

It's really funny to me that people ask me for my secrets of balancing and prioritizing work and family, because so many days I feel like a duck that looks serene on top of the water while it's paddling like crazy beneath the surface.

Sometimes, I'm forced to set priorities. I was your typical workaholic, toiling until 10:00 or 11:00 at night with no life outside the office. I'd like to say I had some epiphany, but it was my doctor, when I was pregnant the first time, who said I had to start realizing that work has its place but it isn't the end-all I thought it was. Sure, I had thought about how I might balance my life, but it was the doctor's constant threat of bed rest that finally slowed me down.

I had to make my actions reflect the words that were coming out of my mouth. It's easy to say, "My family comes first," but harder to make it true when you also love your work. I finally decided I wanted my kids to have my prime time, and that's when I took action.

I don't think mothering and a professional career are mutually exclusive. Many of the skills and values are the same—coaching, mentoring, sharing information, integrity, honesty, and, let's face it, managing chaos. In both environments, you reap what you sow in terms of positive relationships, camaraderie, and interesting experiences. Both roles are demanding and difficult and stretch you in ways you never imagined possible.

I found it very interesting one day when a client of mine was shocked that I had kids. He said he just assumed that someone who does what I do successfully has no other life. Not that I try to hide my kids, but I was proud of the fact that I wasn't discounted professionally because I am a mom.

Incidentally, next to mothering as the most visible role for finding balance is fathering. I think men are facing a whole paradigm shift about what it means to be a dad today. Let's also not forget that we are the sandwich generation, caring for older relatives as well as our children. My father had a debilitating stroke two years ago, and while I can't spend as much time as I'd like with him, I certainly need to be more involved now, and can be, with my home-based business.

I think my secret to prioritizing is that I do a lot of planning and searching. This didn't happen overnight. I remember five or six years ago, before I had kids, thinking, "What could I do that would allow me to work on my own someday?" That was my fantasy, until I got pregnant the first time and had to make some hard choices.

DEBBIE WILLIAMS, LET'S GET IT TOGETHER

One of the best ways to reach your goals—whether they are daily, weekly, or yearly—is to group your tasks into categories. I do it this way:

A: Must Do
B: Should Do
C: Could Do

"A" priorities are those that I must do today, such as pick up the cake for my son's birthday party or attend a business meeting at the office.

"B" priorities consist of tasks I should do, but if I don't get to them, the world won't come to an end. Ordering that birthday cake in advance, dropping off clothes at the dry cleaner, and balancing my checkbook are examples of "B" priorities.

"C" priorities are those things that need doing, and I should do them, but it's not crucial to my life if they wait a day or two. Filing paperwork, recaulking the bathtub, and reprogramming the speed dial of the telephone are all "C" items. But be careful to do the items in this category, before they become "A's" or never get done! Consider writing them down on small slips of paper and putting them into a Job Jar. Whenever you get a block of time to spare, pull out a task and do it.

If you want more help on time management, I offer two tele-classes, "The Five Characteristics of an Effective Home Manager," and "Working from Home with Kids" at my online training facility, OrganizedU.com.

Darcy Volden Miller, LittleDidIKnow.com

Setting priorities? I'm still trying to figure that one out! I think the key is to have a space for your dreams. One of the best things I found is a product from Box-is.com. They have the most beautiful keepsake boxes that are "a space for your dreams and the inspiration to make them come true." You define what the box is and then fill it with things that are symbolic of your goals and dreams such as favorite quotes, pictures, and trinkets. You can include anything that is personally meaningful to you. This box was a determining factor in helping me reach my goals. I liked the idea of boxing dreams so much that I created a special box just for mothers who desire to start their own business!

Another idea for focusing on your goals is to hold a Dream Board party. You can do this alone, but it's more fun with friends. You go through magazines and find pictures, words, or symbols of your dreams and paste them on a big poster board. This creates a dimension for your visions and helps you discover and maintain your path toward achievement. Another thing that helps me is having someone to account to. Find someone who is like-minded and supportive of your vision and report to them about how well you are achieving your goals. Sometimes, if you know you have someone to report to, it's easier to reach your goals, because it's hard to let someone else down who's rooting for you.

JULIE MARCHESE, TWINSADVICE.COM

I believe that one of my personal strengths is the ability to set priorities. Actually, I got a lot better at it after I had more than two children. I can easily itemize in my head what needs to be done and in what order, based on importance and/or necessity. Plus, I am always doing at least two things at the same time—folding laundry while talking on the phone, reading e-mail while listening to the kids playing outside.

I've been a list maker since I was a child. The items that I put on my to-do list are tasks that must not be forgotten. For example, Joey—snack helper on Monday, follow up with *Tribune* on Tuesday, call Gram on Wednesday. I don't list things like check e-mail several times each day or do laundry daily. I'm able to automatically include these items without writing them down.

I assign my tasks to the appropriate time of the day. For example, I make all of my phone calls during my children's nap times when the house is quiet. I answer e-mail when my children are either napping, content playing, or at night after they go to bed. I do household tasks such as cooking dinner, making lunches, and cleaning when the children are playing around.

MOLLY GOLD, GO MOM !NC.

My business is based on helping mothers prioritize and manage their business schedules, so I apply my product to my business. The advice I give to other women managing a family and a business is broad but useful. First, you need workspace, and you have to accept the fact that your kids will be in it while you're trying to work. Working from home requires you to renegotiate roles so your work time can be as free from distraction as is realistically possible. At the same time that you must work within your family priorities, you also have to find a release time so you can clear the clutter from your brain and process all that is around you. Work is all-consuming, unfortunately, and you may find yourself sneaking back. Don't! You're better off sneaking over to the laundry basket while the kids are underfoot than writing e-mails, trust me!

62

How do you get your family and friends to respect your time even though your office is in your home?

KIT BENNETT, AMAZINGMOMS.COM

It's tough to get respect when your office is in the family laundry room! Respecting my work time is a constant issue for my family. I've tried absolutely everything. Taking the advice of a friend, I once wore a hat to symbolize I was at work. It did the trick for a while, until the children became used to my hat. Then I tried notes on the office door. That also worked for a bit, but eventually the notes became part of the décor and were ignored. I have learned that my children just want my attention. I give them some of my time and then go off to work. We play with this schedule all day. The most important step was to create my office space. It is only four feet by four feet and is indeed located in the laundry room, but it has walls, shelves, and a desk. It is the "office," and everyone knows it's where I go to work. I do not resolve sibling conflicts there or make snacks or play. When I leave that room, I am available. In hindsight, I should have done this first. When my office was in my bedroom, it was difficult both for my kids and me as well. Even worse, work was always looking at me even while I was sleeping! I recommend you create any sort of divider to separate work from home. Use separate phone lines, computers, and space whenever possible.

Realizing that my home office "schedule" is constantly changing, I have had to be very creative. The first thing a work-at-home mother needs to do is identify the reason she is at home. Is it cost, convenience, or time with her family? For me it was the desire to be available for my children and take care of their needs at home and school. Which meant I needed to be flexible. If I go on a school field trip during the day, I work at night. If the children are sick, I stay with them until rest time. I had forgotten my reason for working at home until my son recently reminded me with the wisdom of a child, "Mom, you spend all your time helping other moms be good moms but you don't spend time with us!" *Ouch!* He was right. That's when I reevaluated my priorities.

SHANNON RUBIO, THESMILEBOX.COM

My husband is a big support. He does whatever needs doing, and I could not run my business without his help. He appreciates that I'm doing what I feel is necessary, although he thinks I work too much. He is probably right, but as long as I am not still in my office at midnight, he is fine with it. I have had to work hard to teach the kids about my working from home, but they understand now. I know they want me to not work as much. My oldest recently asked, "When are you going to be through with these boxes?" I explained that if it were not for the boxes, I would have to get a job, the children would have to go to day care and traditional school, and at the end of the day we'd all come home. After I explained the alternative to him, he said, "Okay, forget it. I like the boxes." I struggle with the balance between working too much and my responsibility of being home with my children.

JORJ MORGAN, COOKBOOK AUTHOR

Often, we work together to get things done. While writing *At Home in the Kitchen*, my husband and three boys were the most critical recipe testers that exist in any test kitchen. If these guys didn't like it, I was sure no one else would. They learned to have a lot of patience. While I was testing recipes for the "Veggies on the Side" chapter, the boys ventured into the kitchen. One asked, "What's for dinner?" They rolled their eyes at the thought of two or more veggies for one evening meal again. They weathered the broccoli with aplomb, knowing that we were heading for chapter 12, "The Dessert Café."

63

How much time do you spend on administrative work for your business?

DIANE DESA, A VIRTUAL ASSISTANT

I spend approximately three to five hours per week doing my administrative work. Since I am a virtual assistant and this is my business, it doesn't take me nearly as long as someone who might not do administrative stuff for a living.

A virtual assistant is a good solution for a small-business owner just starting out. Most virtual assistants have at least ten to twenty years experience in an administrative capacity and are very familiar with the administrative tasks that are associated with setting up and running a business. They can save the small-business owner time and agony by taking care of these tasks, which gives the owner more time and energy to run and market her business.

For my business, I set aside Friday afternoons to handle the administrative work. I make sure to get all my billable time in between Monday and Thursday, and my clients know I may not be available on Friday afternoons. This works well for me, and I haven't had any complaints from my clients with this arrangement.

ROBIN ZELL, BRAGELETS

Although learning to make the bracelets took a lot of practice, I found the paperwork involved in running a business was the most difficult task to tackle and is still my greatest challenge. I hate paperwork, but there's no one else to push it off on when you own your own business. I work on it late at night to get it all done. I'd much prefer to make the bracelets, take orders, and market my product than pay attention to the detail stuff.

JEANNINE CLONTZ, ACCURATE BUSINESS SERVICES

Every week is different in my line of business. My administrative work depends on how many projects I'm working on or if it's time for my next marketing campaign, which I do every sixty days. I've gotten into the habit of invoicing client projects on completion instead of doing them all at once at the end of the week as I used to. It keeps me better organized, and I don't overlook any charges, because the project is fresh in my mind. I do spend two to three hours every Friday organizing myself for the next week, answering correspondence, filing, and paying bills. If I have a project to complete, I do that as well. On those lucky weeks when business is really good, I will do most of my administrative work on Saturday or Sunday.

KIMBERLY STANSELL, AUTHOR

I suggest that business owners use the Web to manage administrative tasks.

I use tools that make it easier for me to run the business and for employees, suppliers, and customers to interact with me. Dot-com firms make it easy for small-office professionals to manage those mundane but vital administrative chores. Here are a few sites to investigate.

- **Bill in the red.** The RedGorilla site offers fast, Web-based methods for tracking and sorting billable hours and expenses. It's free, and so are e-mail invoices to your clients. Premium services are also available. Gorilla Biller lets you send out invoices via fax or U.S. mail for $4.95 per month. Gorilla Go Pack gives you wireless access to the system via a Palm or cell phone for $9.95 per month. The Web address is www.redgorilla.com.

- **Keep your calendar online.** Keeping track of all your daily to-dos can be an ongoing struggle. AnyDay.com is a free, online day-planner service that stores your appointments, tasks, and contacts. You can also schedule meetings with other AnyDay users; send e-mail reminders of due dates and meetings and collaborate on all aspects of your calendar with selected recipients. This tool can be synchronized with your existing personal information manager (PIM).

- **Get a cyber-secretary.** Freeworks.com automates the things you don't want to do, like expense reports, purchase and vacation requests, time cards, phone and employee lists, and other paperwork. The service converts all the paper into electronic memos and Web-based forms that are routed to staffers via e-mail. And it's free.

- **Find a virtual assistant.** A virtual assistant works closely with successful individuals and small businesses without being physically present. They are independent contractors who handle clients' needs via e-mail, fax, and phone, working from their own offices. If you need relief from administrative trivia, then consider what a virtual assistant could do for you.

  Virtual assistants offer a broad range of administrative support, such as handling accounting services, human resource assistance, concierge services, collections, sales and marketing support, travel planning, research, and more. Virtual assistants are convenient and charge $35 to $75 an hour. You pay only for the time they actually spend working for you, and you don't incur any other employment costs. They typically expect you to commit to at least twelve hours of their services per month. Most virtual assistants will offer the first one or two hours free so the two of you can test the relationship.

  Virtual assistants have a vested interest in your business and can literally become a partner in your success. The more an assistant learns about your business, the more she can help you.

LINDA MCWILLIAMS, ONCEUPONANAME.COM

Almost 50 percent of my time involves paperwork or administrative tasks such as maintaining my customer database, printing invoices, ordering products, and controlling inventory. I spend the most time maintaining my Web site. I change, add, delete, and update daily. I really enjoy that part of my company. I have a Yahoo store now rather than just a Web site out on my own, and sales have tripled. I do my own ordering, designing, and maintenance of the store. It takes more work, but my profits have increased, so it's worthwhile. I've gotten so good at running my Yahoo store that I am thinking of starting a second business.

TERESA KIRBY, A GARDEN PARTY

I need to spend more time with administrative work than I actually do right now. Even though I work at least ten hours a day, there never seems to be enough time to do it all. Filing taxes for the company is the biggest hassle, because some are filed monthly, others quarterly, and others annually. When we can afford it, we will hire a bookkeeper to do this unpleasant job. I will gladly hand it all over! Paying taxes, consultants, and vendor bills is not glamorous, but certainly necessary. I also spend a lot of time ordering product and talking to vendors. More often than not, one of my children is screaming in the background or they are fighting with one another, so it is a constant challenge. When you run a home-based business, you have to expect these types of challenges on a daily basis.

LARA PULLEN, ENVIRONMENTAL HEALTH CONSULTING, INC.

I try to set aside Friday for administrative tasks that include paying bills, cleaning my desk, filing, balancing my books, invoicing, updating my Web site, doing taxes, following up with people that I had interviewed and many other things. I think that 20 to 25 percent of your time doing administrative tasks is about right.

When I was launching my company, I interviewed several accountants and hired a good one up front. I think that was the smartest thing I did. My accountant was with me from the beginning and made sure my books were in order and explained everything to me as I went, including taxes.

64

How do you handle the time-consuming task of collections?

MERYL GUERRERO, PARENTING 101

I have a harder time getting vendors to turn in my invoices than getting clients to pay their bills. While it's necessary for tax purposes, it's also fiscally sound to collect all your revenue and have all your expenses logged in the same calendar year. I find time each week to follow through on this financial paperwork.

Because you operate out of your home, clients become familiar with you and sometimes think that you aren't a normal business. For some reason, they forget that I'm really in business and have the same financial obligations a big company has. I find I also must deal with the internal politics and policies of those who owe me money. If you provide services to nonprofits and government agencies, sometimes you must navigate the bureaucracy to get paid.

WENDY HARRIS, NATIONAL ASSOCIATION OF MEDICAL BILLERS

Our members pay fees up front, except for our training services. The members receive a portion of the program each time they make a payment. If they don't pay the fee, they can't complete the program. When billing for training services, I print out invoices from my computer and distribute them monthly.

BECCA WILLIAMS, WALLNUTZ, INC.

For direct sales from our Web site or over the phone, we accept credit cards or we take personal checks. I take inventory weekly at the local toy stores that carry our products on consignment and send them a statement at the end of the month. When we do get a big account in the future, I expect that terms of 60 days net will be the norm.

DARCY LYONS, A GARDEN PARTY

In our business, products are sold to consumers through party hostesses. We ask the party guests to write checks directly to the hostess for the products they purchase. The hostess then writes a check for the total amount and sends it to the consultant. We get this check at the time the merchandise is ordered—this way, we do not have pending receivables for product. We established a policy early on that we don't fill an order until we have payment.

65

What is a normal day for you?

KIT BENNETT, AMAZINGMOMS.COM

I have two sets of days, because my husband works out of town three days a week. When he is away, I wake at 6:30 A.M., make a latte, wake the kids, make breakfast, and pack lunches. I'm not a good limit setter, and my children require constant coaching to get out the door. At 8:00 A.M. our neighbor's daughter arrives on our doorstep, and I drive everyone to school. When I return home, I clean up the kitchen, make beds, do one household chore, then take a shower. At 9:00, I spend time with God, praying, reading, or writing in my journal. My workday starts at about 9:15. First, I check e-mails and then prioritize them into a to-do list. I work on the computer until about 11:30 when I make another latte and make phone calls until 12:30. Then I work on the computer again until 3:30 when the kids come home and don't return to the office until evening. The children and I talk about their day, eat a snack together, and they do homework and chores. I spend the rest of the afternoon making dinner and nagging about the chores. Dinner is at 6:00. At 8:30, I read with my son, and then he goes off to bed. My twelve-year-old and I watch the *X-Files* together before she goes to bed. I return to the office until midnight when I stop. I watch the news and go to bed. None of this is straightforward or routine. Believe me, flexibility is involved, what with errands, sleepovers, school skate nights, and special projects.

KAREN WILKINSON OLTION, EBUBBLES.COM

My typical workday starts with checking e-mail and phone messages and making responses on a priority basis. Then I check the activity on my Web site and work other pending projects like responding to customers, helping out in the warehouse, and checking on stock levels. Next, I check our search engine listings where we primarily use the "pay-per-click" model.

I usually set aside a half hour a day to cruise the Internet to see what's happening in body and skin care and to look for ideas in magazines. I don't read the newspaper on a daily basis, but subscribe to the *Wall Street Journal,* the *New York Times,* and Internet World News e-mails.

Most days, I have work to do related to new products. I do all the photography myself in a modified closet that is my "digital studio." I shoot pictures, do color correction, masking (cutting the images from their background), and optimization to every picture before it goes out live on eBubbles. I also do the copywriting, using information from the manufacturers. Adding new products is quite time-consuming and complicated compared to bricks-and-mortar retailers—they simply remove items from their boxes and set them on the shelf!

I rarely take time for lunch—I usually eat at my desk. This is not a good habit, and I'm trying to work on it. If I take even fifteen minutes to stop and sit down, I feel refreshed. Almost every day at 5:00, I stop and take our dogs, Bella, a golden retriever, and Woody, a chocolate Lab, for a hike in the hills up behind our house. Within the hour, I'm usually back at my desk working for at least another few hours. We eat a lot of take-out for dinner!

We're quite lucky with our setup here in Laguna Beach. Our house, built in 1927, is on an acre of land and there is a little guest cottage, originally the outhouse, where I have my office. Our garage is as big as a barn and doubles as the warehouse. The best thing about having these separate structures is the psychological advantage of being able to separate work from our home. At the end of the day, I can close the door to the cottage and "go home."

NANCY CLEARY, WYATT-MCKENZIE PUBLISHING

After my three-year-old wakes up about 7:30 A.M., I run into my office to boot up the computer, and cook breakfast. I am in and out of the office for the next hour, checking e-mail, looking at my deadlines, changing a diaper, finding matching socks and pants and tops that fit, although not necessarily "match." My daughter and my husband get up around 8:30. I make sure their breakfast is ready, and clothes are somewhere Dad can find them and dress the two of them. Then I head to the office and shut the door.

The first two hours are always crazy. Most days I work on new input from a design job, making the changes, getting final approval, and preparing the FedEx package to send to the printer in California. The phone rings nonstop until noon, when I let my voice mail take over and I "create" some lunch. Dad and the kids head out to do errands, including stops at the bank and the FedEx drop-off box, a fifty-mile round trip. Then it's time for *Oprah* and my time. I grab my journal and usually that week's copy of *Publisher's Weekly* and *Advertising Age* and scan them for publishing opportunities. I listen, study, and observe Oprah's guests. For every author, guest, and celebrity I find myself doodling in my journal. At 2:00, I head back into the office for three to four hours of straight design time on motivational seminar company materials. I work through a design rep in California. Her clients imagine she has a great big design studio when in reality it's just little old me up here in Oregon. Dad and kids return in time for dinner, which I cook while checking e-mail and preparing the post office package. If it's Monday, I have to watch *Boston Public* and *Ally McBeal*, but then I go back to the office to work on my publishing projects. I never shut down before 10:00 P.M., and some mornings I work until 4:00 A.M.

SHANNON RUBIO, THESMILEBOX.COM

I'm not sure any day is "normal" by any standard, but we do have a routine that works for us. The kids usually are up and about by 7:30 A.M. That is a real benefit to homeschooling and all of us being at home. None of us is rushing to get out the door or dressed for school, so mornings are easy for us. This freedom allows the children to eat breakfast, play the computer, and sometimes watch television until about 8:30 or so. At that time, they get dressed and make their beds. My two oldest children are enrolled in video homeschool. By about 8:45 or so, they are starting school while I do things with my youngest child. So, for most of the morning, I have two kids on videos, with breaks in between, while my three-year-old plays with toys, games, or the computer. There are no real time limits, except I really like to get the school videos done by noon so that I can focus on my work in the afternoon.

From noon until 3:00, three days a week, our one employee, a seventy-year-old lady, comes over. She does a lot of the paperwork and organizing for us. Also, while she is here and can watch the kids, I run errands if I need to. Often during this time, my second grader is still doing his videos, usually until 3:00 or so. During the afternoon, my three-year-old sleeps. Most of the afternoon, I spend working. I am usually finished about 5:00, and we wait for the UPS man to come get the boxes.

Part of the reason this works so well is that my husband works on a tugboat and is home two days, then gone two days. Today, when he is home all day, I am free to run errands. If I have any meetings or lengthy phone calls, I schedule them for the days when he is home. Housework I fit in when I can, and my husband helps. Because I work from home, the business pays for a housekeeper to come twice a month and help clean up, which is a huge relief. Somehow, this whole schedule works.

JEANNINE CLONTZ, ACCURATE BUSINESS SERVICES, INC.

There really is no normal day, because our business entails so many different skills sets: word processing, desktop publishing, mailing services, and Internet research.

This past week, I completed work on a client newsletter that involved moving some ads around, contacting an advertiser for ad changes and information for a "spotlight" article, invoiced products, handled statements and collections calls, worked on conference plans, transcribed some tapes from meetings, and spent six hours at clients' offices working "on-site." Sometimes I'm working on three or four projects in a day. Sometimes I'm paying bills and updating my company expenses. There's no set time or day to do them, as every week is different.

Tomorrow, I'm taking the completed and approved newsletter to the printer. After I pick it up on Wednesday, I'll spend the next two days folding, sealing, labeling, and heading for the bulk mail center. After that, I won't be doing that project for another sixty days.

ROBIN ZELL, BRAGELETS

I was not blessed by being a morning person, so I normally have to drag myself out of bed in the morning. From 7:00 A.M. until 9:00 A.M., the morning is filled with dressing and feeding the children and preschool activities. I begin the day with returning phone calls and then spend time with my little ones. Mid-afternoon brings the return of my high schoolers and the start to my crisis management sessions for adolescent girls! I try to "power nap" on the couch for forty-five minutes sometime in the afternoon. I begin my nagging to get chores done, check and answer e-mail, and make dinner. We start homework, and I try to exercise two days a week. Everyone goes to bed by 10:00 P.M., when I start making bracelets. I eventually go to bed around midnight. Somewhere in there I do laundry and constantly pick up, purge, and sort through what is my home. Whew! Anyone want to be me? There are days when I'm not sure I do!

CHAPTER TEN

Marketing Your Home-Based Business

G o yell it from a mountaintop: You've built a company. Now it's time to market your business and acquire customers. This is one of my favorite parts of running a business. Perhaps that's because it's so easy to see the results of one's efforts. There is nothing like the feeling of seeing your company's name in the newspaper or suddenly hearing the phone ring more frequently because a flyer you distributed has reached its target.

No matter how much money a business owner spends, successful marketing is built on one important element: word of mouth. The goal of every marketing initiative you launch should always be to get people talking about your services or product. Word of mouth is the most powerful form of marketing. Whether it's a compelling offer in a direct mail piece, a professional looking brochure, or the best Web site, you should make every effort to get people talking about you, your company, and your product. I've been fortunate enough to work and learn from two marketing geniuses during my professional career. One was Tom Gruber, who is famous for the "Two all-beef patties, special sauce" McDonald's campaign and the other was John Costello of the "Softer Side of Sears" slogan. The one thing that both of these men recognize is the power of word-of-mouth marketing. Can you think of anyone who doesn't still remember what goes on a Big Mac because of Tom's jingle? I'll reflect later on some of the other lessons these two men taught me during our short time working together.

Just how do you get people to talk about you? First, of course, you must have a plan. Although your business plan should have included a marketing plan from the beginning, it is important to broaden the plan to include specific initiatives and strategies now that your company is up and running. A good marketing plan should include: research information, including the demographics of your target market; strategies; benchmarks to measure results; expenses; and execution details.

The first thing I do when writing a marketing plan is draw a picture of my customer. Yes, that's right. I borrow one of my children's crayons and literally draw my customer. In order to acquire customers, you have to know who they are. Although your research gives you some insight, you need to know your customers personally to learn how to acquire them. In the case of BlueSuitMom.com, my drawing showed a mother with a child on her hip and another holding her hand while on her shoulders were lunchboxes, backpacks, and a briefcase. This picture provided me with other details I needed to know about my customer. I knew my customer was an executive working mother weighed down by children and the heavy briefcase symbolizing the demands of her profession. Her day included making lunches, doing homework, parenting, and going to work. My marketing plan must get me in front of this busy mother.

The next step in developing my strategy was to walk myself through her day in order to determine when I could "touch" her. Stop and think for a minute how many marketing messages you receive during the course of one day. In your car, it's a radio commercial; reading the newspaper, it's an ad; eating your morning cereal, it's a sweepstake or promotion for a theme park; opening the mail, it's endless coupon packets. As a business owner, you don't want your marketing message to get lost among the hundreds of others your customer will see during the day. Therefore, on the back of my picture, I wrote out an hour-by-hour timetable of my customer's day. Here's what my BlueSuitMom's day looks like:

Morning

>   7:00: Pack lunches, drop children at day care or sitter, stop for coffee, get to work

>   8:00: Log onto Internet, check schedule for meetings, begin to-do list at the office

>   9:00: Make pediatrician appointments around work meetings

>   10:00: Consider promotion, look for new job, or manage office peers

>   11:00: Plan family vacation or business trip online

>   Noon: Go to the gym, think about daughter's upcoming birthday, grab a quick lunch

Afternoon

>   1:00: Sneak out to a school play

>   2:00: Conduct corporate conference call, check on children coming home from school

>   4:00: Manage children's after-school schedule and homework and begin to think about dinner

>   5:00: Commute home, stop for a few errands, still think about dinner

Evening

>   6:00: Feed the family, return calls, make next-day lunches

>   7:00: Manage family finances

>   8:00: Organize bedtime routines

>   9:00: Go online and order baby shower gifts, books, or chat about concerns online

>   10:00: Maintain relationship with husband or significant other

>   11:00: Bedtime

Drawing a picture and writing down her schedule reassured me that I knew who my customer was, what things were important to her, and where she was during the day. The challenge of writing my marketing plan was how to get her attention. The fortunate thing for BlueSuitMom.com is that women like to talk to each other, especially if they find something that helps them with their daily task of balancing work and family. Our strategy was to leverage the strong word-of mouth network among working mothers. To do this, our marketing initiatives included e-mails asking for referrals, online articles to share with coworkers, and rewards for sending a friend to our site.

Once you know who your customers are and your strategy for reaching them, select the vehicles to deliver your message. There's a marketing smorgasbord to choose from: direct mail, database marketing, public relations, online marketing, advertising, event sponsorship, sampling, to name just a few. Each one varies in cost and effectiveness depending on the magnitude of your budget and the value proposition of your product or service. "Value proposition" is a term that I will refer to frequently, so here is a quick definition: Value proposition characterizes how your customers or potential customers perceive the importance of your product or service to their needs. A working mother would value parenting information more than advice on traveling to the Orient. Why? Because parenting information is useful on a daily basis, while a trip to the Orient, though nice, probably isn't something she does every day. You as a business owner present a value proposition that is compelling and interesting, and the consumer determines if it is important enough to pursue. You want your customer to react to your offer, so it's essential to include a call to action in all your marketing initiatives. The call to action might be "Buy now," "Order now," or "Hire me." It is not enough to just present a compelling business proposition: You must also tell your customer what you want them to do. You will find that the higher the value proposition, the less you will have to spend to get the word out about your product. The reason is, if people see value in what you are offering, they will talk about it. As we all know, the more people talk, the better it is for your business. This is true for your public relations efforts as well. In that case, the media is your customer, and your offering to the press is a good story. The better the story, the more press you will receive.

When creating your marketing plan, take an honest look at your value proposition. Is your product a must-have or is it a luxury item? How can it help your customers in their daily lives and what is that help worth to them? Is it worth giving up something else in order to buy your product instead? If you aren't sure how your customers feel about your service or product, ask them. Conduct informal focus groups of strangers or friends. You might be surprised to learn that there is more than one way to look at your product.

Direct your marketing efforts and budget toward initiatives that will create results. If your service or product carries minimal value proposition, you will be forced to buy advertising to make up for press coverage you may not be able to obtain. If you have a good story to tell, concentrate your greatest efforts on networking and public relations. The best part about marketing is that you can easily see what works and what doesn't. One lesson I learned, from John Costello of Sears' fame, is Don't be afraid to test. Try different offers, slogans, and value propositions until you find the one that produces the results you are seeking. If you are printing brochures with an offer for one hour of free service, try printing half with a "get two hours free" offer instead and see which one gets customers calling. Your marketing plan will be a dynamic document that you will want to continuously maintain, based on the results of your efforts.

A major part of the BlueSuitMom.com marketing plan was to present ourselves to customers, vendors, partners, and the media in the most professional manner possible. Part of that strategy was the need to reflect the professionalism of the women in our market. The other part was, if we wanted to play on the same field as the big guys, we had to look like a big guy. You will see later how we applied that strategy to our public relations effort, but we also practiced it throughout our business. I'll give you some examples. To look big, we had to appear to have more than two people in the company. The first rule of our office was to throw out all singular pronouns when we spoke. Whether we were talking to a potential partner or a writer, we always used words like "we," "us," "our team," and "the staff." That gave the impression there were others who made up our team. Think about it. No one wants to be part of a wimpy enterprise! In this same vein, we never made hasty decisions on the phone. If a decision was required on ordering equipment, signing a partnership contract, or buying advertising, we always gave the response "We will discuss it at our weekly staff meeting and get back to you with the opinions of our team." Even though the team was only the two of us, our words gave the appearance that we were larger. One of the funniest stories is how, at first, we could not afford a fancy phone system for our office. I've always believed that you can tell the size of a company by its phone system. We were working with your basic $10 phone, no hold button, no conferencing abilities. We wanted to look like a big company and play music while the caller was on hold. I found a way. Each time I needed to have the caller wait for a minute, I set the phone in front of my compact disc player. Of course, we tested the plan a few times by calling each other before we tried it on our callers. We laugh about it now that we have a real phone system. My point here is that your business has to reflect the clients you intend to serve. If you want to be taken seriously by executives in large companies, you need to think like a big company.

66

How did you create your marketing plan?

BETH BESNER, TABLE TOPPER

If you think all the other stuff was hard, wait till you get to marketing. It's the hardest yet the most rewarding part of being an entrepreneur, particularly when your product begins to sell.

In developing my marketing plan, the first thing I did was to create a price list and sales materials. Then I set up an accounting program and hired sales representatives to take the product around to stores. Pricing was tricky, so we worked with a consultant to get advice on our margins. Our plan also called for public relations, so I sent out press releases and samples to the media.

AMILYA ANTONETTI, SOAPWORKS

Owning other businesses allowed me to discover my marketing strengths. Guerilla marketing is what I am best at. Also, I have always partnered with the media to help me get my business and message talked about. One of the best marketing events I've done was a Back-to-School Bash with a local radio station. We threw a kids' fair in the radio company's parking lot. Participants were the local Chamber of Commerce, the public library, the San Leandro Boys' and Girls' Clubs, and a parking lot full of potential customers. Word of mouth has always been key in all my businesses. The Yellow Pages, cable television advertising, and direct mail have never worked for me. I choose to spend my dollar where I am sure I can make a dollar. Eventually, as cash flow becomes less strained, I will gamble a little bit more with my marketing budget.

JORJ MORGAN, COOKBOOK AUTHOR

My marketing plan is very straightforward. Before publication of my book, I contacted Web sites that market to working women and/or food enthusiasts and offered them food-related articles in exchange for a link to purchase my cookbook. I retain ownership of what I write and can offer it to more than one Web site. I then created a Web site of my own (www.jorj.com) to interact and promote the book and all of the other Web sites that I write for. Phase two of the marketing plan incorporates the same strategy with printed materials, including newspapers and magazines. Phase three of the plan includes marketing to corporations. I offer special promotions such as my services teaching a cooking class or giving a cooking demonstration to their employees in exchange for purchasing books to give as corporate gifts. I use the same strategy for community fund-raising events and specialty bookstore signings.

GWEN MORAN, MARKETING EXPERT AND WRITER

My best story about creating a marketing plan has to do with a business owner I'll call Seth, a highly respected interior designer. After reading an article about successful home-based businesses, Seth decided to quit his nine-to-five job to launch his own corporate office design consultancy. He turned a spare bedroom into an office, ordered a batch of business cards, and called colleagues to let them know about his new venture. Then Seth waited for the phone to ring. Six months later, he had only one client and his business was failing miserably.

While some entrepreneurs crow that they have achieved success without planning, stories like Seth's are much more common among businesses that don't have an ongoing marketing program. Just as a winning football team always goes onto the field with a solid game plan, a successful business has an outline of how to reach out to prospective customers.

If the word "plan" makes you sweat, fear not. It is possible to create a simple, effective marketing plan in less than twenty-four hours. By following a series of steps, you will be able to schedule your marketing activities as part of your everyday routine and reach your growth goals that much sooner.

Hour 1: Taking Stock

Before you map out where you want your marketing plan to take you, you need to find out where you are. How is your business positioned in the market? Is this how your customers see you? You may want to ask some of them for feedback. Be as objective as possible and write four or five paragraphs that summarize your business, including philosophy, strengths, and weaknesses. Don't worry if it's not neatly organized—it's more important to get everything down on paper.

Hours 2 to 3: Setting the Goal

Now that you have a sense of where you are, you can decide where you want to go. Ask yourself what you are trying to accomplish with this plan. Do you want to increase sales? Change the perception of your business among target audiences? Generate more store traffic? Do you want to enter a new market where you may not have much experience? The right marketing tools can help you in a variety of ways.

Outline each of your goals, being as specific as possible. While you should be optimistic, use a healthy dose of realism to keep yourself grounded. Remember that the best marketing plan in the world is not likely to increase sales 80 percent next year unless there are special circumstances, such as an outstanding new product introduction or the sudden disappearance of your competition. While it's fine to have multiple goals, be sure to prioritize them so that you can create a realistic plan to achieve them.

Hours 3 to 4: Hitting the Target

Who are your target audiences? If you say "everyone," you need to rethink the answer. Even the largest companies don't market blindly to every individual. Rather, they break their audiences down into distinct profiles, or niche audiences, and create messages and vehicles to reach each segment.

Define your niche audiences as clearly as possible. If you are reaching out to businesses, describe what type, including industry, revenue level, location, and other important characteristics. If consumers are your audience, describe their age, sex, income level, marital status, and other relevant facts. Be as specific as possible. You will probably have several audience segments, but be sure to rank them in order of priority.

Hours 4 to 9.5: Researching Your Plan

Now that you've outlined where you are and where you want to go, it's time to play private detective to find the best route to get there. Nothing provides a clearer look into the path of least resistance than research.

Information about your target audiences is available from a variety of resources, many of them free. Take some time to find out about demographics (the physical characteristics of your audiences) and psychographics (the psychological characteristics of your audiences). Demographics outline such factors as age, geography, and income level. Psychographics offer insights into trends, buying habits, market segments, and the like. *American Demographics* has an outstanding Web site that offers access to many articles about various consumer and business market segments (www.demographics.com).

Trade associations and publications are often great places to start your research, especially if you are reaching out to businesses. Use your own and your target industries' trade resources for audience information. Many associations and publications are available on the Internet. For information about consumer audiences in your region, try your state or county department of economic development. The Small Business Administration offers limited help with market research. Find out more about their capabilities at www.sba.gov.

Once you have lined up this information, write a detailed profile of your audience segments. Include all of the demographic and psychographic information that you can. For instance, if you are selling a product to homeowners in Anytown, USA, find out what percentage of people own their homes in Anytown. What is the average household income? Do most homeowners have children? The more specific you can be, the better.

Hours 9.5 to 18: Planning the Action

This is the heart of your game plan. For each goal that you have outlined, you will need to create a strategy, key messages, and a series of steps that will help you accomplish the goal. You have many tools at your disposal.

As you examine each of your goals, conduct a mini-brainstorming session. Consider what the best vehicles for your message may be. You may decide to use newspaper, radio, television, magazine, or outdoor advertising; direct marketing programs, including postcards, sales letters, flyers, business reply cards, newsletters, and toll-free response numbers; and public relations elements such as publicity, events, speaking engagements, sponsorships, opinion polls, and the like. Perhaps you can accomplish your objectives and cut your costs by teaming up with related, noncompeting businesses for in-store promotions or cross-promotional outreach. Online promotional opportunities are more abundant than ever, and you may want to consider designing a

Web site or uploading information into a news group or special interest forum.

Write each strategy and list the key messages and tactics below it. For example:

Strategy: Position myself as the leader in home inspections in my community.

Key Messages: Homer Wright Home Inspections is a reputable, trustworthy name in home inspections.

Tactics:

1. Approach area community college about teaching home-buying class.

2. Propose feature story to local paper called "'Ten Things to Look for When Buying a Home," with me as the source.

3. Create brochure titled "Secrets of Home Buying" and offer it free to people who call in.

4. Issue press release about free brochure to local media.

5. Send informational brochures to real estate agents and mortgage brokers who refer home buyers to home inspectors.

For each step you plan, keep asking yourself, "Why should I do this?" Don't get trapped into big splashy promotions just for the sake of doing them. It's much more effective to have smaller, more frequent communications if your budget is limited. Let's say a small accounting firm wants to increase publicity in local newspapers. The owner makes a $10,000 donation to a local charity's annual gala, believing this will make a great news story. While the gesture was greatly appreciated by the charity and its supporters, that money represented the majority of the firm's annual marketing budget. In return, the owner got one small story in the local newspaper. If the organization's goal was to become more philanthropic, the donation would have been an effective gesture. However, because the goal was to increase publicity, the money would have been better spent on a diverse marketing program with more components.

Finally, be sure that your promotions project the right image. If your audience is conservative, don't create a flamboyant promotion. Similarly, if you need to project a cutting-edge image, be sure that your promotion is smart and sophisticated.

Hours 18 to 21: Budgeting Your Resources

Some business owners believe that marketing is an optional expense. This is one of the most tragic mistakes in business. Marketing expenses should be given priority, especially in times of slow cash flow. After all, how are you going to attract more business during the slow times if you don't invest in telling customers about yourself?

Take a realistic look at how much money you have to spend on marketing. While you do need to ensure that you are not overextending yourself, it is critical that you allot adequate funds to reach your audiences. If you find that you do not have the budget to tackle all of your audiences, try to reach them one by one, in order of priority.

For each of your tactics, list each expense. For example, producing a brochure includes writing, photography, graphic design, film, printing, and delivery. You should outline the estimated cost of each. From there, you can beef up or pare down your plan, depending on your situation.

Hours 21 to 23.5: Timing Your Projects

Now that you have developed the steps involved in each activity, allot a segment of time and a deadline to each. Again, be sure that you are not overextending yourself or you may get burned out. It's better to start with smaller, more consistent efforts than to begin with an overly ambitious program that you discard a few months later.

Hours 23.5 and after: Go for it!

What you now hold in your hands is probably the most effective to-do list that you will ever write. You have prepared a document that will help you reach your audience segments from a point of knowledge and expertise instead of "shoot-from-the-hip" hunches.

Don't put the marketing plan on a shelf and forget about it. Your marketing plan should be a living document, which grows and changes over time. As your business reaps the benefits of your initial marketing strategies, you may want to increase the scope of your marketing. If you find that something is not working, discard or change it. Consistency and continuity, delivered with a dash of creativity, give you the formula for successful marketing.

LARA PULLEN, ENVIRONMENTAL HEALTH CONSULTING, INC.

Getting government contracts was a big part of my original marketing plan. Unfortunately, the strategy hasn't opened up as much business as I anticipated. I found that as much as the government says they want to help small women-owned businesses, it isn't the reality. Government agencies tend to be large and inflexible. If I need to expand in the future, however, I may spend some time trying to get government contracts. At this point, though, it doesn't seem worth the effort. They have certified me as a woman-owned business, but it hasn't seemed to do much for me. The only government contract that I have is actually a sub-contract. I would suggest that small businesses find out from government agencies the names of the companies that have been awarded large contracts. Then, instead of dealing with the agency, go straight to the main contractor to see if they need your expertise on a special subject. In my experience, the big companies would rather use in-house than outsource, but in some instances they can be persuaded. Here are some actions you can take to help you get government contracts for your company:

- Register with the Procurement Marketing and Access Network, PRO-Net, a searchable database of contracts up for bid.
- Consult the Small Business Administration's Web site (www.sba.gov).
- Subscribe to the *Commerce Business Daily*, which alerts companies to relevant government solicitations.

- Look at Sellingtothegoverment.net, the portal of the Government Marketing Association for procurement assistance.
- Investigate the Federal Procurement Data System, the site that tells you who bought what and for how much from over sixty executive-brand agencies (www.fpds.gsa.gov).

REBECCA HART, PUBLIC RELATIONS

A big part of my marketing plan was figuring out what to call my company and how to position my business. Ultimately, I decided to use only my name, Rebecca Hart, APR, because I've spent ten years in the business, and I decided to leverage that instead of starting from square one with a generic name.

When considering using your own name for your company, there are two schools of thought. The first is that your good name can be one of your best business assets, so why not apply it to your company? The second is that if you ever want to sell the business, you need to have a stand-alone enterprise that isn't dependent on you.

ROBIN ZELL, BRAGELETS

My market is new mothers, so it is important for me to be where they are, which is the maternity wards. The majority of my $8,000 a year marketing budget is spent on inserts in hospital bags distributed free to new mothers in the maternity wards of hospitals. There is a company in St. Louis and Chicago that fills bags with items targeted to new moms, such as coupons and infant product samples. The Chicago hospital bags did not do well after a year, so I redirected those funds to print media advertising. I bought a small classified ad in a prenatal book given to newly pregnant moms, and I have bought classified ads in *Baby Talk* and *Parenting*. These are very expensive, costing about $30 per word. The results were not as good as I had hoped. I got a lot of calls from low-income people who wanted a free catalog, which I do not have. I can assume that some people with Internet access went to the site, but not a lot of orders came from that. It's important to realize it's okay to try new things until you find one that works for your company.

RESOURCES FOR DEVELOPING YOUR MARKETING PLAN

- The Small Business Administration (SBA) has a number of Small Business Development Centers, Women's Business Centers, and Business Information Centers throughout the country. The SBDC counseling program assigns a consultant to meet with entrepreneurs on a regular basis to monitor progress in any area from marketing to human resources. Free. Find the nearest center by calling 800-827-5722.

- The SBA's Service Corps of Retired Executives (SCORE) is a group of retired executives with various areas of expertise. The organization offers free counseling to start-up or established business owners. Request someone with a marketing background to help you write your plan. Free. Call 800-634-0245 or visit their Web site at www.score.org.

- College marketing departments. See if the marketing professor at a nearby college will make it a class assignment to develop a marketing plan for you, or find out if there is a marketing or related business club on campus which would handle the project. Free.

- Internship programs. A marketing student may help you write your marketing plan in exchange for the experience or a small stipend. Call the marketing departments of colleges in your area or your state college and see if someone can recommend a student. Free or small fee.

SHERRY MAYSONAVE, EMPOWERMENT ENTERPRISES

One of our key strategies is to create strong partners with other companies. Once we identify a target company, we apply tactical strategies. They include:

1. Finding companies that can clearly and measurably benefit from a strong connection with our company's products and services.

2. Going to the top executives, the presidents or CEOs, and articulating how they can easily leverage their business via a relationship with us. When they refer us down the management chain to lesser executives, we make it a point to convert them into "champions" for our company. We do this by convincing them that this partnership not only will be good for the company but will also enhance their careers.

3. Focusing on one initial project we and the target company will do together. We make it easy for them to form the partnership. We do everything possible to make this project a bigger success than expected and then leverage this into other areas to further expand the partnership. The targeted company wants a "win" from the partnership, but we don't sell our souls or do anything unprofitable for us. The situation has to be win-win. We recommend targetinging five companies where the leverage you can bring is obvious, real, and measurable. Then make a professional and aggressive approach.

67

What was your most effective marketing initiative?

DARCY VOLDEN MILLER, LITTLEDIDIKNOW.COM

We assembled a most wonderful mailing of samples for both the *Rosie O'Donnell Show* and *Oprah*. It consisted of ten very large boxes (five for Rosie, five for Oprah) that contained all the mothers' products from our site. Standing five-feet tall, the boxes were hard to miss. We designed the sides to look like a child's block, showing the mother, the products, and the story. Both Rosie and Oprah gave on-air mentions to particular products, and we are still seeing the results of our efforts. We are looking forward to future spots.

So much hard work and time, not to mention some incredible graphic design, went into the boxes that we didn't want our spectacular efforts to die after their TV appearances. We developed the LittleDidIKnow.com print catalog, featuring all the mother-owned businesses that are part of our site. The sides of the boxes became the catalog pages. We wanted to print 15,000 catalogs, except that the printing charges would have cost each mother $400. Although this seems like a minimal investment for the amount of exposure, it was a large amount for some of our eighty home-based moms. To raise the $20,000 we needed, we put together a fund-raiser and sponsorship package. Our moms all over the country asked their friends, families, and constituents to help them either by making a donation or purchasing advertising space. We referred to our campaign as using our "Mom Power" and "Guerilla Girlfriend Marketing." Within forty-five days, we raised the $20,000 we needed to print the catalog.

SHERRY MAYSONAVE, EMPOWERMENT ENTERPRISES

Our most creative marketing effort is our partnership with Casual Corner Stores. Causal Corner contacted us when their e-commerce executive saw me on the *Today Show*. Their name obviously had synergy with my book, *Casual Power*. National publicity pays off! Our first partnership project was in conjunction with Casual Corner's planned e-commerce offering of clothing and accessories for working women. They were focused on providing a high-quality line of products that were very affordable and professional. This was a perfect match with my philosophy.

My husband, Stephen, our marketing mastermind, scheduled a meeting with Casual Corners's head of Internet marketing and their president at their corporate headquarters to discuss potential projects, including the Internet. We had a strong match in business philosophy and vision and discussed a variety of projects but agreed to start with one and make it a success. Both groups were mutually supportive, and we let the head of Internet marketing know it was a pleasure to work with her and hear her good ideas on how we could work together for our mutual benefit.

We held a follow-up meeting with the chairman/CEO and key executives. I presented a short-form version of my corporate seminars, which focused on the importance of nonverbal communication and business attire in creating a first impression. This was so well received that the chairman/CEO wanted to hire me full time! We explained that we could better leverage Casual Corner by remaining independent and in a nonexclusive corporate partnership. They understood, and we agreed to finalize an agreement within thirty days. They were aware that we were in discussions with other companies. We did our part to make these meetings easy for Casual Corner. We paid the travel expenses and accommodated their schedules.

The elements of our partnership included the following

- Press release on our relationship.
- *Casual Power* for sale in over 400 Casual Corner stores.
- *Casual Power* available on Casual Corner's Web site.
- *Casual Power* leveraging Casual Corner clothing and accessory sales. These successes are being communicated to the store managers and are creating more excitement and positive results for everyone.
- Empowerment Enterprises's presentations made to all Casual Corner U.S. district managers. Photographs show makeovers of EE clients wearing Casual Corner clothes.
- Casual Corner direct mail catalogs give frequent quotes from Sherry, feature *Casual Power,* and list the book for purchase.

We are now in the process of launching multiple campaigns, including direct mail to Casual Corner's gold credit card customers, corporate presentations, book signings and presentations in their flagship stores, and extending the sale of *Casual Power* into additional stores. The partnership is a mutually beneficial relationship.

Dee Ennen, Ennen Computer Services

In marketing my book, my most effective promotion was a free booklet I created from the advertising section of the book, showing how to acquire new clients. Through the booklet, I developed a relationship with the reader and increased my credibility as a writer. Most people find out about my booklet through my Web site, www.gate.net/~gregnn, although it often becomes a topic of discussion when I participate in online chats or message boards, too. There are no costs involved, because I send e-mail copies to people who request it, and they just download it. It's hard to determine exactly how many books I've sold using it, but I would definitely say a lot!

Nancy Cleary, Wyatt-McKenzie Publishing

When I took the leap and volunteered my time, talent, and energy to a group project, I created a sales force that now includes all of the women I was helping. Using your talent to help others works, and it comes back to you tenfold. I can't say I will recoup the $10,000 a client would have paid for a piece similar to the one I donated to the group, but I now have ninety women devoted to me.

The cooperative marketing plan that grew out of donating my time is now multiplying my marketing efforts. Cooperative marketing is a proven method of getting the word out about your product. I studied the success of *Chicken Soup for the Soul* when I first researched publishing and discovered they had a powerful cooperative marketing plan. Each author included in those first *Chicken Soup* books was asked to do five things a day to promote the book, however small or huge. I adopted this as the basis of my cooperative marketing plan. Any topic or business can apply it: Just create a group project, newsletter, booklet, or Web site describing the project, idea, program, or facility and then ask everyone involved to promote it.

Robin Zell, Bragelets

I launched a Mother's Day promotion that produced a lot of results for Bragelets. I gave a Chicago hospital distributor four gift certificates for free strands of Bragelets to offer to new moms. The distributor gave out one certificate a week during the month of May.

When you do such a promotion, you can expect what's called break-age, that is, a number of people will never redeem their certificates. Your liability thus is actually lower than your offer. Only one mother cashed her certificate in that promotion. So, for the cost of one bracelet, I got my name out to a lot of new moms. I also deepened my relationship with the hospital.

BETH BESNER, TABLE TOPPER

I'd say our best marketing to date has been placement in catalogs and mentions in public relations efforts and the media. All the business books tell you not to spend money on advertising, but to get as much free media as possible. As to catalogs, I always felt that our product was well suited for catalogs because it's an innovative product that needs some explanation. Catalogs generally don't charge you, and they provide a tremendous opportunity to be visible to your target market. Another marketing strategy we use is to combine sampling, printing our URL on all our materials, and listing store locations on our Web site.

I have found the best way to get parents hooked on our product is to let them try it once free. As part of our initial strategy, we sold the Table Toppers to the food courts in malls. It was an easy way to get the word out about our product, and I got paid by the malls on top of it. We use the same strategy selling our Table Toppers to restaurants. Unless your product is very expensive to produce, the best way to sell people on it is to give them one for free and let them try it!

JULIE MARCHESE, TWINSADVICE.COM

The number one thing drawing traffic to my site is my listing in the Yahoo directory. Ninety percent of my traffic comes from Yahoo, and 5 to 8 percent from AOL. People find me by doing a search. I used to do a lot of radio talk shows. In retrospect, I don't think they did that much for me, because my market is so small. I do think that people starting businesses should focus their efforts on public relations. One good story helps to spread the word. The best advertising is still word of mouth.

JEANNINE CLONTZ, ACCURATE BUSINESS SERVICES

The most creative marketing I ever did was sending out packets of seed with a "seeds of change" message on it to my direct marketing list. The cost of the seed cards at $2 each limited the number of people I could afford to send them to, so I sent them to my A-list prospects only. I also had expenses for letterhead, envelopes, and postage. My database of 200 prospects is compiled from Chamber of Commerce members, the Yellow Pages, and larger companies that advertise regularly in the newspaper for administrative support. Of these, fifty are my A-list prospects. I've done additional research on them and found that they are interested in outsourcing and are looking for the services that are my specialty. For this effort, I composed a letter and said I was enclosing the packet of seeds to kick off my "seeds of change" promotion. I went on to outline how more businesses were outsourcing their core administrative tasks to allow their staffs to do what they did best, promote and grow their businesses. I got five calls from it and landed one new client. I still have those same 200 people on my prospects list. We'll see how well I do with it next time!

GWEN MORAN, MARKETING EXPERT AND WRITER

I like creating a seminar that targets my market. Anyone who has ever attended an interesting and informative seminar knows that it is one of the best ways to train staff, keep up-to-date on industry changes, and learn new skills. Seminars are also a powerful way to build awareness about your company, market your products or services, and possibly create a new revenue stream for your business. Follow this checklist to make your seminars great:

- **Fee or free?** When determining what or if to charge for your seminar, consider two rules of thumb:
    1. Most people will attend events if they have already paid the fee.
    2. The more you charge, the less overt in selling you should be.

If your seminar is meant primarily to showcase your expertise, you may charge higher fees. However, if you're trying to create an environment to sell a specific product or service, you need to charge less or waive the fee. In either case, make sure that you deliver timely, interesting, and worthwhile content.

- **Partner up.** Consider defraying your costs by teaming up with a business related to yours. An attorney and an accountant may deliver an informative small-business start-up seminar to attract new clients for both.

- **Check your date.** Do some homework before you book your date to avoid competing with another event that may reduce your attendance. Call around to other facilities and find out what they have planned for that day and check with a few of your colleagues to see if there are industry events scheduled.

- **Oh, won't you stay?** Before you determine the length of your seminar, consider your audience, your topic, and other related factors. If you're planning on speaking to a room full of accountants, don't schedule a half-day seminar during tax season. Conversely, if you have a lengthy, complex topic to discuss, don't try to cram it into a two-hour luncheon.

- **Location, location.** Most hotels and conference centers routinely host seminars and have the process down to a science. If your budget won't allow for such accommodations, check out renting space at a local college or training facility.

- **Have good handouts.** Handouts are one of the most overlooked tools in seminar marketing. Give your attendees professional-looking handouts that support key points in your presentation.

- **Do mini-marketing.** Create a concise marketing plan for your seminar. Include publicity, direct mail, advertising, and other appropriate promotional vehicles. Remember, the more you get the word out, the more people will attend your seminar.

- **Require an RSVP.** Advance registration gives you a good idea of how many people to expect and how many handouts you'll

SEMINAR COSTS

Creating seminars requires an investment of time and money. Here is a quick budget checklist to make sure you have considered your main expenses:

Location rental

Refreshments/meals

Fees for additional speakers

Promotion/advertising

Creation and printing of handouts

Audio-visual equipment rental

Microphone and podium rental

Name badges or tags

Additional lighting

Decorations, banners, signage

Equipment and materials shipping

Travel and accommodations

Personnel to staff the event

Information provided by Moran Marketing Associates

need. Always ask how the registrant heard about the seminar as a way to track your marketing results.

- **Don't understaff.** Be sure you have enough staff at the event to handle registration, last-minute errands, product sales, distribution of handouts, and other event essentials.

- **Capture your attendees.** Be sure you collect names, postal and e-mail addresses, and other important contact information from your attendees for follow-up purposes. (Remember, most attendees are prospects.) You may also wish to develop a seminar evaluation form to distribute and collect to help you make your seminar even better next time around.

Customer Service

We started this chapter by discussing the importance of the word-of-mouth ripple effect, so I would be remiss if I didn't conclude the chapter on the marketing plan with a few words about customer service. Nothing will attract or deflect customers to your business quicker than a good or bad experience. Think about the last time you had to wait an extra day for your car to be repaired or had a terrible meal at a restaurant. I bet you told at least two people about the experience. People like to talk about their experiences, particularly if they are extremely good or terribly bad. Take the time to include a customer service strategy in your marketing plan. Identify ways to show your appreciation to loyal customers, to reward referrals, and to fulfill the promises you make in your advertising. Get your customers talking about you to their friends as quickly as possible by providing exceptional customer service. Word of mouth will grow your business faster than any other marketing initiative.

68

What best describes your feelings about customer service?

KIMBERLY STANSELL, AUTHOR

Customer service is the least expensive way to make more money. Nothing helps you grow faster than to be perceived as a service leader in your customers' eyes. You can find some great ideas and information on how to create or revamp your customer service program. Check out Service Quality Institute at customer-service.com, International Customer Service Association at www.icsa.com, and Outrageous Customer Service Tips at online newsletter at www.pitt.edu/~pirrs/cust/cust.html.

JORJ MORGAN, COOKBOOK AUTHOR

In my business, customer service is all about response time, especially since I am hoping to be a "companion in the kitchen" to my readers. I feel that it is extremely important to return telephone calls and answer e-mail questions, within twenty-four hours if possible. I want my readers to know I am there for them when they have cooking questions. The more successful they become, the more enthusiastically they will cook my recipes.

SHANNON RUBIO, THESMILEBOX.COM

I think good customer service is critical, especially with Internet businesses! It seems as if people today, online or not, expect bad service. I mean it's sad, but people think it's normal to wait days for a response. I reply right away to the needs and questions of my customers. It can be morning, noon, or night, and I reply right away. Boy, does it pay off. I have had people be so mad, but when they get a reply in two minutes from a real person, they calm down instantly. I may not eliminate the problem, but their mood changes. We have had lots of UPS errors that are totally not our fault and have overnighted boxes to fix the error, even though it costs us money. Our philosophy is, one happy customer is worth a hundred! On the other hand, there have been people we just could not please, and I have had to learn that some people will never be happy.

LINDA McWILLIAMS, ONCEUPONANAME.COM

I developed my views on customer service from my days at Xerox. I spent so much time listening to people complain about service that I promised myself if I ever owned my own company it would be a priority for me. Today, as a business owner, I am customer driven. I think it's not just good but excellent customer service that is the key. I believe in the power of word of mouth—it is my best means of advertising, and it's free. Few people are dissatisfied with our product, because we aim to please. We ship for free because customers want it, and we are always available. We list our phone number all over our Web site so they can contact us. Whether you are a $2 million company or a small company, I believe customer service is very important.

Public Relations and Advertising

The goal of each initiative is to get your business recognized. Public relations and advertising are the best vehicles of communication to spread the word to the masses about your company. A good public relations effort or advertising campaign can have a snowball effect on the prevalence of your name in the business community. It's an important way to gain recognition of your brand by consumers, business partners, or potential investors.

The costs of public relations and advertising can vary greatly depending on the amount of professional input you seek. Advertising space can come with a big price tag; big agencies tend to charge high retainers but bring contacts within the industries that prove to be invaluable later. It's important to weigh the costs of public relations and advertising that reach broach markets to more targeted efforts such as database and online marketing. In this chapter, we will evaluate the pros and cons of public relations and advertising.

Public Relations

Nothing propels your company forward like one good public relations story. Let me assure you that the old adage about the power of the press is true. The list of businesses that have grown out of one good newspaper article or five minutes on *Good Morning America* includes the Rubix cube and Baby Einstein video, to name just two. The best part of getting good press coverage is that it often comes with a small price tag. A single well-written press release can spawn an avalanche of media attention. One rule to remember is that the press is no different from anyone else—if others have it, they want it. Your challenge is to create the media buzz about your product or service and gain their attention.

There are several tricks to rising above the pile of press releases that arrive each day to newsrooms. The first is to treat members of the media as customers. You should respond quickly to their needs, deliver the best product possible, maintain a good relationship, research your market, and respect their time. Just as you would target the right customers for your business, it's important to focus your efforts on writers in the media. I can't tell you how many times during my career at the *Miami Herald* people sent us letters addressed to another newspaper or to a writer who no longer wrote for the *Herald.* Spend time discovering the writers who cover stories like the one you plan to present, and remember that each news organization usually has more than one area you can approach. When we launched BlueSuitMom.com, we sent materials to the technology writer as well as the lifestyle editor. To gain additional exposure, we sent personnel appointment announcements to the business section. You can't imagine how many people skim the Promotions column to see who has changed jobs in the business community. Take any mention you can get, even if it's just an item in the Personnel or New Businesses columns.

Keep in mind the needs of your customer, who in this case is a reporter looking for a good story. The product the reporter needs is a unique story with an interesting angle. Don't just write a press release saying, "We are proud to announce our new business." That won't do it. What's unique about you? What is interesting about you or your business? Think about what hooks you to read an article in the newspaper or stop to watch a news segment on television. Personal stories, heroic efforts, first-of-their-kind products, or a solution to a commonly known problem are all good angles. We launched BlueSuitMom.com with two press releases that included different messages. Our headlines were "BlueSuitMom.com Launches First Web Site Targeting Executive Mothers" and "First Women's Site to Offer Virtual Classes Launches on Mother's Day."

In the first press release, we identified ourselves as the first to market a unique niche. In the second, we focused on what set us apart from other women's sites: virtual classes. Although some reporters received both releases, each release went only to the appropriate writers.

Seasoned public relations executives will tell you that their relationship with members of the press is their most valuable asset. Keep in mind that reporters always need stories. If you give them a good story, you have made their job easier. A way to develop a good reputation with reporters is to position yourself as a resource for future stories. Make it known that you are available to them to provide a list of industry contacts or statistics, even if you aren't included in the article. I make it a habit to always offer additional angles to every story I pitch to the press. I also provide names and contact information for other people who can be part of the story, even if they are competitors. This practice allows me to exhibit the objectivity that journalists admire and respect.

Sometimes, even with good relationships and an interesting story, you have to find some other way to rise above the clutter and get noticed by the media. I credit our extra efforts in public relations to the early success of BlueSuitmom.com. Our strategy was not only to deliver interesting story ideas but to get noticed. To do this, we created a unique press kit. Being a start-up business with a limited budget, we designed, printed, and assembled the kits ourselves. In honor of our launch date, we decided to go with a Mother's Day theme and designed the kits to look like expensive Mother's Day gifts.

I've always believed presentation is everything. I call it the Tiffany's blue box approach to public relations. Although we assembled our press kits on the office floor, we wanted them to look like they came from a large company. We used oversized white boxes large enough to lay several unfolded press releases in them. On the computer, we created large gift tags that said, "On Mother's Day, 11 million

RULES OF WRITING AND
DISTRIBUTING PRESS RELEASES

1. Include contact information, name, and phone number, at the top of the page.

2. Include a release date if the information is time sensitive. Otherwise, write "FOR IMMEDIATE RELEASE."

3. Type the headline in all caps.

4. Use an italicized subheading to present an additional story angle or highlight the uniqueness of your news.

5. Include Who, What, Where, When, and Why in the first paragraph. Keep it short and concise.

mothers will receive the same gift." Notice how we called attention to the magnitude of our market and created a sense of curiosity as well. When the recipients opened the boxes, they found neatly creased blue tissue paper with our company name, BlueSuitMom.com. Included in the box were the press releases, bios of our management team, and promotional items designed for busy executive mothers. We included a school notepad, pen, a small box of crayons, and a chocolate bar. The boxes were imprinted with our logo. Our tactic was that, even if they didn't read our releases, who can resist using free stuff or eating chocolate? We knew our name was catchy, and if they took a minute to go to our site, we were confident they would find a great product. On our media list as a matter of strategy we included mainly female members of the press. This selective process gave us a fifty-fifty chance of landing our press kit in the hands of a working mother.

6. Use good grammar and spelling.

7. Limit your story to one page.

8. Include a boilerplate paragraph at the end of the press release.

9. End the release with the word, "End" or the characters "###."

10 Never send a release as an attachment. Paste the copy into the body of the e-mail.

11. Never fax a press release unless you follow it up with a phone call.

12. Send only black-and-white photos.

Our strategy worked. Within the first week of launching our site, BlueSuitMom.com's story appeared in the *Fort Lauderdale Sun Sentinel,* the *Philadelphia Inquirer,* the *Denver Post,* the *Salt Lake City Tribune,* and the *Lincoln Nebraska Star.* Within a month, twenty print publications gave us coverage, including the *Wall Street Journal, USA Today,* and three electronic news segments. The most startling thing was that the entire effort, including sending the packages by Federal Express, cost only $1,800. We could not have bought nearly enough advertising to produce as much traffic to our site for the same money.

The final step in gaining media attention is a well-written press release. This obvious step is often ignored or done carelessly by business owners. They omit contact information, the location of their business, and other vital facts. There are industry-recognized standards to follow when drafting your press releases. Always include the five Ws in the first paragraph: who, what, when, where, and why. Provide a good quote in the body of the press release and add supporting statistics with full credit to the source. The final paragraph will be a boilerplate paragraph that you will use in all your press releases. It is a mission-statement-like description of your business that clearly and quickly tells the reader who you are.

There are services available to help you distribute your press releases. If you decide to hire a public relations firm to do this distribution, make sure they have established relationships with the organizations on your media list. However, you don't have to be a public relations professional to gain access to the same services.

69

What distribution channels do you use for your press releases?

GWEN MORAN, MARKETING EXPERT AND WRITER

You can distribute press releases in several ways. PRNewswire distributes news releases and photos to the media, the financial community, and even consumers. PRNewswire's "wire" is leased from the Associated Press and delivers information directly to newsrooms via satellite. The service also delivers directly to more than 1,400 Web sites and databases via its Web site, www.prnewswire.com, e-mail, and fax, and to thousands more through third-party syndication and redistribution. Membership in PRNewswire costs $100 per year, and there is a fee per release. Local distribution begins at $550. Other "wire" services include:

- Business Wire: www.businesswire.com
- Internet Wire: www.internetwire.com
- Internet News Bureau: www.newsbureau.com
- URLWire: www.urlwire.com
- Xpress Press: www.xpress.com

70

What has been your most successful public relations effort?

SHERRY MAYSONAVE, EMPOWERMENT ENTERPRISES

Our best public relations decision came only after we hired a publicist who was referred by my publisher. She set up my book tour and some engagements. I'd advise business people to establish in their own minds what they are trying to accomplish and then select a PR person or firm who specializes in that area. We later chose another PR person, Stacey Miller who specialized in book promotions, used current technology, had Internet contact with media, and who was very excited about the book. The results were excellent. Publicists usually charge a monthly fee or a per package fee. It is well worth the expense.

We found Stacey Miller on the Internet. She only promotes books. She told us that we had gone about the initial book PR and book tour in a backwards fashion. Her idea was to get national publicity first and then set up a book tour, not regional publicity first, as our first publicist had done. I vote for Stacey's plan. Doing the book tour as an unknown author was grueling! A week after I hired Stacey, she pitched me to a *USA Today* reporter who had sent out a request over Profnet.com. I had a successful interview with the reporter and was mentioned in her article, along with the title of my book. Other publicity sprouted from there, and the momentum continues.

The other lesson I learned is not to be afraid to try new PR ideas or approaches. I tried advertising in a publication that is targeted at talk radio stations, and I have had dozens of live interviews enabling me to reach a broad audience. In interviews, go out of your way to be accommodating, available, and entertaining. Most of all, try to appear knowledgeable, because this gives you an aura as an "expert" and elevates your products as important problem-solving aids. Advertising in the *Radio & Television Interview Report* can cost between $400 and $600 an issue, but they offer volume discounts. More information about *RTIR* is available on their Web site, rtir.com.

Position yourself as an expert not only to the press but to your corporate partners. We currently have three key partners and are working on two more. The benefit is that you can leverage their marketing, advertising, and sales promotions. For example, Kayser Roth, the manufacturer of No Nonsense and Calvin Klein leg-wear products, quotes me as the expert on all of their new packaging, on their Web site, and are offering special retail promotions on *Casual Power.*

Invest in a high-quality Web site, even if you are selling a product directly over the Internet. It is great advertising and becomes a virtual brochure.

All of these approaches will dovetail and create momentum for your business. Soon, people will begin to call you, because you, your company, and your products are so visible in so many different ways.

DARCY VOLDEN MILLER, LITTLEDIDIKNOW.COM

The success of our public relations campaign is based on a cooperative effort we call "Mom Power." We have almost a hundred moms from coast-to-coast out there telling everyone they know about our site. In a group this large, it is inevitable that somebody somewhere has a contact we can leverage. It is amazing the kinds of connections that surface in a large group such as ours.

Our printed catalog also serves as a media vehicle. Not only does it showcase the products of our moms, but it also tells their stories. We have pushed it into the hands of targeted media as their desktop reference for stories on work-at-home moms. Anytime any one of our moms gets any media attention, they mention LittleDidIKnow.com, not only helping themselves but all the other mothers who are part of the site, too.

As far as handling the media, we just say, "Bring it on!" The biggest challenge is getting the media to take an interest in your story. Timing is very important. It's almost impossible to know what story a writer or producer is working on at the moment and the only ideas they're looking for that develop that story. If you send a press release to them about "MomPower" and they're writing about "Web site design," you'll get overlooked that week. The good news is that the media keep stories of interest for future use and with good luck something may "pop" for you soon. One big challenge is finding out who the media people are and how they operate. On top of learning everything else about your business, learning how to write effective press releases and getting them into the right hands is a serious challenge.

GWEN MORAN, MARKETING EXPERT AND WRITER

One way to get the attention of the press is to use the retail calendar as a promotional tool. The retail calendar is made up of special days like Martin Luther King Jr.'s Birthday, Valentine's Day, Presidents' Day, and so on, and is the marketing tool of choice for many merchants.

Sure, that's great, you might think, but how does it apply to my business? Actually, the retail calendar offers opportunities for many businesses to create innovative and effective promotions. The following steps will help you look at this marketing tool in a new light.

1. Look for publicity opportunities around various holidays. For instance, Nathan's Famous, the renowned hot dog maker, holds an international hot dog eating contest at Coney Island each Independence Day. The wiener master hosts entrants from around the world in a fight for the title of International Hot Dog Eating Champion. The Independence Day tie-in is perfect for a patriotic push in the event's publicity materials. Similarly, announcing a search for the most romantic couple in time for Valentine's Day or for the messiest house in time for spring-cleaning season could give your business a nice bit of attention. Be sure, however, that your efforts are appropriate for your target audience and marketing goals.

2. Make your own holiday. If you're tired of the same old celebrations, check out Chase's Calendar of Events (www.chases.com) and find a new one. This comprehensive listing contains more than 12,000 entries including celebrity birthdays, astrological phenomena, culinary

celebrations, and festivals around the world, fully indexed by location, date, and category. From Dr. Seuss's Birthday on March 2 to Elephant Appreciation Day on September 22 to Peanut Butter Lover's Month in November, you can be sure to find a holiday that tickles your fancy. If you still can't find one, declare your own—Chase's Calendar shows you how.

3. Plan ahead. Regardless of how you use the retail calendar, it's important to look ahead and give yourself enough time to create effective promotions. Start by looking three to six months ahead and determining how you can capitalize on what's coming up.

4. Think creatively. Even if you sell only to other businesses, taking advantage of timely opportunities can keep your business front-of-mind. Ask yourself what your business can offer to support your clients during their seasonal changes.

LESLEY SPENCER, HBWM.COM

I have sent out many news releases over the years and have generated some great publicity. Our very first publicity mention was in *Baby*, and that helped us get national attention and get HBWM off the ground. We've also been featured or quoted in numerous newspapers, magazines, television news programs, and radio programs. Some of the publicity we've received has come from writers finding the HBWM.com Web site on their own. Many media people know they can come to HBWM.com and find all types of home-based working moms in particular industries, locations, and backgrounds. Our members appreciate the opportunity to get national publicity. It's been a great win-win situation.

MOLLY GOLD, GO MOM !INC.

My financial return from PR comes from an article in *Redbook* magazine. When a *Redbook* writer inquired about our company, I sent two planners to her and received national exposure in my target market, moms in their thirties, for free! We get orders every day that cite *Redbook* as their source. In terms of television, our "Working Woman" segment in January 2000 was a local hit, generating the highest number of visitors in one day to our site.

Our public relations strategy is to tell people about our product, but I have found their interest is as much about me as it is the planner. I'm not that comfortable with this attention, because I still think of myself as a stay-at-home mom.

We purchased target lists of press contacts at national women's magazines and local parents' publications from a PR service. At the launch of our company, we did a local press release about our launch and our participation in a trade show. Fortunately, the *Washington Post* picked up the story, which spawned a story in *Newsweek,* which yielded the phone call from *Redbook.* We've done basic press kit mailings to go along with our attendance at the Baby Faires last spring. In addition, over the past year, we've sent to women's interest reporters at the top 100 city papers and top 25 television markets nationally. We always tie into an upcoming holiday or event, like back to school. We've been written up in almost 20 of the national parents' papers, and more will come with our Mother's Day round. These big guys reprint good press releases, a discovery that allowed us to get our foot in the door with them over the past year.

The best advice I have is to make public relations campaigns your first priority. Mailings aren't free, but they are so much cheaper than advertising. A well-crafted press release has a huge impact. A very seasoned momprenuer reminded me to view PR campaigns as the bricks and mortar that help build your business. The fanfare is fleeting and brief, so you must tell your story repeatedly to the press. They can do more for you to reach your target audience than you ever can for yourself. When dealing with reporters, remember to make it easy for them to write the story. Give them everything they need to plug you in when they have a hole. Finally, don't ever quit sending out your PR communications: The effort will pay off over time. In the past month, I made two great contacts that were a year in the making!

Advertising

Advertising is more expensive than public relations. Most industry professionals divide advertising into electronic and print. The former includes radio, television, and online ads. We'll discuss online advertising in the next chapter when we focus on online marketing efforts.

For a small-business owner with limited advertising dollars to spend, radio may prove to be the more affordable electronic medium. Radio rates are based on the time slot and the number of minutes you purchase. Every market is different, but radio airtime usually runs from $25 to $100 a minute in midsize markets. This expense is in addition to the cost of producing the ad you will run. Most marketers include a catchy slogan, mention the company's name at least three times and offer an irresistible bargain to the listener. Think of the ads you hear on the radio. How many times do you hear "Limited time only," "Act now," or "Today only"? Radio advertising allows you to send an urgent message to an audience with a common interest in music or talk. When buying radio ads, ask the station about value-added elements. Often, radio stations will kick in tickets to local events, disc jockey appearances at your place of business, or concert tickets for use in customer promotions. If you'd like to host your own advertorial radio talk show, you can hook up with many radio stations that broker this kind of space. They allow you to buy blocks of time for whatever type of programming you'd like to conduct.

Television advertising tends to be more expensive than radio, but it gives you a larger audience. Add production costs to the cost of airtime just as in radio. A more affordable way to advertise on television is to purchase airtime on cable networks. By using cable, you can narrow the market that you will reach with your ad. Ad representatives should provide you with demographic and saturation numbers. Choose wisely before you shoot your entire marketing budget on one national television ad. This was the mistake made by Internet start-up companies during the 2000 Superbowl. A year after many of them spent millions on a thirty-second Super Bowl ad, most were out of business!

Print advertising includes newspapers, magazines, the Yellow Pages, and ads in programs. Newspaper advertising has many affordable options. We'd all like to take out a full-page ad in the *Wall Street Journal*, but, for most of us, this isn't the best use of our advertising money. In fact, when we launched BlueSuitMom.com, we considered advertising in the *WSJ*. To our disappointment, the ad carried a $25,000 price tag and, in addition, wouldn't have reached our market. Just in time, we learned from our media kit that less than 50 percent of the *Wall Street Journal*'s circulation is female. The lesson here is to choose carefully and make sure you review the demographics of all publications you are considering.

Buying newspaper advertising gives you many choices, including the day of the week the ad will run, the size of the ad, and the section in which it will appear. Ask the advertising representative to describe the trends in readership and benefits among all these choices. Compare the information they provide with your marketing goals. You would never, for instance, place an ad for baby products in Sunday's sports section.

Smaller local weeklies are good marketing vehicles. You may reach fewer readers, but the cost is much more affordable.

Whether you choose to buy national magazine space or a full-page local ad, the elements that appear in the ad are similar. Every ad should include at least your company's name, logo, location, and how to contact you. Most marketers today include both a phone number and Web address in their ads. Give your customer as many ways as possible to reach you so it becomes convenient for them to buy your product. Present consumers with a compelling value proposition that entices them to react to your offer. It might be a reduction in price, additional value, or a free item. The only rule about print advertising is to use the white space well. Translated, that means not to clutter your ad with unnecessary copy or graphics. Keep it easy for your potential customer to read.

Many small-business owners look to the Yellow Pages for their print advertising. Although effective for many businesses, the cost can be high. The elements of the ad are similar to magazine and newspaper ads, with one exception: Omit the compelling urgent call to action in favor of the reason why your product or service raises you above the offerings in the hundreds of other listings.

71

What kind of advertising do you use for your business?

JEANNINE CLONTZ, ACCURATE BUSINESS SERVICES

My best results come from a Yellow Pages ad. It costs me $72 per month for a one-inch bold ad, but I get lots of calls, and it's worth it. I've gotten a few as-needed clients and some resumes. I suggest placing ads in as many categories as you can afford. In fact, next year I'm going to follow my own advice. Right now, I have a large ad under "Secretarial Services" and a smaller one under "Transcription" that was a free listing given to me by my Yellow Pages's representative. Next year, I'll add a one- or two-line ad in a few more categories. The thing that works best is the one-inch ad, even though it's expensive. However, it does separate me from the crowd. I've had prospects tell me they thought I was a larger, more established company because of the larger ad.

LINDA MCWILLAMS, ONCEUPONANAME.COM

I participate in a co-op advertising program that has been very successful for my company. I was invited to join this co-op by its two owners about a year ago. There are nine business owners in the group and each of us contributes $150 to $200 every two months. I've participated in similar groups that are larger, but you tend to lose control with too many participants. Collectively, our co-op group decides how and where to spend our money. If someone sees a good advertising opportunity, they tell the group, and we vote on doing it. We have used Web cards that feature all our logos. We have tried advertising on Must See Sites, which also placed us in big magazine ads like *Parenting* and *Baby Talk*. That ad didn't do as well as they said it would. We have also passed out flyers and promos for each other in our outgoing packages and tried contests to attract customers. Some work, some don't, but the info that we share, the support we receive as a group, and the teamwork we have is wonderful. I have learned so much from many of the ladies in this group! This is so important in any type of business where support is half the battle. Many times we have felt like throwing in the towel, but the group support keeps urging us on! Selecting the right co-op depends on the people who are behind it. Look around first, or start your own. Remember big doesn't always mean better.

JULIE AIGNER-CLARK, BABY EINSTEIN

We only began advertising in 2000, when we moved our products into the mass market to support our retailers, Target and Wal-Mart. This new marketing strategy carried a budget of $800,000. We chose to run several full-page, four-color ads in the top parenting magazines. Although our advertising campaign appears to be working, we seem to get the word out best when parenting magazines write us up in product reviews.

Direct Mail

Direct mail delivers your message individually to consumers. Most direct mail advertising is done through mass mailings to a targeted group of people. Direct mail campaigns may include simple postcards illustrating your product or elaborate tri-folded brochures describing your services. Once the promotional material is produced, you will then select a group to receive it. Direct marketing list companies sell names and addresses to business owners seeking a certain demographic of consumers. You can be very specific on the characteristics of the audience you want to reach. For instance, when we launched BlueSuitMom.com, we bought a list of employed females with children and incomes over $50,000 who lived in Chicago, New York, Atlanta, and Miami. The mailing can be designed exclusively for the market whose mailbox you intend to hit. Professional marketers will segment or divide their lists into groupings and test different offers within their campaign. By measuring the response of each offer, they are able to determine which promotions drive the behavior they desire in their customers. The cost for direct mailing can vary depending on the number of pieces you decide to print, the required postage, and the complexity of producing the actual printed material. Remember, just because you mail out 1,000 brochures doesn't mean that you will acquire 1,000 new clients. In fact, a typical response rate to a direct mail piece is 1 percent to 3 percent. This means that if you send out 1,000 brochures selling your widgets, you can expect to sell about twenty widgets.

72

How do you create direct mail advertising for your business?

NANCY CLEARY, WYATT-MCKENZIE PUBLISHING

I design direct mail pieces both for my company and for my clients. My first piece of advice is to hire a professional graphic designer—perhaps one you can trade your service or advertising space with. Bartering is alive and well in the design business: That is how I got to where I am today! Perhaps you could offer the bottom quarter of the last panel on your brochure to your designer in trade for part of the design fee. Under this arrangement, you pay for the production and mailing costs, and they benefit from the exposure and the personal referral. You can add a note, "This brochure created in cooperation with DesignScapes Studio. Visit their site for all of your promotional design needs, online and in print: www.designscapestudio.com." I say this because my average design fee for an 8½ × 11, two-sided, high-end brochure is $1,500. You can also offer your printer an advertising byline for a reduced printing fee (the average cost for 1,000 full-color, two-sided brochures is about $800 with proofs).

As important as a good-looking direct mail piece, however, is what you do with it. Your mailing list, or the event at which you will distribute these brochures, must be in line with your market. The piece also has to move the reader to action–with an offer, a coupon, a request for submissions—anything to take your customer a step further. Web sites are invaluable for this. If you can get customers to your site to subscribe for a free newsletter or download a coupon, then you've got their e-mail address. You'll use it for your next marketing effort online, which can be done at no cost.

Also use cooperative marketing ideas. If you can find others who are reaching the same market you are, collaborate! Create a piece that offers valuable information while leading customers to buy your products or services. By joining forces, you not only have more to offer, but you can split hard costs and combine mailing lists.

Robin Sterne, Wow! Designs, Inc.

I believe creating a successful look for your direct mail pieces begins with branding the look of your company. The first part of this process is conveying your image through a logo. Your logo will hopefully represent you for many years, so you want to create the right balance between your image and your industry. The first thing I do in creating logos for companies is to become familiar with their competitors' logos. You want your logo to stand out. It is also important to understand the main reason for a logo. Is it to use mainly in print, on signs, or on the Web? A small, tightly designed logo may not produce well and could deliver the wrong impression to your customer. Yellow and blue are the most pleasing colors for outdoor signage, and you see many storefronts using this combination. Blockbuster is a good example. I usually like to create two or three ideas and show them to clients to gauge their reaction. It's important to see how people react to the colors, tag lines, and shape as well as finding out how it makes them feel. Since a logo should tell the customer what your business is about, I often ask people what kind of business they think the proposed logo represents, without disclosing the name of the company to them. It's a great way to determine if the logo indeed illustrates the business's image.

Gwen Moran, Marketing Expert and Writer

Often dubbed "junk mail," direct mail can be considered the Rodney Dangerfield of marketing. However, this "don't-get-no-respect" medium is actually one of the most effective, precise, and economical ways to convey your message to key audiences. Consider these tips:

- **Converse first.** If your mailing is a team effort requiring a printer, list broker, mailing house, graphic designer, and/or writer, be sure you consult with each one at the start of the project. Discuss your goals for the project and invite their feedback. Ask the mailing house whether they want the list to arrive on disk or on labels. Make sure your graphic designer knows the size and weight restrictions for the postage classification you need to meet.

- **Buy from a broker.** Because selecting the right list is the single most important element of your direct mail effort, consult a reputable list broker. Check the Standard Rate and Data Service's (SRDS) direct mail volume, which can be found in many libraries. A knowledgeable broker will help you find a list that meets your criteria with minimal waste. Be sure to ask what the "deliverability guarantee" is. Usually, it's 93 percent. If your return rate from incorrect addresses is higher, find out if the broker will compensate you.

- **Check the list.** Most lists are rented for one-time use and have minimum purchase requirements. That means you pay for the minimum number of names, even if you use fewer. However, many lists can be used multiple times by paying two or three times the one-time rental rate, so discuss your needs with your broker. Don't even think about poaching a list. Most are "salted" with dummy names that allow list companies to track who's mailing without authorization. Brokers for subscription lists and lists of parents of young children may want to see a sample of your mailing piece before they release the list.

- **Be careful with creative.** It's important to be creative when you are competing for a prospect's attention. However, you also have to watch the size and weight of your piece to meet standard postal service classifications. If your piece is an eighth of an inch too long or a fraction of an ounce too heavy, you will waste big bucks in extra postage. Be creative, but run unusual sizes, colors, or shapes by your local post office first.

- **Be benefits-oriented.** Too many direct mail pieces get bogged down in details that don't sell the prospect. Be clear, show your prospects what's in it for them, and make sure that your response procedure is easy for them to understand.

- **Testing one-two-three.** Test different lists, mailing pieces, and offers and don't be afraid to try new approaches. Columbia Records is an example, By changing its offer from ten records for $1.99 plus free shipping and handling to ten records for a penny, plus $1.98 shipping and handling, the direct music seller increased its return 23 percent.

- **Check your timing.** Mail local, first-class mailings on Monday. Most pieces will reach prospects on Tuesday, the lightest mail day of the week. Different industries have different times of the year that work best for them. Check with your trade association or list broker.

- **Get help.** The United States Postal Service has business centers in every state to assist businesses with direct mail marketing. Contact your local post office for the location nearest you. You may also contact: Direct Marketing Association, 1120 Avenue of the Americas, New York, NY, 10036-6700, 212-768-7277 (www.the-dma.org).

CHAPTER TWELVE

Database and Online Marketing

There are few marketing initiatives as targeted as database and online marketing. In fact, when the Internet emerged in the early '90s, it was touted as the database marketers' dream. Targeting a specific market allows you to speak directly to consumers that fit the profile of your customers. This is important for two reasons. First, it allows you to minimize the wasted advertising dollars spent delivering your message to consumers who just don't care. If you sell baby shoes, it is unproductive to send a discount offer to a home owned by a single young man or a retired male. Targeting your marketing efforts to mothers of children less than three years of age hold a much better chance for a return on your investment.

Second, target marketing is also important because it allows you speak in a meaningful way to your prospective customers. Let's use the same baby shoe company example. By targeting mothers of children with boys under three years of age, the store owner can create promotional materials that spotlight the most popular little-boy styles and describe the features that make them last longer than most other boy shoes. Before the Internet, asking the consumer for their information was what created databases. As you can expect, many people do not wish to supply strangers with this information and often provide incorrect or incomplete answers. The Internet gave marketers a way to track the interests, buying patterns, and online behaviors of individuals almost immediately.

On BlueSuitMom.com we can view hourly what stories are the most popular with our readers, what topics readers are searching for, and what products they are buying. You can imagine how valuable a list reporting 1,000 new mothers read an article entitled "Fitting Your Child for Shoes" would be to our fictitious shoe saleswoman. Online marketing allows you to be as targeted as database marketing. Our shoe saleswoman might want to buy ads on site, that cater to mothers of newborns, such as babyuniverse.com.

Amazon.com is the best example of a company using online marketing and database mining to deliver individualized messaging to each and every customer. The site remembers which books you purchased, your favorite authors, and when you need to be reminded of a book's debut. Chances are, you'll develop a relationship with Amazon.com and eventually translate your loyalty into sales.

Database Marketing

Once you have customers, it's time to create a database so that you organize the information you obtain about them. These data can prove to be your most important marketing tool. By properly organizing details about your customers, you can confirm that you indeed know what your customers look like, analyze their buying habits, and retain their business. Database marketing when done correctly allows you to maintain a one-on-one relationship with your customers. The goal of database marketing is to create a lifetime value customer through repetitive sales. Other marketing initiatives simply try to gain as many new customers as possible by casting a net of special offers or multiple exposures to the masses. Database marketing focuses on selling a product to one customer over and over again at the same time you are increasing the amount of the sale.

Omaha Steaks does a great job at database marketing. Several years ago, I ordered steaks for my father. The next year, I received a letter from Omaha Steaks asking me if I'd like to send steaks to him again, and, while I was at it, perhaps I'd like to order some for myself. They remembered not only who I sent steaks to but the kind and number I sent as well. They made it so easy for me that I not only reordered for my father, I added three more people to my list. This year, I once again received my Omaha Steaks' letter complete with every person's name, previous order, and delivery address filled out. All I had to do was say yes. I assure you that their efforts in maintaining a relationship with me cost them much less than sending out 100,000 direct mail catalogs to noncustomers. It is a fact that it costs less to maintain a customer than to acquire a new one.

When done correctly, database marketing can help you identify your best customers and develop relationships that keep them coming back for years.

73

What are your suggestions for database marketing?

Gwen Moran, Marketing Expert and Writer

Mention database marketing, and many entrepreneurs will shoot you a "been there, done that" look. In fact, even the newest business owners have likely taken a stab at sending a mailing or two, learning early on that some work, and some don't. However, advances in computer software, an increased understanding of relationship marketing and a shifting marketplace that demands more personalized attention have all combined to form an environment where database marketing deserves a new look on a more comprehensive level.

In a nutshell, database marketing is simply using the information in a database to more effectively reach out to your customers. Although it is sometimes used interchangeably with the term direct mail, database marketing is actually much more far-reaching. Just a few years ago, most in-house databases offered no more than random names and addresses. Now, off-the-shelf software packages costing about $200, such as ACT! 2000 (Symantec) and GoldMine 4.0 (GoldMine Software Corporation), make it easy to capture vast amounts of information about your customers and organize it so that it's effective for day-to-day use. Those data let you communicate to your customers through traditional methods such as mail, fax, and telephone. On a more sophisticated level, the information allows you to develop a "model" of your customer to more specifically target your advertising and marketing dollars, create interactive online services and promotions, predict trends, cross-sell, and build stronger relationships with clients and prospects.

Some level of database marketing is critical for all businesses from small retailers to large multi-national corporations. Maintaining a database allows you to say, "This is my customer." The secret of success, according to industry leaders, is the depth of information you are able to capture.

Depending on the size of your database, you can likely manage it in-house. Whether you use a contact management program such as ACT! or GoldMine, an off-the-shelf database software package such as Microsoft's Access (it costs about $300), or a custom-designed program, you'll need to decide what information will be useful to you. The most basic information for all entrepreneurs includes the company or person's name and address, contact name, phone, fax, and e-mail numbers. Other important information includes sales history, seasonal needs, and preferred products or services.

Entrepreneurs are wise to go a bit further in their fact-finding. For businesses that market to consumers, it's important to also capture information about the size of households, occupations, hobbies, favorite media, likes and dislikes, and lifestyle information. For business-to-business marketers, capture information about the size and industry of the customer, level at which buying decisions are made, and other specifics. This information allows you to understand who is buying your product or service and where to find them.

Gathering the data can be as simple as an on-site questionnaire, a form on your Web site, or having your sales or customer service staff collect information. If asking so many questions makes you uncomfortable, you can find much of this information, for a fee, through large information services companies like Experian Information Solutions (www.experian.com) or Harte Hanks (www.hartehanks.com). These companies warehouse huge national databases compiled from such varied information sources as warranty cards, online questionnaires, magazine subscriptions, telephone surveys, and public records. Often, you can provide a name and address, and these services will provide you with the person's interests, shopping habits, type of credit card, magazine subscriptions, and the like. Such information is usually priced on a cost-per-thousand basis, which can range from $50 to $200 or more, as the criteria get more specific.

As your database grows, it is important to limit access to it for several reasons. Having too many employees who don't fully understand the format of the database or the protocol of entering information could potentially damage the integrity of the data. In addition, a good database is an important company asset and should be treated as such. If an employee moves on to one of your competitors with a copy of your database, the consequences could be devastating. Similarly, if you contract with an outside database management or marketing company to manage your database, have your attorney add a confidentiality clause to the contract.

Once you've built your database, the process of analyzing the information that's in it is called "mining." Data mining is a process wherein businesses look for patterns within the data that they've collected. By capturing the right information, companies can provide the very personalized service that is becoming the standard today. Database marketing can actually serve as a sales force for smaller companies by finding the right customers to make an initial purchase and then by helping companies communicate to these customers when it's not possible to do it face-to-face.

There are some "miner" cautions, however. Your results will only be as good as the data going into your file. It's important to find the right people to manage the database—those who understand the reasons for the database as well as the complexities of maintaining it. Additionally, make sure that common sense is the main ingredient in developing your models. If you build a bad model, you can spend big bucks chasing the wrong customers.

All of the best data in the world won't help you unless you actively put your database to work for you. In addition to creating customer profiles and models, you can search your database for trends. Some of the off-the-shelf contact management programs have templates to assist you in predicting customer needs before they arise, that is, when customers are likely to reorder a product or need to stock up on a seasonal item.

As a result of several court rulings, it has become a common practice to gain your customers'permission before reaching out to them. Such "opt-in," or permission marketing, can increase your effectiveness dramatically. Opt-in marketing begins with asking customers about the products and services in which they are interested, then gaining their permission to send them more information. This way, they are more likely to respond to your follow-up messages.

Your subsequent outreach mechanisms may take many forms. In addition to mass mailings, which traditionally have low response levels, you can use your database for a variety of applications, including:

- Sending very specific e-mail notifications of new products, Web site updates, or special offers

- Mailing customized price or information sheets

- Conducting phone outreach based on reorder trends for your customers, reminding them to reorder products before they run out of inventory or to schedule a service appointment on time

- Using a simple questionnaire on your Web site to ensure that products or services of interest to a customer are brought to his or her attention each time that customer logs on to the site

- Capturing a sales history to examine what sales offers have been most successful and eliminating or changing those that have little result

- Assisting you and your salespeople in adding a personal touch to your outreach efforts like sending that A-list customer tickets to see her favorite sports team play

---

DATABASE MARKETING RESOURCES

- *Data Mining Techniques: For Marketing, Sales, and Customer Support* by Gordon S. Linoff and Michael J. A. Berry (John Wiley & Sons, 1997). $49.99. How to turn the information in your database into gold.

- *Permission Marketing: Turning Strangers into Friends, and Friends into Customers* by Seth Godin (Simon & Schuster, 1991). $24.00. The strategies of companies that practice permission marketing, including Amazon.com, American Airlines, Bell Atlantic, and American Express.

- The Direct Marketing Association, New York, NY. 212-768-7277. Offers a number of publications on direct mail, database marketing, and related topics (www.the-dma.org).

Database applications will become increasingly important as the Internet and electronic communication play larger roles in interfacing with customers. Start capturing this critical information now so that you're ahead of the competition and can maximize opportunities as they arise.

Online Marketing

The birth of the Internet was a marketer's dream come true. The Internet presents businesses with a way to interact with customers one-on-one in a real time environment and allows them to evaluate customer response to their marketing efforts almost immediately. In the past, a neighborhood bookstore might send out a postcard announcing a sale on a particular book and wait several days to see if sales increased. Today, a bookstore on the Internet can put up a "Sale" banner on its site and within hours determine if the value proposition is enough to get people to buy. Advancements in technology allow business owners to send out multiple messages to customers with similar needs. For instance, ClikVacations.com sends different travel deals to its customers based on vacation preferences. If you prefer warm weather travel, your ClikVacations.com e-mails will highlight destinations such as Mexico and the Carribbean. Ski buffs receive travel deals for Aspen and Vale. The capabilities of the Internet allow this site to test its pricing by offering different deals to various customers. Within minutes, they can determine if $100 off a trip to Las Vegas is more appealing than an offer of a free extra night at a hotel.

The challenge of the Internet is in getting customers to find you. By the year 2002, it is estimated that there will be more than three million pages on the Web. So how do your customers find your Web site? This is where a strong online marketing strategy becomes important, particularly if yours is a Web-based business. When I was launching BlueSuitMom.com, I went to Michael Egan, as I mentioned earlier. At the time, he was chairman of theglobe.com, a company that enjoyed the largest IPO of 1999 and was experiencing the Internet slump of April 2000. I went to him to ask for his insights about what it took to be successful with an Internet business. As the founder of Alamo Rent A Car, Nantucket Nectars, and other successful companies, he knows his business. His three-hour conversation with me was full of important lessons, but the one word that he repeated over and over again was "distribution." Distribution. He said it was the single most important thing to obtain on the Internet. I believe he is correct. The only way to build a brand online is to be in as many places and in front of your customers as much as possible. Fortunately, there are many tactical strategies that cost you more in time than money and will help you meet this goal. Search engines, content syndication, e-newsletters, banner exchanges, link swapping, and online community involvement are just a few of the marketing initiatives that will create distribution for your company.

74

What types of online marketing have you applied to your business?

DARCY VOLDEN MILLER, LITTLEDIDIKNOW.COM

We do mostly linking and have our own Little Did I Know banner-exchange program. The banner of each member of our group goes into a rotation on our site, and the moms follow the same rotation on their own sites. It's all about helping each other succeed. Search engine placement is also a big factor in traffic to our site and is perhaps even more successful than banners and links. It's a close call.

I would recommend hiring someone who knows the tricks of the trade to do search engine management. It is a very time-consuming task that has to be monitored almost daily. Every search engine has different standards by which they catalog sites, and they change them often. There are people at the search engines whose job it is to engineer your site and the code on each page in a way that is more attractive to the search engines. It's also critical to be listed on the first couple of pages of a search engine—otherwise, you'll be buried in a sea of a zillion other Web sites, and customers won't take the time to find you.

Without search engine traffic, you are left to rely on the links that you've scattered throughout the Web. The trick is to scatter your links anywhere and everywhere you can. In fact, some search engines even assign higher placements based on the number of links to the site. Since it makes you more attractive to the search engines, make it a habit to list your site in at least three places a day. A great place to find literally thousands of places to list your site is at www.the1000.com.

We make it very easy for our visitors to link to Little Did I Know if they desire. A lot of times people have their own home page or maybe even a business site, and they will want to put a link to your site, especially if it is interesting for their visitors. So, make it very easy for them to link to you. Have a special place where they can easily get to your buttons and banners, because those will stick out more than just a little text link.

We also have an opt-in e-mail list so that we can send our visitors updates, specials, and newsletters to increase repeat traffic and buying.

DEE ENNEN, ENNEN COMPUTER SERVICES

I manage boards on Bizymoms.com Web site and also on the Home-Based Working Moms Web site. I also host one-hour chats every week on Bizymoms.com. Managing the boards normally takes thirty to forty-five minutes, three times per week. I found these opportunities through my online correspondence when people sent me e-mails saying they were members of these groups. I researched them further and decided to become involved.

I have generated several new customers through the contacts I've made through communicating on Bizymoms.com. It also positions me as an expert in my field.

TAMMY HARRISON, THE QUEEN OF PIZZAZZ COMPANY

I started writing articles for HBWM.com after working with them for about six months. During that time, I learned the ropes of the business and networked with members and nonmembers. I took notes about the topics other home-based working moms wanted to hear about. In the beginning, I only published my articles on the HBWM.com Web site and in our e-newsletter. My exposure on HBWM.com produced interest from other sites, and soon others started asking permission to publish my articles. I try to write four articles a month on mothering and parenting, budgeting, working from home, and household humor, all areas I specialize in.

I receive the best responses from the HBWM.com e-newsletter and Gary Foreman's Dollar Stretcher eNewsletter (www.stretcher.com). Gary runs most of my budgeting articles.

LESLEY SPENCER, HBWM.COM

Our most successful online marketing initiative has been search engine listings. The highest amount of our traffic from any one source has come from Yahoo, about 13 percent. The next highest at 11 percent is from folks choosing our domain from word-of-mouth referrals, publicity, and bookmarks. I'd say that 40 to 50 percent of our traffic is from search engines.

We manually listed ourselves with the main search engines and used a service to submit our URL to several of the smaller ones.

Our e-newsletter enables us to keep in touch with persons who visit our site. We offer articles, tips, and information regarding parenting and working from home. A good newsletter should feature content relevant to the site, have value, and be fairly short. E-newsletters are offered so freely all over the Internet that you need to give customers a reason to subscribe and stay subscribed. We send out an e-newsletter on Mondays and Fridays. Our Monday edition focuses on home business success, while our Friday edition focuses on parenting and family success.

To encourage sign-ups, we have a registration box on our home page and subscriber information in the e-newsletter. We also put subscription information in the signature line of our e-mail.

KIT BENNETT, AMAZINGMOMS.COM

Our e-mail newsletter has been a great marketing tool. A successful e-mail newsletter goes beyond advertising and provides the reader with something useful. Amazingmoms' newsletter offers crafts, parenting tips, and recipe ideas. Our goal is to get readers to click through to our Web site, so we don't put the entire article in our newsletter. I suggest introducing your information with a luring sentence or two and then adding a link to "read more." Write for your site and your readers' interests. If yours is a sewing site, don't write articles showing how to replace bathroom tiles. Use a consistent format, and send your newsletter regularly. You want to create habits in your readers so that they learn to depend on the information you provide them. Also, create interaction with games and contests. People receive hundreds of e-mails each day, so you don't want to overwhelm them by sending your newsletter too often. Weekly seems to work well for Amazingmoms.

To get viewers to register for my e-newsletter, I apply different tactics. I promote a monthly prize drawing for new members, include sign-up notices within the first screen on my site, and I add my newsletter ad to my e-mail signature. Make it easy for people to subscribe to your newsletter by asking for a simple response via e-mail. Send them a welcome message as confirmation.

It is important to choose the right newsletter management system. I use a list management company that charges about $30.00 per month to send 5,000 newsletters. In the beginning, I attempted to manage the Amazingmoms' list in-house. However, I vastly underestimated the amount of work involved to handle the list efficiently with my own software. The small investment was worth it. I eliminate the hassle of trying to do it myself. Choose your list management company carefully from the beginning, and it will save you hours of work. Look for a company that can manage all subscriptions and unsubscribes, has the capability to gather demographics, allows the list owner to add several e-mails at one time, and has HTML format capabilities.

Search engine submissions are also an important part of our online marketing efforts. My husband does this job, using submission software. We have gone through a lot of trial and error with keywords and meta tags. It seems that sometimes the search engines love you, and sometimes they don't.

Linking to other sites is another way to attract visitors to your site. I do searches for sites within my target market that are not direct competitors. I take the time to get to know the site, find contact information, and get a name, if possible. I take notes about the site so that I personalize my correspondence. For example, if I'm at an education site, I might make note of a particular lesson plan I liked. After I've gathered 100 or so e-mail addresses of prospective partners, I send the following letter:

Hello, [Person's Name]

My name is Kit Bennett, editor and founder of Amazingmoms.com (www.amazingmoms.com). I just stumbled onto your site and wanted to thank you for providing an exceptional resource. I particularly liked the information you provided about [Subject]. I will be adding your site to our resource pages and hope it can improve your visibility. Please take the time to review Amazingmoms as well and consider returning the favor. If there is any other way I can be of help to you, please feel free to ask. Thank you again for your time and talent!

Kit Bennett

Although this takes time, it's worth the effort. I have found that all of my links have provided lasting relationships and improved my standings on the search engines. I do not recommend mass mailings. As the webmaster of Amazingmoms.com, I ignore most of the generic mailings but always respond to letters with a personal touch.

RACHAEL BENDER, BLUESUITMOM.COM

The options for online advertising are unlimited, and as a small business you'll get a lot more for your dollar if you focus on the opportunities that require time but not a lot of cash. You can stretch your online marketing dollars through reciprocal links and advertising swaps, search engines, newsletters, articles appearing on other Web sites, joining a banner exchange, posting on message boards, and using ideas like "Refer this page to a friend." Here are the methods that have worked best for BlueSuitMom:

- **Newsletters:** The most effective way we've found to get people to come back to our site is through our weekly newsletters. Within twenty-four hours of sending out a newsletter, we typically see a 30 to 40 percent spike in traffic, especially to the items mentioned in the newsletter. What makes our newsletters so successful? Every issue delivers useful information about topics important to working mothers, and we never include information that isn't pertinent to our readers. I would rather send out a newsletter with two good items than waste the time of our readers with filler. It's great content that makes a newsletter successful. Whether you are selling seminars, candy, or jewelry, what will set you apart is the valuable advice you include along with your sales information. In a newsletter for a baby products online store, for instance, we might give advice about caring for your newborn, with clues on how to know when your infant is sick. Along the way, we'll recommend a good thermometer you might need. Or, if we were giving advice on how to lose weight after pregnancy, we might recommend a jogging stroller. Even if the person isn't interested at the moment in buying a thermometer or stroller, she will still read our newsletter for the valuable information it contains. This approach reinforces our brand, and the next time that subscriber is looking for a childcare product, BabyUniverse will be the first company she thinks of.

Another bonus of newsletters is that your readers are people who have already been to your Web site and are interested in your product. They are a pre-qualified group of people for your advertising message.

We've also been fairly successful at attracting new users by advertising in other people's newsletters. This can be very cost effective, because advertising rates range anywhere from $50 to $500 an issue, depending on the number of subscribers. When looking for newsletters to advertise in, remember to focus on the ones that hit your demographics. If you know most of your customers are new mothers, it will not be effective to advertise in a newsletter that has a 60 percent male audience. Before buying any advertising in any newsletter, I suggest subscribing to a couple of issues to determine if the tone of the newsletter fits your advertising message.

- **Articles appearing on other sites:** Most Web sites are constantly looking for quality content. If you have a lot of knowledge in a particular field, you should consider writing articles or columns for other Web sites. Ask the site to place a short blurb about your site or product and a link to your Web site at the end of the article. If you run a PR company, you can do this to get your press release How-Tos listed on small-business Web sites, or if you own a candlemaking business you can list your gift suggestions on sites geared toward women.

- **Reciprocal links and advertising swaps:** Developing a network of other small businesses who are willing to add a link from their Web sites to yours and vice versa is a great way to get free advertising and develop relationships with other entrepreneurs. Perhaps you can swap advertising space in your newsletters or put banner ads on strategic places on your Web sites. If you run a mail order gift cake company, you could add links from your order confirmation page to a florist. The florist then adds a link from their confirmation page. You can find companies to exchange links with by finding out where your competitor is getting links. Just type in link:url in a search engine to find all the pages linking to that Web site. Example: link:bluesuitmom.com.

- **Refer this page to a friend:** If you have a great product or Web site, people will want to share it with others. By adding a "Send this page to a friend" feature you make it easier for them to do so. You can either use a free version hosted by another Web site like www.recommend-it.com, or create your own cgi script. Add the "Send this page to a friend" feature to every page on your site.

- **Search engines:** Search engines are one of the greatest sources of Web traffic. The trick is to get your site listed near the top. There are many methods to do this. For more information about search engine positioning, check out the Web site, www.searchenginewatch.com, and and also look at articles about search engines at ClickZ (clickz.com/column/seo.html).

CHAPTER THIRTEEN

Managing Growth

W hether you are reading this book because you are contemplating launching a business or you are already a home-based business owner hoping to get a few tips, you are probably wondering why we need to talk about managing growth. Many business owners will tell you that the most surprising reality about launching a business is how quickly it can grow. When you find yourself on the brink of great growth, stop and give yourself a pat on the back. Your hard work and personal spirit have made your dream come true. Although there are people who find themselves in the right place at the right time with the right product with businesses that grow overnight, they are rare. Most business owners must see their companies through growing pains.

Being prepared for the rapid growth of your business is extremely important to maintaining customers, as well as your sanity. One would think that once your company is up and running you can sit back and enjoy all the benefits of being self-employed. Not so. The challenges of managing growth can be more difficult than obtaining your first clients.

The day will come when you must decide whether to grow your business or maintain it at its present level. Two elements of growth demand a business owner's attention. The first is managing the daily operational issues of your company. When your company grows, so do all the moving parts that make it up. If you are making more money, chances are you require a greater number of invoices and accounts payable functions. More income also means you probably have more clients to maintain, which means more phone messages to answer and more e-mails that need responses. Everything grows proportionally in a business.

As your business grows, revisit the topic of time management as it pertains to how you are spending your day. Are you spending more time doing administrative work than servicing customers? Is this the best use of your day? Are you working on things that put money in your pocket? As you experience growth, it might be wise to outsource some of your work. There are always talented individuals or small-business firms looking for project work. It's important to find the right chemistry with whomever you hire to help you manage your tasks. An independent contractor or professional firm allows you to avoid the liabilities of a full-time employee but means you lose the control you would have over an employee.

The second and perhaps greater challenge in managing your company's growth is the question whether to grow the company or not. As a neophyte business owner, your mantra may be "Grow the Business," but, as the old saying goes, "Be careful what you wish for." Growth is what most business owners hope for, but few take the time to figure out what to do when they reach their goal. What happens when you have more clients than you can service? How do you produce more product if it's only you running the machines? A sole proprietor is just one person, and there are only twenty-four hours in the day. To grow your company more often than not means hiring help, which means delegating. Ironically, delegation sometimes isn't easy for a self-motivating, energetic business owner. For many of us, it's hard to imagine anyone else can do as good a job as we do. Our company becomes our baby, as we said in the first chapter. Now, in this last chapter, we must learn how to let go, just as with a child. It's not an easy decision but one we choose for the good of the child or, in our case, the company.

Another dimension to growing the company is the personal side. The struggle to balance work and family becomes more intense and may require a switch in priorities. As a mother and wife, you elected a home-based business for increased freedom. It can be frustrating to know that growing your business may mean abandoning the very reasons you started your company. It is also difficult to impose limits on the company you've worked so hard to grow because of home commitments. You will have to sacrifice something. You must make a challenging decision. Most business owners agree it is healthy to reassess personal goals and priorities regularly, just as you consult your business plan periodically to make sure you are on target to meet your goals. Whether or not to grow your business may depend on your family situation.

75

How do you manage your company's growth?

DIANE BALLARD, DKB ASSOCIATES

My goal in launching my business was to earn twice as much as I did when I was with the Environmental Protection Agency. I am pretty much there right now. I managed my business from the beginning to reach this goal, and now I cannot expand unless I hire employees. In order to grow my company, I will have to decide whether or not to bring in a partner. I need to determine if acquiring a partner will increase my earnings.

At present, I spend very little time looking for new clients. Most of my business is repeat customers or those who come by word of mouth. My short-term goal in managing my client base is to develop a good group of clients who are easy to service and pay well. I am in a holding pattern right now.

REBECCA HART, PUBLIC RELATIONS

It's difficult to figure out what one person can and can't do and whether to hire staff or let opportunities go. Sometimes I miss the challenge of running a yearlong national product launch or something else consuming and visible like that. It's a challenge because I know that I'm good at it, and the skills I have are in high demand. But some projects simply require more resources than I'm willing to commit right now.

I've made a conscious decision to put my family first and let my career revolve around them. It's funny to me that people ask me for mothering/balancing advice, because so many days I feel like a duck that's got it all together on top of the water but is swimming like crazy underneath the surface. I was once your typical workaholic, working until 10:00 or 11:00 o'clock at night, no life outside the office, etc. I'd like to say I had an epiphany, but easing off was really forced on me by my doctor when I was pregnant the first time. I had to start realizing that work has its place and isn't the end-all I thought it was. Sure, I had thought about how to balance my life, but I would probably have kept procrastinating without the constant threat of bed rest if I didn't slow down.

Despite all this, my inclination is to grow, grow, and grow. If I had taken all the business I've been approached about, I would have hired ten people and had a viable agency. There are even days I wish I had stayed in Chicago in my corner office in the Amoco Building, working on national clients that are everyday names, the whole deal. I have to remind myself that I'm just not in that season of life anymore. I finally decided that I didn't want my kids to have just my left-over time, and that's when I took action.

I don't think mothering and a professional career are mutually exclusive. In both environments, you reap what you sow in terms of positive relationships, camaraderie, and interesting experiences along the way. Both roles are demanding and difficult, and they'll both stretch you in ways you never imagined possible.

Managing your business to your priorities takes a great deal of planning and soul-searching. I remember five or six years ago, long before I had kids, thinking, "What could I do that would allow me to work on my own someday?" It was just a fantasy until I was pregnant the first time and had to make some hard choices.

Not that she's any kind of role model for me, but I think it was Ivana Trump who said, "You can have it all. Just not all in the same day." That sums it up for me. I take it very seriously that I'm raising a future husband and father—it's just as important a role as any other and can't be discounted.

DEBBIE WILLIAMS, LET'S GET IT TOGETHER

I think a growing business goes through numerous transitions. When I launched, I was a consulting business, but last summer I made the decision to expand. Now my consulting business includes an online training facility for professional organizers. I'm in the transition stage of contracting help to fill orders from my site. I will most likely use a virtual assistant for these tasks. The next step will be to acquire a webmaster to run both of my sites for me. Acquiring help will free me to work on marketing and networking, which is extremely important for my customer-oriented business.

I recognize that growth will eventually catch up with me again, particularly if I expand into selling more products. My plan then includes enlisting volunteers to help me manage my e-zine publication and additional virtual assistants to fill orders.

DARCY LYONS, A GARDEN PARTY

We allowed our company to grow naturally from the two parties we held with our friends and families. However, it was difficult trying to grow the company with no other party hostesses, especially for our husbands, who came home from tough days at work and had to manage the households. I tried to repay my husband on the weekend with lots of golf time and dinner with the boys every now and then. Managing growth for us means acquiring not only customers but party hostesses and consultants as well. We include information on how to become a consultant in all our printed materials and on our Web site. Presently, we have consultants in six states with possible candidates in ten others.

Inventory management is another growth issue. We recognize that someday we will need a warehouse for storing inventory. At that point, we will begin hiring people to do receiving and shipping of merchandise. Terry's living room can't be our merchandising center forever!

Kit Bennett, Amazingmoms.com

Luckily, Amazingmoms grew slowly at first. I was able to stumble and learn along the way. When my business started to speed up, I drank more coffee, got less sleep, and screamed! Seriously, I created a more structured schedule for my work to create a balance and avoid becoming a workaholic. I started having dreams that my computer was running programs as if it were a living being. Freaky!

I get help for free or through trade and have developed some wonderful relationships this way.

The biggest limitation I've experienced is financial, which should come as no surprise. I think I did not dream big enough when I made my business plan. Like many women, I undervalued my worth and possibly never thought my talent would interest investors. Shame on me! I could have avoided the self-funding road and started out with the team of qualified women that I needed.

Amazingmoms has been the steepest learning curve I have ever climbed. I'm still climbing and I won't ever give up. I hope my story provides inspiration to other moms ready for the journey.

Beth Besner, Table Topper

The hardest element of managing the growth of my company was bringing in employees to help me with the work so that I can continue to grow. Once you add employees, your job gets significantly harder because other people are now counting on you. You have to learn to handle payroll and have to become an effective manager. You have to come up with employee benefits, you have to develop a corporate culture and philosophy, and you have to find a suitable location to work where the rent is reasonable. I had an employee in my home for two years and found it intolerable. I had to work every day she was here, and I couldn't be efficient because she was in my workspace. Another problem that you encounter with hiring employees is deciding what roles you need filled and then finding someone who can wear many hats. Your first employee is the hardest to find, because they need to do many things and do them well enough so you can rely on them.

The only thing I would do differently is to find a partner early on to share the burdens, work, and success with. It's a little lonely when you are doing so much of the work on your own. Women can support and encourage one another and share success better than many men. Women understand that you want to share the work in order to be available to your children.

TAMMY HARRISON, THE QUEEN OF PIZZAZZ COMPANY

When my business started taking off, I was spending more and more time in the office on the weekends, which is taboo around my home. My husband and I sat down for a heart-to-heart discussion about what I wanted from the business, what I wanted for our family, what he wanted for our family, and what we were both willing to do to make all things possible. I firmly believe I am home to raise my children, nothing else. The work is additional income, additional learning, knowledge, and additional fun.

Once we both knew where we stood and what we wanted for our family, I was able to put together a work schedule. The schedule was flexible enough that I could participate in school activities, take time off just to play with the kids, and do the usual "mom" things like grocery shopping and errands so I wouldn't have to spend our family weekend time running all over town.

I choose clients and projects based on the learning curve they offer me. I have no trouble controlling the growth of my business. By being choosy, I keep my services exclusive and have time to focus on each and every client and account to give them the best that I can.

Turning Away Customers

Part of managing the growth of your business may require you to turn away customers, either because you cannot service their needs or they do not meet your business goals. As contrary as it sounds, it's okay to turn away customers at times. However, it's important to do so without burning any bridges. A particular customer may not fit your needs right now, but she may have a friend who does. Time also has a way of changing things, and you never know when you might welcome that customer back. As with anything in life, there is a right way and a wrong way of handling a situation. Be honest when turning away business. If you simply cannot take on any new clients because of time restraints, explain to your customers that a service provider who can give them more attention could better serve them. Explain that, although you would like to accept their work, you do not want to give them less than 100 percent, and your time is committed to other customers at the present time. Most people will admire your honesty. You might provide them with the name of someone to do their work. Make sure it's someone you trust and inform them that you have passed along a client. It's a good way to create a network of referrals and still serve the needs of customers you turn away.

There will also be times when you just don't want to accept a client for personal reasons. Maybe the chemistry between you is wrong. That's okay, too. Here, too, honesty is the best policy. You don't need to explain your dislike of his father's second cousin, but you can say that you don't feel comfortable with creating a professional relationship at this time. We all have some people we choose to limit our relationships with. My parents' next-door neighbor was a well-known gynecologist. All my friends adored him, but I chose not to go to him when I returned from college. I just didn't want to have a professional relationship with our friendly next-door neighbor. I think this illustrates the point that it's not uncommon to choose to limit one's relationships with certain people.

76

Have you ever turned away customers?

MOLLY GOLD, GO MOM !NC

We haven't turned away customers, but we have had to avoid retail relationships in our start-up phase due to limited funding. We learned quickly that selling our planner through gift shops and bookstores was very costly to the bottom line, because of the profit margin retailers require. Our financial resources also restrict our ability to produce the quantities we need to sell wholesale. To overcome this, we focus on direct sales through our Web site. The Web is currently the most profitable and efficient way for us to conduct business.

DEBBIE GIOQUINDO, PERSONAL TOUCH TRAVEL

I've turned away customers who refuse to listen to my advice as a travel expert when I am giving them good information. I once had a customer who insisted he could drive from point A to point B in one day when the trip actually takes three days. Sometimes there comes a point when the customer is not worth the time and aggravation. Even when you'd like to try to satisfy certain customers, you have to realize that, ultimately, they will never be satisfied.

JEANNINE CLONTZ, ACCURATE BUSINESS SERVICES

I've turned away customers more than once. When a prospective client asks for a bid and then comes back to tell me the provider down the street can do it for less, I politely tell them what they can expect from decreased service. I express my best and hope that things work out for them. On more than one occasion, the person has called me back weeks later and hired me. In the end, they not only paid my price but also paid 25 percent more, because now it was a rush job! I also had a client ask me to do something that wasn't really my forte, so I referred him to someone who could help him. It's not always about making a buck. I have to consider that the work I do for clients has a direct impact on the way I am perceived by other business people.

JULIE AIGNER-CLARK, BABY EINSTEIN

When I launched our product, I spent the first two years establishing the brand with The Right Start stores as an exclusive retailer of my products. It was a good move, because they helped grow the brand and gave both videos great visibility in the stores and in the catalog. I turned away many other chains those first two years, then took on specialty markets the third year. Sales were so tremendous that I turned away two major mass retailers. This year, we began selling into the mass channels with great success. It was all about building the brand and creating awareness.

Diane DeSa, A Virtual Assistant

I have only turned away one customer, an inquiry that came through the AssistU Registry. I turned him down because the majority of his work required use of software that I did not know. It would not be fair of me to charge him for my learning curve on a piece of software that I did not feel comfortable working with.

Becca Williams, WallNutz, Inc.

The only customers I've turned away are ones that have requested special design services without being willing to pay more than the price for a volume product. I try to offer these people suggestions for other ways to accomplish their projects so that they feel there has been some value provided to them.

Alex Powe Allred, Author and Gold Medalist

I actually turned down two book assignments this year and never thought that would happen. Man, I would have written a book on belly-button fuzz if someone had asked me when I started my business. Now, I am actually selecting my work and having a blast.

Exiting Your Business

Although planning for the sale of your company may seem lightyears away, it's important to consider it from the start. It's hard to believe today when you have so much passion for your business idea that the day will come when you want to sell it or close the doors. If you just want to close up shop, then you don't have as many things to consider at the onset of your company. For those of us who want to build a business that will allow us to retire one day, setting the groundwork for its sale should be a priority.

As we discussed earlier, a good business plan will contain an exit strategy. This gives you a clear goal as well as a benchmark to apply to your day-to-day marketing and operational initiatives. I advise you to look quarterly at the direction your company is going and determine if you are on course to achieve your ultimate objective.

There is no best exit strategy for a home-based business. It is all based on the individual business owner's reasons for starting the business in the first place. It's okay to say that you intend to run your company until your children enter grade school, at which point you plan to close the doors. It's equally acceptable to admit that you want to build your brand recognition to the point that a large corporation will want to integrate it into their operations. It's even okay to express a desire to make a million dollars by selling your company to your biggest competitor. As a business owner, you must apply your good judgment to your company. Just as your business plan is a dynamic, ever-changing document, so is your exit strategy. Opportunities that you are presently not even aware of may surface at any time. When we launched BlueSuitMom.com, I had two targets on my list as far as possible companies who might want to eventually buy us. Both were women's publications that I felt we could be folded into easily and that we would fill a niche for. In the end, it was Certified Vacations, a travel company, who, fortunately for us, saw the appeal of our market. I never would have anticipated being acquired by a travel company until I later learned that the same women BlueSuitMom.com attracts buy most of the travel sold today. My message to you is: Set a goal, but know that it may change along the way.

I recommend that when you get to the point of selling your company, you do additional research and consult a professional about executing the sale. My focus here is to help you prepare your company for acquisition and touch on a few of the processes involved, in hopes that magical opportunity springs up sooner than you expect.

The first step in preparing your company for a buyer requires some soul-searching that can be done while writing your business plan. Consider what you want out of selling your company for yourself, your employees, and your brand. Determining this will allow you to target the people you want to become familiar with your business. If you simply want to build the company and get out with a lot of money, then a strategic buyer is someone you want to attract. Strategic buyers are looking for companies that have commonalities with their own goals and operations.

There are also financial buyers, who are in the business of making deals. They look for companies making money and in most cases want to maintain the daily operations of the company to protect the cash flow. This buyer relieves you of the fiduciary responsibility of the business but requires you to continue your management role. This can become a problem. You need to consider the personal challenges created when you go from being the boss to having a boss. I read somewhere recently that the average time that entrepreneurs stay with their companies after they are acquired by financial buyers is six months.

Regardless of the type of buyer you plan to lure to your business, it is helpful to know what other companies are looking for in buying another business. Elements they look for are:

- **Synergies:** Your company serves a common market with theirs, shares operational issues that can be consolidated, or presents efficiencies that can be leveraged to improve their performance or market penetration.

- **Positive Cash Flow:** Your company offers a lucrative new revenue stream to complement their existing business model.

- **Niche:** Your company fills a niche in their business model or gives them access to a niche market within their customer base.

- **Existing Business:** Your company is a business they like, and it's cheaper to buy it than build it themselves.

- **Marketing Tool:** Your company provides a marketing vehicle that can support their product or business.

Knowing what the buyer needs helps you to determine what you have to offer. What assets does your company have? Start by looking at tangible property such as computers, machinery, and inventory. Next, consider your contracts and sales agreements and the potential value they present to the bottom line of the buying company. Finally, consider the goodwill of your customers. A loyal customer base represents future revenue for the buyer's company, particularly if they can increase your customers' spending by offering them additional products.

Let's pretend you own a baby blanket company with a large database of customers who are loyal to your brand. Along comes the Totally Toddler company that manufacturers everything else parents need for toddlers. To Totally Toddler, your customers are a readymade group for their products, and they don't have to spend money on advertising. Best of all, your customers have demonstrated a loyalty to your brand. Suppose each of your customers spends $10 a year on your products. By introducing them to their products, Totally Toddler could get them to spend an additional $15 a year on new products. That's a lot of value for Totally Toddler. By purchasing your company, they not only acquire a business that is making money but also a loyal group of customers with proven spending patterns.

Identify your group of potential buyers early on. Your list might include competitors, companies outside your industry, corporations with a niche to fill, or individuals with means who desire to acquire your company. Take the initiative and make them aware of your company as you begin to grow. When we launched BlueSuitMom.com, I actually sent press kits to everyone on my list, even our direct competitors. Some people questioned this strategy. Why would I want our competitors to know what we were doing? My answer was, I want to make sure they know who we are! I figured they would read about us in the press, and it was all public information anyway. Some press kits included a short handwritten note of introduction and always ended "If there is anything we can ever do together, please let me know. I am willing to work with your company."

I remember Steve Berrard, a former mentor, once told me there is no such thing as competitors in business; there are only players in the marketplace. He's right: You have to be willing to work with other players in the marketplace, especially if you'd like them to acquire your company. There is no better way to prove your value than to demonstrate it through a strategic partnership. If you provide enough value, the day will come when other companies will want to bring your company inside their organization. Establishing relationships as you build your business will help you execute your exit strategy when the time is right.

Should you be required to sell your company before you've nurtured the appropriate contacts, there are businesses that facilitate the sale of companies. Online, there are sites such as www.businessforsale.com that lists companies that are on the market. You can also list your business in other places where buyers are looking, such as the Business Opportunities section of the classifieds, local business organizations, Chamber of Commerce newsletters, or with business brokers. You can also consult with accountants and lawyers who specialize in the sale and purchase of companies. Often, buyers looking for acquisitions contact them.

What are your thoughts on exit strategy?

BETH BESNER, TABLE TOPPER

It is hard to say what a good exit strategy is except to build value in your business by developing a good reputation for customer service, shipping, goodwill, and selling the heck out of your product. I think that the best strategy is to meet people in your industry at places like trade shows and keep an eye on companies that would be a good "home" for your business or product. Focus in on companies that are small enough to need the boost that would come from purchasing your company but large enough to successfully grow it. Generally speaking, the best buyer for a business is a strategic buyer—someone who will save time and resources by buying your company. Also, I think it's important to create added value to your company by acquiring patents, trademarks, a Web site with loads of traffic, and lots of good accounts in major retailers.

SHERRY MAYSONAVE, EMPOWERMENT ENTERPRISES

Often, a single business owner is "the business." When this is the case, particularly if that person is the acknowledged expert in a field, the attraction of the company to a potential buyer may not be as great. To overcome this, you must create other value. In my situation, by training and certifying other communication-image consultants, I am opening up a variety of opportunities. I have individuals who operate under Empowerment Enterprises and use my training materials to work with individual clients and corporations. This creates value and revenues that are independent of me. Empowerment Enterprises thus becomes larger than Sherry Maysonave as a consulting company with inherent value. My future plans include licensing training materials directly to corporations and creating training videos.

JULIE AIGNER-CLARK, BABY EINSTEIN

My exit strategy has been in place for quite some time. I plan on selling the company in the next few years to the right larger corporation. I define that corporation as one that really understands how to grow and manage this amazing brand. We have several huge companies that have indicated a strong desire to acquire us. They all seem like good candidates. Although the company is my "baby," I realize that I have two real babies at home. They are far more important to me than my business success. Bill, my husband, and I sat down and discussed at what point the money would be enough so that we wouldn't later look back and say, "I wish we'd held on for more money." It's that time. We're coming off a hugely successful year of $11.6 million in sales, and our selling price is really high—way more than I ever thought I'd see in my life!

I think you just have to know when enough is enough. I have my health, a wonderful husband, and two amazing little girls. I don't want to spend the rest of my life working for more money than I'd ever have time to spend. We've spent the past few years cultivating relationships with potential buyers. Today, we have great relationships with several companies that are interested in buying us should Artisan, our current partner, not exercise their option to do so. Everyone is just waiting to see what Artisan will do. Should they not "pay up," we'll go with the highest bidder!

AMILYA ANTONETTI, SOAPWORKS

I have sold several companies in the past. Some I sold at a profit and others at a loss. Including an exit strategy within your business plan is very important. From day one, SOAPWORKS was built to fit with a local competitor. I think that laying the groundwork for your exit should be part of building the business. I always build my models with my eye on my competition. I have a future buyer in mind along with my own visions. What would be important and valuable to them?

For me, the right time to get out is when it isn't fun and fulfilling anymore. I bring passion and vision to a company, and when that is no longer there for whatever reason, then it is time to move on.

My accountants and my attorney have always been a huge part of the building, running, and selling of my businesses. You need these members of your team to be strong and trustworthy.

In conducting the transaction, I have become stronger at speaking for myself and more confident of my worth and value. In the beginning, I left most of this in my lawyers' hands. Now, we discuss ahead of time what the goal for each meeting is and who will lead the meeting. Keeping control in your corner is key.

Exit Advice

Just as my business plan had an exit strategy so does my outline for this book. I consider my exit strategy for *The Women's Home-Based Business Book of Answers* to be as important as the exit strategy for BlueSuitMom.com. My exit goal is to deliver to you the most value for the money and time you spent on this book. In contemplating that, I realized that passing on the hindsights, insights, and lessons learned by my veteran home-based business owners is the most valuable asset I have to offer. Wow! If I only had the same 20/20 vision when I launched my company, I know I could have saved myself many costly mistakes and a whole bunch of time along the way. Although I can't give you access to a crystal ball and the power to look into your business future, I can relay some final words of wisdom from our experienced entrepreneurs.

78

What last words of wisdom or advice do you have for our readers?

KIT BENNETT, AMAZINGMOMS.COM

If you are holding this book in your hands, you are already considering self-employment and possibly a home-based office. You dream of an income not contingent on petty office politics and mandatory meetings, and, above all, freedom. I believe in this dream as well. Self-employed women are strong and willful and are quickly becoming the backbone of American business.

Do not make this decision lightly or treat it as a whim. Self-employment is not for everyone. Yet the rewards are numerous. If you need a day off, you can take one. When your little one becomes ill, you can be there. If money is tight, you can work harder to give yourself a raise. The flip side to these benefits could range from long odd hours, small inconsistent salaries, and in my case, an office space where I type to the thump-thump of my clothes dryer. Think of some worse-case scenarios and ask yourself, "Will I still be happy?" My answer is undeniably *"Yes!"* I love my work. I believe in my purpose and feel very fulfilled.

As you think about it, I recommend asking yourself these questions:

Do I enjoy the business I'm thinking of creating?

Has this business been done before? Could I do it as good or better, and how can I make it my own?

Do I work better alone or with a group? If your answer is alone, get enough funding to hire consultants. If a group is your thing, hire one or two people.

Are there aspects of my business that I don't know? Get help and learn the necessary skills. I hate to do my financials but know how to do them if necessary. Remember, the proverbial "buck" will stop at your door.

My motto is "Be bold. Ask for help. Make mistakes and learn from them. Forgive yourself and others and then move on."

LESLEY SPENCER, HBWM.COM

Don't let your business become more important than your family. Strive for balance and remind yourself often what you want in life. If it's more time with your family, don't let your ambition interfere with their needs and your time together. Success is different for everyone. You decide what success is for you and set your priorities and goals accordingly.

A home business can consume you. The thought of success or making a ton of money can cause us to forget what's really important. In five years, will you be most proud that you made a certain amount of money or that you enjoyed your children while they were young? Will you think back to all the rushing around and quick meals and wish you'd spent more time enjoying life? Will you have spent time together with your spouse building a strong marriage? We know good marriages don't just happen. They take work just like everything else. Will your family life be healthy, or will everything be on the back burner while you make millions and become "successful?"

My husband believes a person is truly successful when he or she is happy. I think he is right. Some of the most "successful" people who are rich and famous are not truly happy. Happiness is about being content with what we have. I find I must often take a look at my life and how I'm living. It is so easy to let our businesses consume us. I need to remind myself why I choose to work at home and make sure my priorities are straight.

Don't put your happiness and your family on the back burner. Family time together is too precious to waste.

GWEN MORAN, MARKETING EXPERT AND WRITER

There are six things that I wish someone had told me before I started my business:

1. **You don't have to know everything.** When I started my business, I was twenty-six. I felt like my age was a barrier to getting bigger clients, so I acted as if I had all the answers in order to prove myself. A few years later, I went to a conference where business owners twenty years my senior were talking about issues that I was facing. Epiphany! I wasn't alone. Had I learned to start asking questions sooner, I would have saved myself a lot of anxiety and needless effort.

2. **It may not be funny now, but someday it will be.** As controlling as we often need to be as small-business owners, there is a certain amount of "letting go" that is necessary. When bad things happen—and they will—you need to take a deep breath and solve the problem as best you can. Then, once you've done your best and taken the lessons you need from the situation, you have to let go of it. Haunting yourself with second-guessing and hindsight only serves to weaken your effectiveness. Some of my funniest stories today were absolutely horrific when they were happening.

3. **Remember that you have the right to walk away.** Whether it's a client from hell or an unreasonable employee, you don't have to stand for it. When you work for someone else, you have to work under the conditions they provide or else leave the job. When you work for yourself, you set the boundaries. It's easy to forget you're the boss. When a relationship stops being beneficial, you can choose to discontinue it.

4. **Your business is not your life.** As business owners, we confuse our lives with our businesses. Wrong. We wrap our identities up in our businesses. Wrong. You are a unique and important person in your own right. Your business is what you do to make money or serve some other need. If it struggles from time to time that is not a reflection on you

or your ability. Don't sacrifice your life—your health, your family, your friends, your peace of mind—to your business. It doesn't deserve it!

5. **Be professional.** One of my pet peeves is people who are in home-based businesses who don't present a professional image. I think this is a make-or-break issue for these businesses. I actually worked with a woman who let her five-year-old answer her business line. It was so unprofessional that I had to wonder if she really was serious about her business. Finally, I stopped using her service.

6. **Be sure that you have at least the basics of technology.** Fork over the extra $10 a month for a dedicated fax or modem line. It's inexcusable that a client needs to call you before he or she can send you a fax. Also, in this day and age, there's no excuse for a busy signal, so sign up for one of those answer-call services from the phone company. You need e-mail. You need to have an overnight courier account. You probably need a mobile phone, copier, and other office equipment. If you don't invest in the proper technology to service your clients, they will go elsewhere.

JEANNINE CLONTZ, ACCURATE BUSINESS SERVICES

My final words of wisdom? Be sure that this is what you want to do, and be serious about your business. I run across many people who think that because they can type, they can run a business support service. It's much harder than that. It's also not something that's going to make you rich overnight. However, if you're looking for something rewarding that will make you feel good about yourself and your talents, your business can do that. I must admit my business has mostly brought me joy, and I consider myself very fortunate. I certainly wish I had thought to do it years ago. It is very rewarding. I hope you will find it rewarding, too!

KAITLAND THORSTENSON, CERTIFIED PUBLIC ACCOUNTANT

If you want it enough, then you have to be willing to work, to pursue, to research, to learn, to persevere, and to utilize all those wonderful strengths that you have as a woman. Most of all, have faith in The Power, regardless of your belief system, that controls our lives. Then have faith in yourself. The greatest strength we have as women is our belief that we are equal to and almost always better than what we think we are. No matter what, do not let another person's criticism stop you from your goals. Those who second-guess you are not your friends. They may be jealous of your strength and wish to bring you down to their level. When I made the choice to become my own woman and change my lifestyle radically, I found a total lack of support from friends, family, and coworkers who all had come to depend on me to be there 24/7 for them. In being strong enough to go my own way, I have become an even more successful and rewarded woman. I now have their respect and their acceptance, even their encouragement to become even more.

Linda McWilliams, OnceUponAName.com

Be persistent! I have seen many businesses on the Internet come and go. They went under probably because they didn't have the right support, encouragement, and drive. Surround yourself with people who will support your business ideas and efforts, not put them down. It's a strange thing, but sometimes the people you rely on for support are the ones who try to make you feel you are wasting your time or trying the impossible! Distance yourself from their negative attitudes and move on. Be persistent, and you will succeed! No one is an overnight success. It takes time and a lot of hard work. If you think anything else, you won't make it.

Robin Zell, Bragelets

My final advice is: Do your homework to launch a business, and then double it. And don't think that working at home will give you abundant free time with your kids. Quite the opposite. Just remember, you will get back what you put in. I often spend time feeling bad because I am torn between working more and spending more time with my children. Unfortunately, this guilt doesn't leave you.

Jorj Morgan, Cookbook Author

My final words of advice are to make sure you love what you do. The more personal fulfillment and happiness your hard work yields, the more pleasure you bring to your family and friends. Make sure that each workday is a blessing, not drudgery. View success as it is measured in your heart. The monetary rewards will follow close behind.

PRISCILLA HUFF, AUTHOR

Wisdom? I do not know how much wisdom I have, but here are some thoughts:

1. Make sure you have some sort of business plan—either in your head or on paper—and use it as a weekly guideline from which you plan your daily and future goals.

2. Market yourself and your business (after all, you "are" the business) on a daily basis. This is the fun part, seeking out new and creative ways to get the word out, as well as noting the marketing techniques that work best for you.

3. Network daily with others in business. I try to help pass a lead to at least two other entrepreneurs each day. It really does reap many rewards. Give back, too, to your community on behalf of your business. It is good PR for your company, and you will be a role model for young people.

4. Care about your customers. Always give them a little more than they expect. Be honest and always treat them with the respect you demand for yourself. Look for ways to attract new customers, so your business will continue to grow.

5. Finally: Enjoy the entrepreneurial ride! Owning a home business has more ups and downs than the wildest roller coaster and is just as exciting! If you can survive the downs as well as the ups, you will have a sense of accomplishment that few nine-to-five jobs can ever give you. And no one can take those experiences from you!

SHERRY MAYSONAVE, EMPOWERMENT ENTERPRISES

I have nine short thoughts as my final words of advice.

1. Expect everything to be harder than planned for.

2. Expect everything to take longer than you planned for.

3. Focus—don't try to do too much.

4. Promise a lot to your clients, and deliver more. In today's world, people are used to being promised a lot and receiving less. Your customers will become your best sales team if you exceed their expectations.

5. Be prepared for your business to cost more than you expect.

6. Every person you hire is critical, especially in the beginning. Make certain your philosophies, standards, goals, and vision are a match. Hire the best people you can.

7. Plan time to have fun.

8. Be intellectually honest with yourself. If something is not working, admit it and change.

9. Don't get "analysis paralysis." Make decisions quickly.

BETH BESNER, TABLE TOPPER

The best advice I have is to carefully set out your goals in a business plan and stick with it. I never did that despite reading in all of the books that I should, and I wish I had. I find myself floundering at times because I never set an oar in the water but was willing to go with the wind: possibly to license the product, possibly to sell the business, all the while moving ahead to sell my product like gangbusters. I think if I had thought it out completely, I wouldn't struggle every few months about how to move forward or what to do next. The other thing my husband reminds me of every day is to stay focused. Sometimes it is easy to get carried away about things and go off into different directions because we are so enthusiastic. Know your limits. It's better to do one thing very well than a few things poorly.

NANCY CLEARY, WYATT-MCKENZIE PUBLISHING

My final thoughts are simple: Demonstrate patience, have faith, and believe in what you are doing. It is hard to get your dream out into the world. Some days it is even painful. Only if you believe wholeheartedly in what you are doing will it work. And you will hear it from people trying to bring you down. Know that these people have probably not fulfilled their own dreams and seeing you fulfill yours causes them to react in a way that has *nothing to do with you,* only with themselves. Doubters say to me, "You are selling empty boxes?" I proudly declare, "Yes, I am." The philosophy behind these "empty boxes" is a space to devote to your dreams.

I had a mentor who said, "These boxes hold your magic—I can tell you believe in them with all of your heart. Everyone who holds one in their hands, and who fills it up with their dreams like you have, will feel that magic too."

Molly Gold, Go Mom !nc.

My last words of advice? Don't rush into business without having your infrastructure mapped out both personally and professionally. The business plan is just the tip of the iceberg and doesn't address how you will cope with the ups and downs. Remember the three years to success rule: Even in these wild times of dot-com success and failure, business is still business. It takes staying power and the ability to forge on in the face of unknowns. I mean this about business and about parenting. You have to be a risk taker and be able to manage the chaos of bouncing back and forth in your two roles. We don't think we take risks in our parenting, but we take a huge leap of faith that mother and child will succeed in their relationship. Make no mistake about it: Your personal balance journey will be more complicated than the success or failure of your business. Honestly, that is what it is about. Your own personal desire to start this venture represents the other side of Mom, her side. Go for it!

Julie Aigner-Clark, Baby Einstein

Remember what's important. Children grow up so fast!

Rachael Bender, BlueSuitMom.com

The best advice I can give about starting a small business is to do thorough planning. If you know that your family depends on your income, make sure you save months' worth of income to prepare you for the lean times. If you are a real people person, make sure you plan activities with friends so you aren't isolated in your office. Remember, as all-consuming as your business is, it isn't your whole life. If you become too obsessed by business and don't find balance in the rest of your life, you will end up feeling resentment toward your company. So, take time to plan for activities that make you happy and do some financial planning, too.

DEBBIE WILLIAMS, LET'S GET IT TOGETHER

Don't be afraid that you're not the best out there—just do it! Not even the most trained and experienced people run their businesses perfectly. We all make mistakes. The most important thing is to learn from them and try not to repeat them. Follow your instincts, always be professional, and try to return your phone calls and e-mails within twenty-four hours. Today's customer wants information now, so try to get them an answer as soon as possible.

AMILYA ANTONETTI, SOAPWORKS

You can learn from the mistake I made early in my business. of allowing other people to steer me away from my core vision. I got caught up on going international before I was ready. I got caught up on representing other products before mine was completely built. Stay focused and true to your passion

The Last Word

I'm not the type who always wants to get the last word in a conversation, but I feel the need to do so here. Not because it's my book: The book is really the product of forty-one very talented businesswomen. Let's just call it an author's prerogative.

My final word of advice is "commitment." Be committed. In all stages of your company, demonstrate commitment to the process. First, you need commitment to follow your dream, pursue your vision, and find personal balance if that is one of your reasons for launching a home-based business. You will need commitment to find the funds to launch your company. Commitment will lift you up when the most recent no gets you down. It will push you forward when the mental fatigue from long hours of work makes you think you can't go on. Commitment will create the determination you'll need when you have to ask a retailer to sell your product or you have to cold call a list of potential clients. It is the characteristic your children will learn from watching you demonstrate it on a daily basis. It is the thing that you will have to instill in the people who are closest to you, like your spouse and friends. Luckily, it's contagious, and the more you exhibit it the faster it will spread. Commitment to your market will drive you to test advertising, sampling, and promotions. It will keep you focused on your goals when the day-to-day operational issues pile up and seem overwhelming. Your commitment will enable you to network with strangers and to tell and retell your story. Commitment will enable you to dig deep down inside and find the courage to take the risks necessary to launch your company. If you are truly committed to launching your own home-based business, what are you waiting for? Get out there and demonstrate your commitment.

Good Luck! We are all cheering for you.

Index